"Jason Meyer offers a st(
preaching—not only affi:
how to interpret each asp
Bible's whole message. Expository preaching can get lost in microscopic
examination of a particular passage. Meyer keeps the redemptive context
in view, not only providing many 'aha' moments for experienced expositors, but also giving a new generation of preachers even more incentive to
expound the Word in a manner true to the text."

Bryan Chapell, President Emeritus, Covenant Theological Seminary

"My friend Jason Meyer has a firm grasp not only on the theology of
preaching, but also on the theology we're called to preach. He is gripped by
the Christ-centered plotline of the Bible and understands something that
desperately needs to be recovered in our day if the church is ever going
to experience the kind of reformation many of us long for: the preacher
is *not* called to say many different things—but rather the same thing over
and over, in many different ways, from every different text."

Tullian Tchividjian, Senior Pastor, Coral Ridge Presbyterian Church,
Fort Lauderdale, Florida; author, *One Way Love*

"Jason Meyer's work cuts a new swath in the plethora of books on preaching. Meyer grounds his view of preaching in biblical theology, showing that
the proclamation of God's Word fits within the story line of Scripture. The
reader will find wisdom on a multitude of other topics, such as the nature
of expository preaching and the role topical preaching should play in the
pulpit. The book breathes out a passion for God and a joy in Jesus Christ,
so that the weight and gladness of preaching pulsate throughout the work."

Thomas R. Schreiner, James Buchanan Harrison Professor of
New Testament Interpretation, The Southern Baptist Theological
Seminary

"Here Jason Meyer takes us on a sure-footed journey through the whole
of Scripture, from Genesis to Revelation, unfolding for us what the entire
Bible reveals about preaching. The result is a luminous, deeply grounded
biblical theology for the ministry of the Word, and a winsome, compelling apologetic for expository preaching! *Preaching: A Biblical Theology* is a
very important book that will be read and discussed by serious-minded
Christians far and wide."

R. Kent Hughes, Senior Pastor Emeritus, College Church, Wheaton,
Illinois

"Going . . . going . . . gone. Jason Meyer hits it out of the park."

C. J. Mahaney, Senior Pastor, Sovereign Grace Church of Louisville

PREACHING

PREACHING

A BIBLICAL THEOLOGY

JASON C. MEYER

Foreword by John Piper

CROSSWAY

WHEATON, ILLINOIS

Trade paperback ISBN: 978-1-4335-1971-0
Mobipocket ISBN: 978-1-4335-1973-4
PDF ISBN: 978-1-4335-1972-7
ePub ISBN: 978-1-4335-1974-1

Library of Congress Cataloging-in-Publication Data

Meyer, Jason C. (Jason Curtis), 1976–
   Preaching : a biblical theology / Jason C. Meyer.
     pages   cm
   Includes bibliographical references and index.
   ISBN 978-1-4335-1971-0 (tp)
   1. Preaching. 2. Bible—Homiletical use. I. Title.
BV4211.3.M49   2013
251—dc23   2013018041

Crossway is a publishing ministry of Good News Publishers.

VP		23	22	21	20	19	18	17	16	15	14	13
15	14	13	12	11	10	9	8	7	6	5	4	3	2	1

To John Piper

I cannot calculate the depths to which
I stand in your debt. I learned much about
true preaching from the electric shock I experienced
while sitting under your preaching. Thank you.

And to Bethlehem Baptist Church

I count it an unspeakable honor to herald
the word as a pastor of the flock that I love. Thank you.

CONTENTS

FOREWORD

by John Piper

I share Jason Meyer's concern that many pastors "no longer tremble at the task of preaching." Our contemporary obsession with being casual at all costs—not just in our dress (which is minor) but in our verbal and soul demeanor (which is major)—obscures crucial dimensions of God's reality.

David Wells's twenty-year-old assessment is still widely true: "The fundamental problem in the evangelical world today is that God rests too inconsequentially upon the church. His truth is too distant, his grace is too ordinary, his judgment is too benign, his gospel is too easy, and his Christ is too common."[1] And taking God's holy word on their lips does not make the preachers tremble.

But God is raising up many younger voices with the conviction that there is a radically God-centered, gospel-saturated, joyful alternative to carefree, breezy, chipper ways of dealing with divine things. This is especially true of preaching. Jason Meyer strikes the refreshing old note: "Preaching is a high calling. It is not just difficult; it is impossible with man."

Whether a preacher is staggered at the task of preaching depends largely on whether he is stunned that God Almighty has spoken in a Book. And that God calls sinful, fallible human beings to herald with authority what he has spoken there. God could have done it without a book and without preachers. But he chose both as indispensable. Wise preachers tremble at this.

Another reason the task of preaching is impossible and wonderful is that the main aim of preaching is not the transfer of information, but an encounter with the living God. The people of God meet God

---

[1] David F. Wells, *God in the Wasteland: The Reality of Truth in a World of Fading Dreams* (Grand Rapids: Eerdmans, 1994), 28.

in the anointed heralding of God's message in a way that cannot be duplicated by any other means. Preaching in a worship service is not a lecture in a classroom. It is the echo of, and the exultation over, God speaking to us in his word.

The faithfulness of the echo will determine the authenticity of the exultation. Which is why Jason mounts a compelling biblical case for preaching as exposition of Scripture. God has spoken in the Book. All of it is marked by grammatical and historical specificity. None of it, by accident. None of it, erroneous. Preaching honors this. Bows before the specificity of this authority. Exults in the explosive power of the particulars. And shows enough of them in the message that people don't have to take the preacher's word for it: *Look! This glorious reality over which we are now exulting is really there.*

Underneath these convictions about preaching, Jason exposes a massive biblical foundation by excavating the whole terrain of Scripture. I know of nothing like what he has done here in tracing the stewarding of God's word from Genesis to Revelation. I commend it for its uniqueness and for its faithful rendering of the heart of preaching.

As many readers know, I have a personal stake in the man Jason Meyer and his message. Jason accepted the call of God to pick up where I left off after thirty-three years of preaching at Bethlehem Baptist Church. I have loved and fed this people for three decades. As you can imagine, it will be a crowning joy to my life if Bethlehem continues to walk in the truth, nourished by the faithful exposition of God's word.

This is why I am thrilled with the message of this book and the theological and expository commitments of Jason Meyer. He wrote the book, and he models the book. God's hand is on him to "to preach . . . the unsearchable riches of Christ" (Eph. 3:8). And he is a faithful guide in how to do this.

Jason Meyer does not take preaching lightly. Paradoxical as it may sound, both he and I rejoice that we have discovered and experienced the truth of God's statement:

> This is the one to whom I will look:
>   he who is humble and contrite in spirit
>   and trembles at my word. (Isa. 66:2)

A WORD FOR
BUSY PASTORS

When I first wrote this book, I had a long and winding path to my main point—complete with a long preface, some soul searching, and something of a brief history of research with regard to evangelical preaching. If these kinds of things interest you, you can find vestiges of them in the appendixes of the book. I realize now that I need to just cut to the chase. I hope many busy pastors are reading this book. I know that your time is precious, the needs are overwhelming, and preaching books are legion. So the question of the hour is, why bother with this book?

BACK TO THE BIBLE: DID GOD REALLY SAY?

The first temptation was a focused attack on God's word. Satan successfully sowed seeds of doubt in Eve's heart concerning what God had clearly spoken. Our ancient foe hates true preaching and has set his sights on scrambling the clear signals of Scripture concerning it. He has good reason to oppose preaching. Spirit-filled preaching is still the church's greatest weapon against Satan's kingdom. I agree with Martyn Lloyd-Jones that "preaching is the highest calling and the greatest need for the church and the world."[1] If it is so important, we had better be clear on what it is. Has God clearly revealed what preaching is in Scripture? Ultimately, no one else can define preaching. It is God's idea. Has he spoken?

God is not silent on this matter. He has spoken clearly and authoritatively. Paul even calls preaching a "charge" (2 Tim. 4:1) from God.

---

[1] D. Martyn Lloyd-Jones, *Preaching and Preachers* (Grand Rapids: Zondervan, 1971), 9. Lloyd-Jones defends this claim in various ways. One argument he gives for the importance of preaching is that a revival of true preaching has been the defining mark of every reformation and revival in church history (24–25).

This charge is to "preach the word" of God (4:2). What does this charge mean? Where would one go to find the answer?

BACK TO THE WHOLE BIBLE

Evangelicals know that the answer is the Bible, but where in the Bible? This is the key question. I fear that most attempts to answer this question have been unnecessarily selective. Some studies narrowly rely on word studies of "preaching" words. Others tip their hat to the Old Testament and then spend the rest of their time looking in the New Testament. *This book is unique in that I think the whole Bible alone can give a holistic answer to what preaching is.* We will strive for a holistic answer by looking at preaching in the light of the larger category to which it belongs: the ministry of the word.

In this study, it is important to emphasize that I did not merely set out to defend a particular view of preaching. C. H. Spurgeon said that the gospel is like a caged lion: you don't have to defend it—just let it out of the cage. In the same way, I do not want to "defend" preaching as much as I want to let the Bible's view of preaching out of the cage.

OVERVIEW: CHOOSE YOUR OWN ADVENTURE

The first five chapters of this book attempt to give a broad overview of what Scripture says about the ministry of the word (i.e., not just preaching). These chapters give the essential introductory framework for the rest of the book. They are vital to read in order to make sense of the whole.

Where you go next depends upon you. When I was a kid, I used to read the "choose your own adventure" category of books. I wrote this book in a similar way. Someone could jump from the introductory chapters of part one (chs. 1–5) to part three (chs. 17–19) without much difficulty. The first five chapters are a condensed biblical theology of the ministry of the word. They form the prerequisite concepts that prepare the reader to make the necessary transition from the preaching we find *in* Scripture (chs. 1–5) to today's context in which we preach *from* Scripture (chs. 17–19).

So what is part two? If someone could skip it, then is it really all that important? It is an eleven-chapter attempt to buttress the condensed biblical theology of part one. I recognize that some readers will be more than ready to make the move from part one to part three. Others, however, will not feel ready yet. They will want to examine the scriptural foundations of part one. Therefore, part two is an attempt to provide structural supports for part one. Structural supports are massively important, but not everyone enjoys examining them to see how sturdy they are. Some will appreciate this attempt to assure them that the supports are sturdy.

One television station advertises that it has movies for guys who like movies. Another way to describe part two would be to say that it has details for readers who like details. These eleven chapters are the meat of a biblical theology of the ministry of the word. Each chapter looks at a different paradigm. One could read straight through them, or they could serve as reference points for later reading.

Therefore, a reader who enjoys big-picture reading could jump from part one to part three and then move on through the rest of the book. A reader who loves double-clicking on details could read the book straight through as it stands.

Part four takes some soundings from systematic theology (chs. 20–21) and then offers reflections on the place of topical preaching (ch. 22). The last chapter wraps up the study with conclusions and applications (ch. 23).

ACKNOWLEDGMENTS

I simply cannot name all the people who helped make this book a reality; the list would be too long, and my memory too limited. Therefore, I want to highlight four sets of people.

First, I want to thank the wonderful team at Crossway for believing in this book. My editor in particular, Thom Notaro, was simply outstanding. The book is better because of his labors. To God be the glory.

Second, I would like to acknowledge the tremendous influence of John Piper. D. Martyn Lloyd-Jones once said that people may help make a preacher less distracting through preaching classes and the like, but only God can really create a preacher. Lloyd-Jones went on to say that the best thing an aspiring preacher could do was to go find the best preacher he could and then spend some time sitting under his ministry. I read those words in John Piper's preaching class as part of the Bethlehem Institute, and they rang true. I realize now that I followed Lloyd-Jones's advice without even knowing it. Pastor John (as I came to call him) has shaped me in more ways than I can put into words. I am dedicating this book to him as one small way of acknowledging the mammoth blessing he has been to me under God. To God be the glory.

Third, I also dedicated the book to my flock at Bethlehem Baptist Church. The way that God has given me a heart for them has been a wonder to me over the last year. It reminds me of the scene from *How the Grinch Stole Christmas* in which the Grinch's tiny heart grows three sizes, breaking the box that houses it. God has done a similar work in my heart for Bethlehem, and a corresponding work in the congregation's heart for me. My pastoral assistant at Bethlehem, David Zuleger, has also been a tremendous blessing in the editing process of this book. To God be the glory.

Fourth, my family is the single biggest influence on me under God. My heart is bound up with my four wonderful children: Gracie, Allie, Jonathan, and David. I have to give them credit for how much they have helped me write this book—especially by asking constantly, "Dad, aren't you done with the book *yet?*" They have been great cheerleaders.

No one on this list can hold a candle to my wife, Cara. She was my greatest encourager along the way as I wrote this volume, and she did so much in so many ways to help make it a reality. Cara, words always fail me when I try to express my thanks to God for you. Let it be known that you have a hold on my heart like no one else ever could. Thank you for loving me so profoundly. To God be the glory.

God has sovereignly orchestrated the influence and blessing of these four groups. The glory is all his. I am simply identifying and celebrating his grace in their lives. All things are from him, through him, and to him. To him be the glory forever.

PART ONE

THE BIG PICTURE: BIBLICAL THEOLOGY OF THE MINISTRY OF THE WORD

THE *WHAT* OF PREACHING

> For if I preach the gospel, that gives me no ground for boasting. For necessity is laid upon me. Woe to me if I do not preach the gospel! For if I do this of my own will, I have a reward, but if not of my own will, *I am still entrusted with a stewardship.*
>
> *1 Corinthians 9:16–17*

THREE CATEGORIES

The central question of this book is, what is preaching? Answering that question forces us to address a broader question: what is the ministry of the word? The ministry of the word flows from the fact that God entrusts his people with his word. His people take that word and faithfully serve others with it. The ministry of the word includes many ministries within the church, such as counseling and personal evangelism, not just preaching. This book addresses questions common to any word-based ministry, but preaching is the main ministry I have in view. Three big-picture biblical categories best sum up the ministry of the word in Scripture: stewarding, heralding, and encountering. This chapter defines them and sketches a very brief biblical overview.

THESIS

My thesis is that the ministry of the word in Scripture is *stewarding and heralding God's word in such a way that people encounter God through his word.* Notice that this thesis highlights three components, which are actually three sequential phases of the ministry of the word.

The first phase is the stewarding phase. It focuses on faithfully receiving God's word. The steward is entrusted with the word of God. The second phase is the heralding of God's word. God intends for the stewarded word to be heralded. The preacher gives a human voice to the divine word so that others will hear from God. The third phase is encountering God through his word. In this step, the responsibility to steward the word passes from the preacher to the people. This phase is a time of great gravity because every word from God demands a response. These three elements are three sequential phases in the dynamic process of preaching God's word: stewarding, heralding, and encountering.

EXPLANATION OF THE THESIS: THREE SUITCASES TO UNPACK

The three parts of the thesis statement are like three suitcases so stuffed with meaning that they are bursting at the seams and demanding to be unpacked one at a time. Let's begin unpacking.

SUITCASE 1: STEWARDING GOD'S WORD

The first phase focuses on the content of preaching, which is the *stewarded word of God*. On this score, it is hard to improve upon Paul's pithy summary in 1 Corinthians 4:1–2. He says that a steward is one who has been entrusted with something (i.e., the *what*) and so he must be found faithful (i.e., the *how*) with respect to what has been entrusted. "This is how one should regard us, as servants of Christ and stewards of the mysteries of God. Moreover, it is required of stewards that they be found faithful" (4:1–2).

Mark Dever offers a succinct definition of a steward: "A steward is someone who is not an owner but one who is entrusted with someone else's property."[1] In other words, a steward is not a master, but a servant—a servant entrusted with something that belongs to his master. John Stott says it well: "Indeed, if the [stewardship] metaphor teaches anything, it teaches that the preacher does not supply his own message; he is supplied with it."[2] God is the Master, the word is his property, and the preacher is the appointed servant entrusted with it.

---

[1] Mark E. Dever, "A Real Minister: 1 Corinthians 4," in Mark Dever et al., *Preaching the Cross* (Wheaton, IL: Crossway, 2007), 18.
[2] John Stott, *The Preacher's Portrait: Some New Testament Word Studies* (Grand Rapids: Eerdmans, 1961), 23. Stott has an excellent study of the *stewardship* word group.

This stewardship of the word may take different forms at different times (patriarchs, prophets, scribes, just to name a few), but the same basic calling ties these stewards together throughout the pages of Scripture.

SUITCASE 2: HERALDING GOD'S WORD

The second phase of preaching is *heralding God's word*. The emphasis on heralding is on *tone* of the delivery. Preaching is not discussing or explaining something with the tone and tenor of a fireside chat. The "herald" is the town crier that speaks with the forceful tone of "hear ye, hear ye." In other words, the herald made his proclamation with a rousing "attention-getting noise" that could not be ignored.[3]

Gordon Hugenberger reinforces the gravity of the herald's task by stressing the political or military associations of the word. He points to the work of Suidas, the tenth-century AD Greek lexicographer, who said, "A herald is in time of war what an ambassador is in peace."[4] The herald would go into "enemy territory ahead of an advancing army to warn the enemy of certain destruction unless they accepted the proffered terms for peace."[5] Therefore, the king would invest the herald with the power "either [to] accept surrender on behalf of his king or to declare war if those terms were rejected."[6] The herald's authority is completely derived and is legitimate only to the degree that he faithfully represents the one who sent him.

Notice how stewarding and heralding go together. Peter spoke of using our gifts to serve one another "as good *stewards* of God's varied grace" (1 Pet. 4:10). He then highlights two basic gifts of grace to steward: speaking gifts and serving gifts. The herald is a faithful steward of a speaking gift of grace when he speaks "as one who speaks oracles of God" (4:11). Paul made the same connection between preaching and stewardship in 1 Corinthians 9:16–17: "Woe to me if I do not *preach* the gospel! For if I do this of my own will, I have a reward, but if not of my own will, I am still *entrusted with a stewardship*."

---

[3] Gordon Hugenberger, "Preach," in *The International Standard Bible Encyclopedia*, ed. Geoffrey W. Bromiley, vol. 3 (Grand Rapids: Eerdmans, 1986), 942.
[4] Quoted in ibid.
[5] Ibid.
[6] Ibid.

The connection between stewarding and heralding is simple. God entrusts the word and then God calls the preacher to herald it. The calling and gifting to handle and herald the word are themselves a stewardship from God. God's calling and gifting are prerequisites for this stewardship, as we will see in the chapters that follow.

Furthermore, the steward needs to stay faithful with what has been entrusted, and the herald needs to stay true to what he has been sent to say. He has no authority to modify the message or insert his own opinions as if they represent the revealed will of the sender. The herald proclaims a message as an ambassador representing the one who sent him.[7]

These two terms, *stewarding* and *heralding*, also help the reader of Scripture to understand the relationship between teaching and preaching. Preaching has an expository dimension because God entrusts the preacher with a specific message. The fact that heralding God's word requires exposition explains why preaching and teaching in Scripture often appear together (e.g., Matt. 4:23; 9:35; 11:1; Luke 20:1; Acts 5:42; 15:34; 1 Tim. 5:17). I believe preaching refers to how something is stated (a heraldic way), while teaching focuses on the content of what is said (unpacking something).

Another reason why people should not sharply distinguish preaching and teaching is that the two are often used interchangeably in Scripture. For example, the response to Jesus's most famous sermon (the Sermon on the Mount) defines the sermon as "teaching" (Matt. 7:28). In the same way, a verse in Romans sheds light on the interchangeable nature of the terms. Paul lays down a general statement for the Jews: "You then who teach others, do you not teach yourselves?" (Rom. 2:21). When he gives an example of this principle, he uses the term "preach": "While you preach against stealing, do you steal?" (2:21).

Therefore, the combination of the terms *stewarding* and *heralding* honors the intricate connection in Scripture between preaching and teaching. One could say again by way of summary that the word *herald*

---

[7]D. A. Carson says something similar in his discussion of what preaching is. He says that preaching has a "heraldic" quality because "in the oft-repeated 'Thus says the Lord' of the Old Testament, or in the proclamation so common to the New Testament, there is an unavoidable heraldic element—an announcement, a sovereign disclosure, a nonnegotiable declaration. As ambassadors, we are tasked with making known the stance and intentions of our Sovereign; we do not have the authority to tamper with his position." D. A. Carson, "Challenges for the Twenty-first Century Pulpit," in *Preach the Word: Essays on Expository Preaching in Honor of R. Kent Hughes*, ed. Leland Ryken and Todd Wilson (Wheaton, IL: Crossway, 2007), 177.

focuses on the preaching aspect or the heraldic tone of the delivery, while the word *teaching* places more stress on the entrusted content that the herald as teacher must unpack.

SUITCASE 3: IN SUCH A WAY THAT
PEOPLE ENCOUNTER GOD

The third phase of preaching brings the burden of God's word to bear upon the hearers. The sequential nature of the first two phases of preaching leads to a moment of truth for the hearers. The preacher in Scripture has spoken God's word. The people now must steward God's word. Properly stewarding the word leads to life and blessing. Improper stewardship of the word leads to death and curse.

We cannot allow our definition of *encounter* to emphasize only positive transformation. I do not use *encounter* as a synonym for what Henry Blackaby has called "experiencing God," which he describes as a positive experience. The encounter can be negative or positive, depending on how people respond to God's word. Consider, for example, Paul's description of the effects of his ministry of the word upon his hearers: "For we are the aroma of Christ to God among those who are being saved and among those who are perishing, to one a fragrance from death to death, to the other a fragrance from life to life" (2 Cor. 2:15–16).

Sometimes an encounter with God through the preaching of the word brings the sweet smell of life, while for others it brings the stench of death. The Scriptures sing with examples of the power of the word to change lives. The word also contains stinging examples of powerful judgments.

THE SWEET SMELL OF LIFE

The great hope of preaching is the power of God. Paul knew that Satan had blinded the perishing (2 Cor. 4:3–4), but Paul kept preaching Christ because Satan's ploys are no match for God's power. God can create light out of darkness by his word and save those who are perishing: "For what we proclaim is not ourselves, but Jesus Christ as Lord, with ourselves as your servants for Jesus' sake. For God, who said, 'Let light shine out of darkness,' has shone in our hearts to give the light of the knowledge of the glory of God in the face of Jesus Christ" (4:5–6).

The Bible makes clear that faith is a gift (Eph. 2:8; Phil. 1:29). God gives the gift of faith through his word. Sometimes this dynamic is encapsulated in a single verse: "So faith comes from hearing, and hearing *through the word of Christ*" (Rom. 10:17).

The new birth comes through the word of God. Peter reminds us that we "have been born again, not of perishable seed but of imperishable, through the living and abiding word of God" (1 Pet. 1:23). James makes the same point: "Of his own will he brought us forth by the word of truth" (James 1:18).

THE STENCH OF DEATH

As strange as it may sound, the ministry of the word can be a ministry of judgment. Paul calls Moses's ministry a "ministry of condemnation" (2 Cor. 3:9). Not only did Isaiah's whole ministry have a negative result upon the people, but God makes it stunningly clear that he intended this result, which means it is not only a result but a purpose. In the famous passage in which Isaiah sees the Lord seated upon his throne, most people stop reading the passage with Isaiah's declaration, "Here am I! Send me" (Isa. 6:8). The next verse, however, which rarely gets preached in connection with "calling" sermons, describes the ministry God is calling Isaiah to do. The people's encounter with God through Isaiah's word will bring judgment upon them:

> And he said, "Go, and say to this people:
>
> > "'Keep on hearing, but do not understand;
> > keep on seeing, but do not perceive.'
> > Make the heart of this people dull,
> >   and their ears heavy,
> >   and blind their eyes;
> > lest they see with their eyes,
> >   and hear with their ears,
> > and understand with their hearts,
> >   and turn and be healed." (Isa. 6:9–10)

This same dynamic appears in Jesus's ministry. His preaching of the parables is a preaching of judgment that reveals the people's hardened hearts:

To you has been given the secret of the kingdom of God, but for those outside everything is in parables, so that

> "they may indeed see but not perceive,
>   and may indeed hear but not understand,
> lest they should turn and be forgiven." (Mark 4:11–12)

Notice that Jesus even quotes the same text from Isaiah. These two texts are statements not merely of effect, but of purpose! Jesus makes the effectual link between speaking and judgment explicit in John 15:22: "If I had not come and spoken to them, they would not have been guilty of sin, but now they have no excuse for their sin." John 8:45 is even more striking in stressing a causal effect between the truth spoken and the unbelief that results: "But *because* I tell the truth, you do not believe me."

Even an anointed ministry of the word can bring death—not only for the hearer, but for the speaker as well. Stephen's sermon in Acts 7 is portrayed as an anointed sermon. No one could resist the wisdom and Spirit with which he spoke (Acts 6:10). His face shone "like . . . an angel" (6:15). However, the encounter between God and the people led to Stephen's death because of the people's hard-hearted rejection. Most people would never imagine that the anointing of the message and the death of the messenger could be put in the same frame of reference. They are both unmistakably there in Acts 6–7.[8]

This discussion on the results of preaching raises the question of the relationship between human responsibility and God's sovereignty. We must be careful not to blur the line between these two biblical categories. How do we know where to draw the line of responsibility?

THE RESPONSIBILITY OF STEWARDSHIP

When the truth is preached, the responsibility of stewardship shifts from the preacher to the hearer. If someone has preached what is false, then judgment falls upon the preacher and the hearer must judge it to be false. This principle is abundantly clear from Scripture. I will limit myself to three examples: Ezekiel, James, and Paul.

---

[8] The peoples' zealous rejection of what Stephen said did not make Stephen's sermon false or a failure on the part of the Spirit or Stephen. Far from it. The text tells us of God's Trinitarian presence at the sermon (the Spirit, the glory of God, and Jesus): "But he [Stephen], full of the *Holy Spirit*, gazed into heaven and saw the glory of *God*, and *Jesus* standing at the right hand of *God*. And he said, 'Behold, I see the heavens opened, and the *Son of Man* standing at the right hand of *God*'" (Act 7:55–56).

Ezekiel 3:18–21 shows that the herald must not remain silent when the Lord summons him to speak. He must speak when, where, and what the Lord wills. If he does not, then judgment falls upon him.

> If I say to the wicked, "You shall surely die," and you give him no warning, nor speak to warn the wicked from his wicked way, in order to save his life, that wicked person shall die for his iniquity, but his blood I will require at your hand. (3:18)

> Again, if a righteous person turns from his righteousness and commits injustice, and I lay a stumbling block before him, he shall die. Because you have not warned him, he shall die for his sin, and his righteous deeds that he has done shall not be remembered, but his blood I will require at your hand. (3:20)

If the steward faithfully speaks the word, then he is not held guilty for someone else's response.

> But if you warn the wicked, and he does not turn from his wickedness, or from his wicked way, he shall die for his iniquity, but you will have delivered your soul. (3:19)

> But if you warn the righteous person not to sin, and he does not sin, he shall surely live, because he took warning, and you will have delivered your soul. (3:21)

The New Testament continues this theme concerning the responsibility of teachers. James states that teachers of the word will receive a stricter judgment: "Not many of you should become teachers, my brothers, for you know that we who teach will be judged with greater strictness" (James 3:1). Acts 20:26–27 clarifies that preachers will not be judged for the unfaithful response of the people if they have faithfully declared the whole counsel of God: "Therefore I testify to you this day that I am innocent of the blood of all [of you], for I did not shrink from declaring to you the whole counsel of God." This is important because Paul explicitly states that some will not respond positively: "and *from among your own selves* will arise men speaking twisted things, to draw away the disciples after them (Act 20:30). Even so, he remains innocent of their blood.

THE CYCLE OF STEWARDSHIP

I have stressed how encountering God through his word can lead to judgment. Let me also emphasize the positive side of stewarding, heralding, and encountering. One of the most important effects of the ministry of the word is the principle of repetition.

God's word → steward of the word → herald of the word ⤸
stewarding and heralding repeated by audience ← audience

The ministry of the word done well on the part of the pastoral shepherd leads to an effective ministry of the word on the part of the congregation. This cycle of stewardship will make an impact at home and abroad.

First, the ministry of the word is needed at home. Hebrews 3:12 warns that some may have an "evil, unbelieving heart, leading you to fall away from the living God." The author calls for congregational action: "*take care, brothers*, lest there be in any of you an evil, unbelieving heart, leading you to fall away from the living God." This action is defined in terms of a congregational ministry of the word practiced daily. "But *exhort one another every day*, as long as it is called 'today,' that none of you may be hardened by the deceitfulness of sin" (3:13). Once the baton of stewardship passes from the preacher to the congregation, the congregation will look for ways to herald the truth of the word within the realm of their relationships (home, work, school, etc.).

Second, the ministry of the word is needed abroad. The happiest thing that can happen to a minister of the word is to see the word do a work of missions mobilization. Jesus said, "And this gospel of the kingdom will be proclaimed throughout the whole world as a testimony to all nations, and then the end will come" (Matt. 24:14). People will hear what Jesus said, and God will do a miracle for the cause of missions by burdening their hearts to go preach the gospel to the nations. Some will adopt Paul's ambition "to preach the gospel, not where Christ has already been named" (Rom. 15:20). The cycle of stewarding, heralding, and encountering at home will lead to stewarding, heralding, and encountering abroad. This cycle says that one cannot spread *a flame* of the word abroad unless people are first *aflame* with the word at home.

CONCLUSION

It did not dawn on me until after most of this book was written that my three categories fit with the perspectival approach of well-known theologian John Frame.[9] The "normative perspective" focuses on the unchanging authority of the word of God. The "situational perspective" traces the changing steward and herald paradigms throughout the word. The "existential perspective" stresses the reality of encountering God through his word.

These concepts give the ministry of the word a balanced and wide-ranging biblical base. This chapter has argued that the concepts of stewarding, heralding, and encountering allow the whole Bible to speak with respect to what preaching is. In the next chapter, I will attempt to show that there is a link between the *what* and the *how* of preaching. We end this chapter on the note of encountering God. Isaac Watts's hymn "How Sweet and Awful Is the Place" strikes the right balance on this score. Some encounter the feast with thankful tongues, while others "make a wretched choice, and rather starve than come." Some may starve, but it will not be because the feast is fake (like a fake fruit basket that looks appealing but does nothing to satisfy one's hunger). The real gospel is a feast of good news. God sovereignly opens our eyes so that we taste and see with the result that we are satisfied for all eternity. All who have tasted the goodness of the gospel long for this all-satisfying Savior to be named where he is not named.

> Pity the nations, O our God,
> constrain the earth to come,
> send Thy victorious Word abroad
> and bring the strangers home.

Let it be, Lord.

---

[9]John M. Frame, *The Doctrine of the Christian Life* (Phillipsburg, NJ: P&R, 2008).

2

THE *HOW* OF PREACHING

> So have *no fear* of them, for nothing is covered that will not be revealed, or hidden that will not be known. What I tell you in the dark, say in the light, and what you hear whispered, *proclaim* on the housetops. And *do not fear* those who kill the body but cannot kill the soul. Rather *fear him* who can destroy both body and soul in hell.
>
> *Matthew 10:26–28*

In the first chapter, I explained my thesis: the ministry of the word in Scripture is *stewarding and heralding God's word in such a way that people encounter God through his word.* In this chapter, I develop the "in such a way" part of the thesis. I will show the link between what the ministry of the word is and how it is to be done.

Stewarding and heralding must be carried out faithfully and fearlessly *because* the preacher has first encountered God through his word. The interplay can be seen in the word pairs shown in figure 1.

Figure 1. The *what* and *how* of preaching

The *What* of Preaching	The *How* of Preaching
stewarding	faithfully
heralding	fearlessly
encountering	reverently

In what follows, I will explain and defend each point briefly from Scripture in anticipation of the fuller survey that comes in the next chapter.

STEWARDING FAITHFULLY

Stewardship demands that the steward be faithful. I chose the word *faithful* very intentionally because of its flexibility in connoting two related concepts: the faithful steward is marked by (1) *fidelity* (faithfulness) and by (2) *faith* (he is full of faith).

The first concept, fidelity (faithfulness or trustworthiness), calls for the person to handle the entrusted word with care. We turn again to 1 Corinthians 4:2. Paul says that a steward is one who has been entrusted with something (i.e., the *what*) and so he must be found faithful (i.e., the *how*) with respect to what has been entrusted. "This is how one should regard us, as servants of Christ and stewards of the mysteries of God. Moreover, *it is required of stewards that they be found faithful*" (4:1–2).

The idea of trust (and being trustworthy) works in two directions when it comes to the ministry of the word. God places trust in a person when he "entrusts" his word to that person. The person must in turn place trust in the word of God because God is trustworthy. This faith is an essential part of his calling to prove "trustworthy" with it (i.e., handle it with care and fidelity). In other words, the idea of trust is a two-way street in this dynamic as the following diagram shows:

God → entrusted word → steward ⤵
trusts both God and his word ← steward

This two-way street prepares us for the next category, heralding. Stewarding, rightly understood, should lead to heralding precisely because has God entrusted his word to a steward for the purpose of heralding. Therefore, stewarding that does not lead to some form of heralding is not true stewarding. Do we have textual warrant to make such a strong claim? Consider the link between believing (i.e., stewarding) and speaking (i.e., heralding) in 2 Corinthians 4:13–14. Believing what we know from Scripture to be true will enable us to speak boldly. "Since we have the same spirit of faith according to what has been written, 'I *believed*, and *so* I *spoke*,' we also *believe*, and *so* we also *speak*" (4:13). Notice that I italicized not only the words "believe" and "speak" but also the little word "so," which shows how they logically relate. Believing is the basis of speaking. Believing is logically prior to speaking—we speak *because* we believe.

The content of that faith is spelled out in the next verse. What compels Paul to keep speaking? He believes and therefore speaks, "*knowing* that he who raised the Lord Jesus will raise us also with Jesus and bring us with you into his presence" (2 Cor. 4:14). Believing must fill the gap between God's promise and Paul's experience. Paul knew of the promised resurrection, but his faith had not yet become sight. Therefore, faith in the God who stands behind his word fills the gap.

This faith caused Paul to remain in the ministry. He did "not lose heart" (2 Cor. 4:16). The reason he did not give up was twofold. First, though he saw death at work in his body (his "outer body wasting away"), he also saw life (his "inner self renewed day by day"). Second, the life that he saw in the present produced hope in God's full and future promise of resurrected life. He looked to the future and saw that death was not the end; it would be swallowed up in victory, and God would use it to usher people into his presence as the path to life.

He looked beyond the things that are seen and temporary (the light momentary affliction) to the things that are unseen and eternal (the eternal weight of glory) (2 Cor. 4:16–18). Therefore, death and hardship could not silence him because he embraced the weight of glory that suffering was actually producing. He believed the word that he was called to herald, so he kept speaking. This leads us to consider our next category.

HERALDING FEARLESSLY

In terms of heralding, the Bible shows that the herald speaks with the authority of the sender. This sense of authority does not create feelings of pride and self-exaltation; it provokes the preacher to fear the Lord and tremble at his word. As a result of fearing God, there is a lack of trembling toward man, a fearlessness that causes the herald to speak up instead of holding back and being silent. For example, notice how Isaiah 58:1 calls for fearless and urgent proclamation:

Cry aloud; do not hold back;
　　lift up your voice like a trumpet;
declare to my people their transgression,
　　to the house of Jacob their sins.

Did you catch the interplay? Crying aloud, lifting up your voice, and declaring are all ways of saying, "speak with urgency and authority." The idea of fearlessness comes across in the call "do not hold back." Heralds must not shrink back in fear of man even though they are confronting men with their "transgression" and their "sins."

Jesus's instructions to the disciples are similar in that they are to take what he says and make it public without shrinking back with fear. "So have *no fear* of them, for nothing is covered that will not be revealed, or hidden that will not be known. What I tell you in the dark, say in the light, and what you *hear whispered, proclaim on the housetops*" (Matt. 10:26–27). The fear of men must be entirely absent from heralding ("have no fear of them"). This fearless attitude should empower the heralds' proclamation. They must not draw back into a fearful whisper; they must stand up with a fearless shout because heralding here is the very antithesis of whispering. The logic of Matthew 10 also pushes us into the realm of our next category.

ENCOUNTERING GOD REVERENTLY

While Matthew 10:26–27 speaks forcefully about the absence of fear, Matthew 10:28 completes the picture by focusing on the need for fear. Ministers of the word should be fearless toward man, but reverent toward God. Jesus does not pull any punches concerning what harm men can do. They can kill the body, but that does not warrant fear because they cannot touch the soul. We should fear God alone because only God can fully destroy both body and soul in hell (10:28). Therefore, all stewarding and heralding should take place in the context of the fear of the Lord. Fearing the Lord should cause faithful stewardship and fearless heralding because if you fear God, you need not fear anything or anyone else.

Other texts testify to the importance of the ethos or the atmosphere in which we carry out our stewarding and heralding. For example, God judges Moses for his failure in this very regard. Notice the link in Numbers 27 between rebelling against *the word of God* and failing to *honor God* as holy in the eyes of the people:

> The LORD said to Moses, "Go up into this mountain of Abarim and see the land that I have given to the people of Israel. When you have seen it, you also shall be gathered to your people, as your brother Aaron was, *because you rebelled against my word* in the wilderness of Zin when the congregation quarreled, *failing to uphold me as holy at the waters before their eyes.*" (These are the waters of Meribah of Kadesh in the wilderness of Zin). (27:12–14)

REVERENT STEWARDING AND HERALDING

These three categories are sequential from the vantage point of the hearer: the minister of the word must steward and then herald the word, and then the people should respond with reverent obedience. From the vantage point of the preacher, the order is different. The preacher knows that reverence must mark every stage of the ministry of the word. The minister must *start* with a reverent fear of God. This reverent fear engenders an aptitude to tremble at his word.

> But this is the one to whom I will look:
>   he who is humble and contrite in spirit
>   and trembles at my word. (Isa. 66:2)

That trembling should define both his stewarding and heralding. The fear of the Lord should put a peculiar stamp on the ministry of the word—the people should know that the word of God is coming from a man who has met God.

Once the word has passed to the audience, the cycle of stewardship begins again in the lives of the hearers. They now have a call to handle the word faithfully, fearlessly, and reverently.

CONCLUSION

The first chapter introduced the thesis of this book. In the second chapter, I have tried to show the link between the *what* and the *how* of the ministry of the word. The next chapter will expand upon a really important point for this study: the Bible is not a textbook on preaching; it is a story. The next three chapters will develop this theme further. Chapter 3 looks at the link between the structure of Scripture and the story of Scripture. Chapter 4 examines the part that the word plays in the story that it tells. Chapter 5 introduces the reader to the stewardship paradigm shifts in Scripture. Chapters 6–16 then examine those paradigm shifts in greater depth.

3

THE LINK BETWEEN
STRUCTURE AND STORY

*Scripture is the royal scepter by
which King Jesus rules his church.*

John Stott

The word of God is the greatest story ever told. Its greatness transcends all other stories in every way because it is a story *about God* (the greatest person) written *by God* (the greatest author). No other book can lay claim to being God's book besides the Bible.

Think for a moment about the story of Scripture. What a wonder to read about the greatest King pursuing the greatest cause (the glory of the Lord filling the earth), vanquishing the greatest enemies (Satan, sin, and death) with the greatest weapon (the word of God). Does this story still capture and captivate you?

Read the last paragraph again. Did you notice that the word of God does double duty in this description? The word of God *is* the story, but it also plays a key part *within* the story it tells. In this chapter, I will analyze the relationship between the structure of Scripture and the story of Scripture. The next chapter will consider the part that the word plays within the story of Scripture.

THE STRUCTURE OF SCRIPTURE

First, we need to take note of the difference between the ordering of the Hebrew Bible and that of the English Bible for the Old Testament. In our English Bibles, the Old Testament has thirty-nine books organized in a loosely topical way: (1) law, (2) historical books, (3) wisdom books and songs, and (4) prophetic books (major and minor). The Hebrew Bible has three main divisions: Law, Prophets, and Writings.

Both the English and the Hebrew arrangements are helpful. Today there is renewed interest in reading the Old Testament according to the Hebrew ordering.[1] I do not think that the sufficiency or clarity of Scripture is at stake in terms of which arrangement we use. I do believe, however, that the Hebrew ordering of the Old Testament is more helpful in tracing the story line of the Scriptures because one can better follow the interplay between narrative and commentary sections. I will assume the Hebrew order in what follows.

Second, in terms of form, Scripture has both narrative and commentary. The Scriptures have six narrative installments: (1) the Pentateuch (Genesis—Deuteronomy), (2) the Former Prophets (Joshua—Kings), and (3) the Writings (Ruth—Chronicles), (4) the Gospels (Matthew—John), (5) Acts, and (6) Revelation. The Bible also has three sections of commentary on the story: (1) prophetic commentary (Isaiah—the Book of the Twelve), (2) poetic commentary (Psalms—Lamentations), and (3) apostolic commentary (Romans—Jude).

By way of analogy, one could helpfully compare the form of Scripture to a sportscast. One person provides play-by-play while another gives color commentary. Think of the narrative sections as the play-by-play and the commentary sections as the supporting color commentary. In other words, the structure of Scripture and the story of Scripture are intertwined. Scripture's form creates clear contours for the content of Scripture's story. We will now examine the relationship between the structure of Scripture and the story of Scripture.

---

[1] Many, myself included, prefer the Hebrew ordering, owing to its more ancient arrangement. This assessment is based in large part upon two texts, Luke 11:49–51 and Luke 24:44: "Therefore also the Wisdom of God said, 'I will send them prophets and apostles, some of whom they will kill and persecute,' so that the blood of all the prophets, shed from the foundation of the world, may be charged against this generation, from the blood of Abel to the blood of Zechariah, who perished between the altar and the sanctuary" (Luke 11:49–51). The reason why this text argues for the Hebrew ordering is that the Hebrew Bible begins with Genesis and ends with Chronicles. Abel is the first martyr (Genesis), while Zechariah is the last (2 Chron. 24:20–22). Jesus also makes reference to the threefold division of the Hebrew Bible in Luke 24:44: "These are my words that I spoke to you while I was still with you, that everything written about me in the Law of Moses and the Prophets and the Psalms must be fulfilled." Jesus's words reflect the common Hebrew ordering even though he mentions "Psalms" as the last division. Sometimes the last division (the Writings) could be referenced according to the most prominent book within it (Psalms).

THE STORY OF SCRIPTURE: A SEVEN-STEP SUMMARY

I will give a seven-step, bare-bones summary of the story in this chapter and then expand upon it considerably in the next.

1. THE FIRST TWO NARRATIVES
(GENESIS THROUGH KINGS)

The divine narration begins with a play-by-play of the drama spanning the creation of all things in Genesis to the arrival of Israel on the brink of God's Land of Promise in Deuteronomy (i.e., covering the Pentateuch). The second installment of the story stretches from Joshua through Kings (i.e., Former Prophets). The play-by-play opens with Israel's entrance into the Promised Land and ends with Israel's exile from the Promised Land. Israel's disobedience makes her like the nations she dispossessed. Therefore, God begins his holy war against the sinful nations in the book of Joshua, but in the end the holy war concludes in Kings with God's judgment against the rebel nation of Israel. The seed of the serpent and its anti-God city "Babel-Babylon" appear to defeat the seed of the woman and its city, Jerusalem. But do they defeat the true seed and the true city?

2. THE PROPHETIC COMMENTARY
(ISAIAH THROUGH THE BOOK OF THE TWELVE)

The voice of the color commentator now comes to the forefront with the first installment of commentary. The prophetic books expound upon the narrative (Isaiah through the so-called Minor Prophets). This commentary highlights how Israel's exile (described in the Former Prophets) comes as a consequence of breaking the covenant with God (i.e., the Mosaic covenant established in the narrative of the Pentateuch). The Prophets also stress a new work of God that will succeed where the old has failed. They foresee a new exodus (note the imagery of exodus drawn from the Pentateuch) and return from exile and a New Jerusalem (images drawn from both the Pentateuch and the Former Prophets). In other words, the real Jerusalem is never defeated. The Jerusalem that falls is just a model of the real thing.

These events will come into being because God will make a new covenant (contrasted with the former covenant) through the coming of the Messiah (imagery drawn from both Pentateuch and Former Prophets concerning the coming King). This Messiah will be the real King and the real seed of the woman. His throne will never be overthrown; his city, the new Jerusalem, will not be leveled to the ground; and the new creation he brings will endure forever.

3. POETIC COMMENTARY

The second installment of color commentary on the narrative comes next in poetic form in the first part of what is often called the Writings. Psalms through Lamentations takes the reader into poetic reflections on the sting of suffering and exile and the renewed hope that can come only with a wise and powerful king like David ruling on David's throne.

4. NARRATIVE THREE (EZRA THROUGH CHRONICLES)

The third installment of narrative then takes the reader through Israel's return from exile and the rebuilding of Jerusalem and the temple. The divine narration skillfully shows that this return from exile pales in comparison to the new exodus and return from exile promised in the Prophets. The narrative then goes through a second telling of Israel's history in Chronicles. Chronicles shifts all the attention to the hope found in the line of David and sets the stage for another return from exile by ending with the decree of Cyrus: Israel will return.

5. NARRATIVES FOUR AND FIVE (GOSPELS AND ACTS)

This decree finds its fulfillment in the Gospels. This fourth installment of the narrative tells the stunning story of how the Word of God took on flesh with the coming of God's Son. Jesus will both proclaim and purchase a new-exodus redemption for God's people as the Lamb of God. This redemption is accomplished through the cross and resurrection of Jesus. Jesus reconstituted the nucleus of the new Israel by calling twelve disciples in the beginning of the Gospels. At the end of the story, he commissions them to bring his purchase of redemption to all the families of the nations. The Gospels close with the promise to empower them to fulfill this mission.

The fifth installment of the narrative in the book of Acts highlights the fulfillment of Jesus's promise of empowerment for mission. Jesus is raised, ascended, and seated on high on David's throne in the heavenly Jerusalem. Jesus leads the disciples to choose a replacement for Judas to bring the number of the disciples back to twelve. The day of Pentecost comes and the Holy Spirit falls upon them. Peter says that Jesus's pouring out of the Spirit is proof that he is ascended and reigning above (Acts 2:33). The disciples are clothed with power from on high so that they can function as Jesus's witnesses, starting in Jerusalem (Acts 1–7), then in Judea and Samaria (Acts 8–12), and then to the ends of the earth (Acts 13–28).

Acts functions in the canon as a new conquest narrative after the pattern of Joshua. This time the conquest of the nations comes by the word of God (the sword of the Spirit), not the physical sword. The disciples do not bring bloodshed upon humanity because their message is that the blood has already been shed for the redemption of the nations. As Jesus suffered rejection and death to accomplish redemption in the Gospels, his disciples suffer similarly in Acts so that this redemption may be applied to the nations by the power of the Holy Spirit.

6. APOSTOLIC COMMENTARY

The third installment of commentary now comes with the apostolic commentary of the Epistles (Paul, James, Peter, John, and Jude). The Epistles interpret the significance of what Jesus accomplished in the Gospels. They comment on the "already and not yet" nature of redemption. In other words, the apostles show that Christ's first coming brought key aspects of redemption to bear that are already on display in the church (forgiveness of sins, the presence and power of the Holy Spirit, etc.). The "not yet" of redemption will come with Christ's second coming from the Jerusalem above, and thus the church eagerly awaits an even greater experience of full redemption from sin (redeemed bodies, new heaven and new earth). The apostles give authoritative guidance as representatives of the risen Christ. They sharpen the focus of the church's mission as she lives in the overlap of the ages and stands in the gap between the first coming and the second coming.

7. NARRATIVE SIX (REVELATION)

This final installment of redemption comes in the final installment of the narrative, in the book of Revelation. The true Trinity (Father, Son, and Holy Spirit) will finally vanquish the false trinity (Satan, Beast, and false prophet). The archetypal anti-God city of Babylon is back, but it will be destroyed by the forces of the true city, the Jerusalem above. Once those forces have been dispatched and the victory over Babylon is complete, then the heavenly city will finally be unveiled. The tree of life found in the beginning of the story in Genesis comes back into the picture in the final chapters of Revelation. All the redeemed will finally see God face-to-face, and there will be no more cursing, crying, or dying. For endless ages in the new heaven and new earth, a new story will be written in which (as C. S. Lewis memorably put it) every chapter is better than the last.

4

THE ROLE OF THE WORD IN THE DRAMA OF SCRIPTURE

> When we read the poem, or see the play or picture or hear the music, it is as though a light were turned on inside us. We say: "Ah! I recognize that! That is something which I obscurely felt to be going on in and about me, but I didn't know what it was and couldn't express it. But now that the artist has made its image—imaged it forth—from me, I can possess and take hold of it and make it my own, and turn it into a source of knowledge and strength."
>
> *Dorothy Sayers*

The last chapter summarized the link between the structure of Scripture and the story of Scripture. This chapter further unpacks the role the word plays in the drama of Scripture. This is perhaps the most important chapter in the book because it is foundational for everything else. I will briefly talk about two vantage points for the story (the view from above and the view from below). Then I will narrate the view from below in ten scenes.

THE WORD IN THE VIEW FROM ABOVE

The view from above sees a Trinitarian God, who was and is and is to come. He is all-powerful and has *no real* rivals. He is "the King of ages, immortal, invisible, the only God" (1 Tim. 1:17). He is "the blessed and only Sovereign, the King of kings and Lord of lords, who alone has immortality, who dwells in unapproachable light, whom no one has ever seen or can see" (1 Tim. 6:15–16).

The view from above sees a God who reigns above the flux and ebb and flow and chaos of creation. No purpose of his could ever be frustrated. No one could ever successfully oppose him or undo what he has planned. There can be no question as to whether his promises will come to pass or whether his agenda will succeed.

What is his unstoppable, overarching agenda? It is a global glory agenda. The King aims to spread the fame of his name so that his creation will be filled with his glory. This sweeping theme helps orient the reader of Scripture to three big-picture questions: *what, how,* and *why.*

Scripture is a story in which (1) God rules (*what* he does) (2) by his word (*how* he does it) (3) for his glory (*why* he does it). All three of these points shine as dazzling aspects of God's unparalleled greatness. A greater King exists than the human mind could even imagine. He is self-existent. He rules over everything that he brought into existence (the *what* of Scripture). This greatest of all kings has a greater weapon than any has ever invented, called the word of God. This word is the means by which God administers his reign (the *how* of Scripture). This great King has a greater cause than any ever conceived: the cause of filling the earth with the knowledge of his glory (the *why* of Scripture).

Notice the role of the word in this drama. Its life-giving power is unparalleled because it brought all into being out of nothing. Its power to kill is also unrivaled. God brings judgment upon humanity through his word. It is often presented in Scripture as a weapon or a sword. This sword is more powerful than a ring of power, an atomic bomb, or any weapon that anyone could invent. The word is the instrument God uses to create the world (2 Pet. 3:5), rule over his world (3:6), and bring final judgment upon the world (3:7).

But there is even more! The word of God has a hinge point that changes everything. Indeed, we could call it the hinge of all history. There comes a point when the great weapon is revealed as a person! In other words, the *how* (the word of God) becomes the *Who* (Jesus as the Word of God incarnate). God administers his rule and reign through the word of God in the Old Testament, and then God's Son comes to reign as the incarnate Word of God that brings God's kingdom to bear in the New Testament (John 1:1; Rev. 19:13).

Jesus will bring the story to a dramatic conclusion with his second coming. The ending is so great that we do not yet have categories to comprehend what it will be like. We have some pictures drawn from our present categories. The Bible says that the earth will be filled with the knowledge of the glory of the Lord as the waters cover the sea (Hab. 2:14). Talk about a thriller! Imagine standing in the middle of the sea. All you see in every direction is water. God wrote a story that will come to its climax when that happens: the filling up of all creation with God's glory. Our joy will be unspeakably great and full of glory!

THE VIEW FROM BELOW IN TEN SCENES: CALL AND FALL NARRATIVES, TWO SEEDS AND TWO CITIES

This view from above is always true because God has no real rivals, but that view is not always clear when one stands beneath the clouds. Conflict makes God's unrivaled reign seem uncertain in this view. Believers must fight the fight of faith. They will walk by faith and not by sight until the faith becomes sight. In what follows, I will narrate the story from this vantage point in ten scenes. It will prominently feature call and fall narratives, as well as two seeds and two cities.

1. ADAM AND EVE

Call Narrative

Remember that the high point of the creation narrative is the *creation* and *commission* of humanity by the word of God. God created all things by his powerful word. He created humanity in his image and then entrusted humanity with a divine calling. This commission was a word of blessing: "And God *blessed* them. And God said to them, 'Be fruitful and multiply and fill the earth and subdue it, and have dominion over the fish of the sea and over the birds of the heavens and over every living thing that moves on the earth'" (Gen. 1:28).

Humanity must multiply so that those made in his image will fill the earth with his reflection. This mission seems to suffer a decisive setback when humanity breaks the word of God's command. A crafty serpent (who we learn later to be Satan—Rev. 20:2) comes into the garden. The thing to stress at this point is that the serpent's strike is aimed at the goodness of *God's word*, not the goodness of God's world.

A war of words begins. Will humanity cling to God's word, or will they succumb to Satan's crafty contradiction of God's word? The original word from God is full of provision (every tree) and protection (lest they die). It is stated positively with only one exception: "You may surely eat of every tree of the garden, but of the tree of the knowledge of good and evil you shall not eat" (Gen. 2:16–17). Satan makes the exception the exclusive thing: "Did God actually say, 'You shall not eat of any tree in the garden'?" (Gen. 3:1).

This story represents Scripture's first example of someone relaying a message from God, both explicitly and implicitly. Eve explicitly "instructs" the serpent concerning God's word, even though in the end she is deceived by the serpent (see the apostolic commentary in 2 Cor. 11:3 and 1 Tim. 2:4). The narrative also implicitly demonstrates that Adam informs Eve about God's word given to him in Genesis 2:16–17. God spoke his word to *the man* (2:16), but Satan goes to the woman. We hear the woman speak for the first time in the attempt to clarify what God has said (Gen. 3:2–3), which she apparently has learned from Adam.

Fall Narrative

The facts of the matter are both clear and tragic. God has entrusted Adam and Eve with a command by his word. Satan contradicts what God has said. Eve's fall narrative consists of three words: "saw," "good," and "took." She *saw* that the tree was *good* for food, delightful to the eyes, and desirable to make one wise, so she *took* of its fruit and ate. She then gave some to her husband, who was with her, and he ate (Gen. 3:6).

Therefore, Adam and Eve fall prey to the serpent's poisonous bite, break God's word, and thus join the ranks of Satan's rebellion instead of crushing it. Conflict becomes a continuous feature of the narrative from this point on. The fall fractures all of creation. We have to first come to grips with the fact that this is a cosmic conflict.

The emergence of the serpent (Gen. 3:1) and the earlier command to guard the garden (Gen. 2:15) allude to a bigger war. One of the angels, Satan, led an uprising against God, along with a third of the angels. God put an end to the rebellion by casting Satan and the fallen angels to earth. Therefore, the cosmic struggle has spilled over onto the earth.

Heaven and earth hang in the balance in this cosmic conflict. Humanity has broken God's word of blessing, and now God's word will break humanity with its word of curse. The King pronounces a curse on everyone involved in this conflict: the serpent, Eve, and Adam. In the midst of the curse, however, God also speaks a word of promise: there will be warfare or enmity.

The Note of Redemption: The Song of the Seed

God will create a division within humanity through warfare. He will cause humanity to divide into two seeds: the serpent's seed and the woman's seed. Judgment will fall on the serpent in a final sense when the woman's seed comes on the scene to crush the serpent.

From this point on, the story is like a musical score waiting for the note of the seed from Genesis 3:15 to sound. An analogy may help at this juncture. Benjamin Zander once gave a lecture on classical music in which he argued that no one is tone deaf. He introduced a piece from the composer Chopin to illustrate his point. Zander played a series of notes: B A G F. He then showed that listeners instinctively know how the next note should sound (i.e., E). But in the piece by Chopin the listener hears false cadences—notes that fail to bring the piece to resolution. Once the note of E sounds, there is resolution. Moving from B to E brings the hearer to a place Zander calls "home." This is the note we have waited for from the composer when the tension within the song is resolved and all is made right.

The fall of Genesis 3 also introduces a "note" of promise in Genesis 3:15. A seed of the woman will come and crush the head of the seed of the serpent. This is the note we are waiting for. The rest of the Bible reads like an audience anxiously listening for that note to be played. People come on the scene in the subsequent narrative that raise our expectations—could this be the one we have been waiting for? This question is answered with a false cadence consisting of a fall narrative as the battle lines are drawn between two seeds and two cities.

2. THE FLOOD OF CORRUPTION AND
THE FLOOD OF JUDGMENT

The Line of Curse

Cain represents the first of many false notes following the fall. Later commentary on the story confirms that he is actually a seed of the serpent (1 John 3:10, 12). Abel offers a sacrifice by faith (Heb. 11:4), but he is not the promised seed, because Cain kills him. God pronounces judgment, and Cain is cast out to be a wanderer on the face of the earth. Cain once again defies the entrusted word that he is to be a wanderer. He becomes a settler and resides in a land east of Eden.

Genesis 4:17–24 is a genealogy for the seed of the serpent, which is really an anti-genealogy. The line of curse consolidates in rebellion against God by building cities. Cain builds a city and names it after his son, Enoch. The genealogy ends with poetry. Poetry is a good created structure that can be turned in a Godward or godless direction. Lamech turns it in a godless direction as he glories in his anti-God rebellion. As Stephen Dempster says, "It begins with Cain, the brother-killer, and ends with the child-killer, Lamech, the seventh from Adam."[1] The downward spiral of sin that starts with an attempt to deny murder (Cain) now descends into celebrating murder (Lamech). The author of Genesis also makes reference to the building of a city, which will receive even more emphasis in Genesis 11.

The Line of Blessing

But the line of promise is still alive and well. Adam and Eve have another son, named Seth. He is a seed that replaces Abel so that the seed of the woman will not be extinct. Seth continues the line of promise with a son named Enosh. The narrator tells us that people begin to "call upon the name of the Lord" (Gen. 4:26). With this encouraging note, the narrator now introduces the reader to the line of promise from Adam to Noah. Enoch, the seventh in the line from Adam, is significant because God walks with him and God takes him (Gen. 5:24). The normal pattern of the genealogy mentions someone's birth and death, but Enoch's lack of death interrupts the structured symmetry

---

[1]Stephen G. Dempster, *Dominion and Dynasty: A Biblical Theology of the Hebrew Bible*, New Studies in Biblical Theology (Downers Grove, IL: InterVarsity, 2003), 70.

of the genealogy. Intimacy with the Lord marks this line of promise. Noah has a name that sounds like the word for "rest," because he is cast as a savior providing rest from the curse.

The Angelic Fall

The fall narrative of Genesis 6 echoes back to Genesis 3 and then back further to Genesis 1. First, there is an echo of Genesis 3 in that the same three terms from Genesis 3:6 appear again in Genesis 6:2 (fig. 2).

Figure 2. Echoes of Genesis 3 in Genesis 6

Genesis 3:6	Genesis 6:2
Eve "*saw*" that the tree was "*good*" (*beautiful*) for food so she "*took*" its fruit and ate.	The sons of God "*saw*" that the daughters of men were "*attractive*" (*beautiful/good*) so they "*took*" as their wives any they chose.

Then the narrator also takes us back full circle to Genesis 1 to show that God's creation has gone from good to corrupt (fig. 3).

Figure 3. Echoes of Genesis 1 in Genesis 6

Genesis 1:31	Genesis 6:12
"*God saw* everything that he had made, *and behold*, it was very *good*."	"*God saw* the earth, *and behold*, it was *corrupt*."

The seed of the serpent has multiplied on the earth. Cain's initial spark of violence has grown to a full-blown wildfire of violence so that "the earth was filled with violence" (Gen. 6:11), not the image of God's glory. God will work to wipe the slate clean of this corruption and start over with Noah as a new Adam.

Noah's Call and Fall Narrative

Noah's call narrative comes in Genesis 6:8–9:17. God brings judgment upon the earth through the flood, but he preserves Noah and his family. The Lord reestablishes the covenant with creation and gives Noah a calling of blessing. He blesses Noah, saying, "Be fruitful and multiply and fill the earth" (Gen. 9:1). This time the people may eat not only the plants, but also the animals (9:2–3). Fallen humanity still possesses the image of God (9:6), and thus the original calling to be fruitful and multiply remains (9:7). God also puts his weapon away in the clouds (his "bow") and promises not to destroy the earth with water ever again (9:8–17).

Noah, the new Adam, has a fall narrative as well. The narrator takes us back to Genesis 3. Noah plants a vineyard and then sins with the fruit of the vine as Adam sinned with the fruit of the tree: "[Noah] drank of the wine and became drunk and lay uncovered in his tent" (Gen. 9:21). The fall is once again followed by a curse, this time pronounced on only one of Noah's descendants.

Blessing and Curse for Noah's Sons

The word "saw" speaks to another problem as one of Noah's sons, Ham, "saw the nakedness of his father." Noah's other two sons, Shem and Japheth, conceal their father's nakedness without seeing it by walking backward and then covering Noah with a garment. Noah realizes what Ham has done to him and pronounces a curse directly (and somewhat surprisingly) not upon Ham, but upon Canaan (Ham's son). The narrator has prepared the reader for this connection all along because he has insisted that Ham be known as the father of Canaan (Gen. 9:18, 22). Noah also declares a blessing upon Shem and Japheth. Noah declares that the Lord is blessed. The blessing comes to Shem because the Lord is described as the God of Shem. Canaan will be Shem's servant, and even Japheth will dwell in the tents of Shem (9:25–27).

The reader does not have to wait long to find out about Canaan and the Canaanites because the narrator describes the family tree in Genesis 10:15–20. This curse upon Canaan and the blessing upon Shem set up the reader for the coming struggle over the Land of Promise. The land is currently occupied by the Canaanites, but it belongs to the Lord, and he will give it to the Israelites. The segmented genealogy of Japheth (10:2–5), Ham (10:6–20), and Shem (10:21–31) helps the reader see the descendants of Noah, while Genesis 11:10–32 identifies the line of promise stretching from Shem to Abram. The tower of Babel (11:1–9) occupies a pivotal place between these two texts (Genesis 10 and 11:10–32). Why?

3. THE FALSE CITY

Beginning in Genesis 11, the satanic seed joins together to build a city. This is not the first city we have seen in the narrative. Cain also has built a city back in Genesis 6:17. Even more emphasis is given to the story of the city in Genesis 11. This city is an archetypal anti-God city. It is a Godless city because it represents a consolidated rebellion against the high King of heaven and earth. The inhabitants of Babel-Babylon try to make a name for themselves by building a tower that will stretch into the heavens. The story has strong echoes back to the fall of Genesis 3. The arrogance of human pride in the garden led Adam and Eve to reach out to lay hold of supremacy on earth. The arrogance of the sin of Babel-Babylon is the attempt to gain control of not only the earth, but heaven as well.

This city is archetypal because the human pride and hubris that energize the activities of the city will show up again and again through-out the narrative. Thus, this city casts a long shadow over the rest of the Bible as the first of many cities that embody the same anti-God function. Therefore, the narrator introduces the city as Babel, which is the same name as the place that shows up so prominently in the rest of the Old Testament as Babylon. Thus, T. D. Alexander recommends calling the place Babel-Babylon to avoid missing the connection. Some translations even render the name of the city as "Babylon" (HCSB, rightly in my opinion).

The Lord brings a judgment upon this city and confuses the languages so that the seed of the serpent will be forced to separate into distinct groups instead of joining together in rebellion against God and the seed of the woman.

4. ABRAHAM

Abram's Call and Fall Narrative

The rest of Genesis 11 introduces the reader to the family of Shem, which culminates in Terah and his son, Abram. They are going to the land of Canaan, but along the way they come to Haran and settle there. Terah dies in Haran, and then in Genesis 12 God calls Abram to go to Canaan. In contrast to the city of Genesis 11 in which the inhabitants try to make a name for themselves, God himself is going to make Abram's name great. In contrast to the five uses of curse up to this point, Genesis 12:2–3 uses the word "bless" five times as a reversal of the curse. Through Abram, all the families of the earth shall be blessed (12:3).

The next story narrates Abram's fall (Gen. 12:10–20). Failing to trust the promise of protection that God has just given, he takes matters into his own hands and puts the seed promise in jeopardy by letting his wife, Sarai, be taken into Pharaoh's harem. God protects the seed promise by bringing plagues upon Pharaoh's house (as God will do again in Exodus).

Seeking the True City to Come

It is important that Abram is a sojourner throughout the narrative and never a settler. That is, Abram does not build a city and does not own any part of the Promised Land—with the magnificent exception of a burial plot. The narrative slows down considerably to describe the purchase of this burial plot, showing Abraham's faith (Genesis 23). Hebrews tells us very clearly that Abraham was not looking for an earthly city that he would build. He was looking for a heavenly city, whose builder and maker is God (Heb. 11:10, 16).

The rest of Genesis documents how the line of promise moves from Abraham to his miracle son, Isaac, and then to Isaac's son Jacob. Jacob's twelve children become the twelve tribes of Israel. God narrows the line of promise to one of these tribes: the tribe of Judah.

5. THE LINE OF JUDAH

Judah's Fall Narrative

Genesis 38 with its fall narrative of Judah makes plain that Judah is not the promised one. Judah fails to give Tamar one of his sons after the first two die while married to her. Tamar resorts to deceit. She tricks Judah into thinking that she is a prostitute. He sleeps with her and (unknowingly) provides a replacement seed for the line of promise. When Tamar reveals that Judah has actually slept with her, he confesses that she is more righteous than he (38:26). This means that Tamar actually believes more in the seed promise than does Judah. God overcomes this threat to the seed promise. Judah's son Perez is the seed that God appoints to carry on the line of promise (Ruth 4:18–22; Matt. 1:3; Luke 3:33).

The Lion King of the Line of Judah

Genesis 48–49 offers the most sustained prophetic message in the book of Genesis. Jacob first blesses Joseph's two sons (48:15–20) and his own twelve sons (49:1–27). The author of Hebrews once again highlights the faith of Jacob in this prophetic stewarding and heralding: "By faith Jacob, when dying, blessed each of the sons of Joseph, bowing in worship over the head of his staff" (Heb. 11:21). Jacob demonstrates faith in not only the Abrahamic promise of Genesis 12, but also the prior promise of Genesis 3:15 because Judah will have his hand on the "neck of his enemies" (Gen. 49:8).

The time frame of this prophecy is set "at the end of the days." This text has many similarities with Numbers 24. Old Testament scholar John Sailhamer describes the parallels between Genesis 49, Numbers 24, and Deuteronomy 31:

> In each of the three segments, the central narrative figure (Jacob, Balaam, Moses) calls an audience together (imperative: Gen. 49:1; Num. 24:14; Deut. 31:28) and proclaims (cohortative: Gen. 49:1; Num. 24:14; Deut. 31:28) what will happen (Gen. 49:1; Num. 24:14; Deut. 31:29) in "the end of days" (Gen. 49:1; Num. 24:14; Deut. 31:29).[2]

There are similarities in grammatical structure (imperative and cohortative), vocabulary (the phrase "in the days to come"), and a messianic focus.

Structure and Vocabulary

> Then Jacob summoned his sons and said, "Assemble [*imperative*] yourselves that I may tell [*cohortative*] you what will befall you *in the days to come*." (Gen. 49:1, NASB)

---

[2] John H. Sailhamer, *The Pentateuch as Narrative* (Grand Rapids: Zondervan, 1992), 36. He sets the stage for this evidence by saying, "At three macrostructural junctures in the Pentateuch, the author has spliced a major poetic discourse onto the end of a large unit of narrative (Ge 49; Nu 24; Dt 31). A close look at the material lying between and connecting the narrative and poetic sections reveals the presence of a homogeneous compositional stratum. It is most noticeably marked by the recurrence of the same terminology and narrative motifs." Ibid. Sailhamer stresses that the person responsible for shaping the final form of the Pentateuch inserted these seams. This claim is difficult to prove, and it is possible that Moses himself wrote them.

And now, behold, I am going to my people; come [*imperative*], *and* I will advise [*cohortative*] you what this people will do to your people *in the days to come*. (Num. 24:14, NASB)

Messianic Focus: The Lion King

> Judah, your brothers shall praise you;
> Your hand shall be on the neck of your enemies;
> Your father's sons shall bow down to you.
> Judah is a lion's whelp;
> From the prey, my son, you have gone up.
> He couches, he lies down as a lion,
> And as a lion, who dares rouse him up?
> The scepter shall not depart from Judah,
> Nor the ruler's staff from between his feet,
> Until Shiloh comes,
> And to him shall be the obedience of the peoples.
>   (Gen. 49:8–10, NASB)

> He couches, he lies down as a lion,
> And as a lion, who dares rouse him?
> Blessed is everyone who blesses you,
> And cursed is everyone who curses you. (Num. 24:9, NASB)

> I see him, but not now;
> I behold him, but not near;
> A star shall come forth from Jacob,
> A scepter shall rise from Israel,
> And shall crush through the forehead of Moab,
> And tear down all the sons of Sheth. (Num. 24:17, NASB)

The final book of the Bible affirms that these prophecies refer to Jesus, "the Lion of the tribe of Judah" (Rev. 5:5). The reader does not see Jesus on the scene yet, however. Attention turns to the people of Israel and many more call and fall narratives.

6. ISRAEL BEFORE THE MONARCHY

Israel's Call

The Lord calls Moses to deliver his people from Egypt. God makes a covenant with Israel. Israel is called to be a new Adam that will bring blessing to the nations. Israel starts with faith, but falls into unbelief. The author of the Pentateuch calls attention to the belief/unbelief paradigm by using a similar structure.

The Pentateuch stresses the crucial importance of faith. In particular there are five texts (Gen. 15:6; Ex. 4:31; 14:31; Num. 14:11; 20:12) that use the faith terminology and share an ordered sequence of problem, promise, sign, and faith.[3]

Genesis 15:6

> Problem: Abram is childless (15:2–3).
> Promise: A son from Abram's own body will be heir (15:4).
> Sign: Abram's seed will be as numerous as the stars (15:5).
> Faith: Abram believes God and it is reckoned as righteousness (15:6).

Exodus 4:31

> Problem: Moses is worried the people won't believe him (4:1).
> Promise: God promises that the people will believe the signs (4:8).
> Sign: The staff becomes a snake; the hand becomes leprous (4:8).
> Faith: The Israelites believed (4:31).

Exodus 14:31

> Problem: The Egyptian army is at the heels of the Israelites (14:1–12).
> Promise: The Lord will fight for the Israelites (14:13).
> Sign: The Red Sea is parted with the staff (14:16, 21).
> Faith: "The people feared the LORD, and they believed in the LORD and in His servant Moses" (14:31).

Abraham has faith, the Israelites in Egypt have faith, and the people after the exodus have faith before the law is given. Exodus 32 becomes a turning point.

Israel's Fall

Israel receives a divine calling, but then falls in unbelief. Israel's fall narrative in Exodus 32 focuses on her idolatry and the consequences of breaking the covenant. Israel's "redemption" from Egypt does nothing

---

[3] I owe this pattern to my former colleague, Old Testament scholar Michael B. Shepherd. He pointed to the work of Hans-Christoph Schmitt, "Redaktion des Pentateuch im Geiste der Prophetie," *Vetus Testamentum* 32 (1982): 170–89.

to deal with her stiff-necked nature. The rest of the Pentateuch keeps referencing how the people are stiff-necked, rebellious, and unbelieving. This lack of faith continues in two prominent examples.

Numbers 14:11

Problem: People are grumbling against their leaders (14:1–4).
Promise: The Lord will bring them into the land (14:6–9).
Sign: The Lord has performed signs among them (14:11).
Faith: the people fail to believe in the Lord and all his signs (14:11).

Numbers 20:12

Problem: People gather against leaders because of a lack of water
   (20:2–5).
Promise: Moses will bring water from the rock (20:7–8).
Sign: Moses strikes the rock with his staff (20:11).
Faith: Moses and Aaron did not believe (20:12).

The first generation fails to enter the Promised Land because of unbelief. God responds in judgment of their unbelief and rebellion and forces them to wander in the wilderness until all of them die. As noted above in Numbers 20, even Moses and Aaron fail to believe, and they die outside of the Promised Land.

Joshua's Call and Fall

Joshua looks like the leader that will lead the people into the Promised Land. God calls and commissions him (Josh. 1:1–9). God promises that as he was with Moses, so he will be with Joshua (1:5). Joshua leads Israel into the Promised Land. The book even records that the promises of God are fulfilled (Josh. 21:43–45). Joshua's fall narrative, however, comes in Joshua 9 as he and the rest of Israel's leaders fall to the "craftiness" of the Gibeonites, just as Adam and Eve fell to the craftiness of the serpent.[4]

---

[4] I owe this insight to Brian Verrett, a student and friend.

The Call and Fall of the Judges

The refrain of Judges highlights the fact that there is no king in Israel, and therefore everyone does what was right in his own eyes. The Lord raises up a series of judges. Samson is the most well known of the judges. He has an extended birth-and-call narrative and an even lengthier fall narrative. The story of Samson is not only a painful narrative of an individual's failure; it is a mirror image of Israel's failure. Stephen Dempster summarizes it well:

> Samson, the supernaturally born Israelite, was set apart as a Nazirite with a distinctive vocation. He constantly breaks his religious vows, is enamoured of Philistine women, loses his identity and physical strength through these encounters, becomes a slave and has his eyes gouged out by the enemy. He represents his own people, who had a supernatural origin, were set apart from among the nations with a distinctive vocation, broke their vows and were enamoured of foreign idols, until finally they lost their identity and spiritual power and became the blind slaves of their oppressors in exile.[5]

Then the narrative takes us to Samuel through Kings. The Lord brings about a series of reversals (anticipated by Hannah's song). The wicked priesthood of Eli falls to the priesthood of young Samuel. Then the wicked king Saul falls to the young David. However, neither of them will play the part of the faithful Priest and King. They are both pictures of the Priest and King to come, as the book of Samuel makes clear.

7. ISRAEL UNDER THE MONARCHY

David's Call and Rise: The True King?

David's rise takes place after Saul's fall. Saul had a somewhat precocious beginning and then quickly crashed and burned. The Spirit of God rushed upon Saul and he prophesied (1 Samuel 10), and then the Spirit of the Lord rushed upon him again as he led Israel against the Ammonites (1 Samuel 11). The Ammonites loom large in the narrative of Samuel. The king of the Ammonites is an ominous figure because

---

[5] Dempster, *Dominion and Dynasty*, 132.

his name, Nahash, is the Hebrew word for "serpent." Saul defeats the serpent king, but any hopes that Saul is the Messiah are quickly dashed when he makes an unlawful sacrifice, thus rejecting the word of the Lord, and the Lord rejects him as king (1 Samuel 13).

David is anointed as king in 1 Samuel 16. The next chapter features David crushing the skull of a Philistine giant and thus evoking the imagery of Genesis 3:15. David's rise as king culminates in his defeat of the king of the Ammonites, named as the son of Nahash. The parallels are striking in that both Saul and David conquer the Ammonite "serpent."[6]

> 1 Samuel 11: Saul conquers Nahash (serpent).
> 2 Samuel 10: David conquers the seed (son) of Nahash (serpent).

David's rise to power throughout Samuel is an amazing story with many feats of faith, not least of which involves crushing and cutting off the head of a Philistine giant (1 Samuel 17). The reader has begun to wonder, "Is this the one we have been waiting for?"

The Rise of Jerusalem: The True City?

The ark of the covenant travels with the people of God and comes to a temporary dwelling place at Shiloh. At this point in the narrative, however, there is no city that becomes the centralized hope as the city of God. Hopes concerning David rise even higher when the ark of God comes to Jerusalem, the city of David (2 Samuel 6). It even appears as if this city will be the permanent resting place of the ark and God's presence. Though David states his desire to build a house for God, God instead promises that he is going to build David a house (2 Samuel 7). David's son is going to build the house and will have an everlasting kingdom.

David's Fall Narrative

Second Samuel 11 will decisively dash any hope that David is the true King. David's reign of righteousness turns into a reign of terror. The author wants to take us back to Genesis 3, but we arrive at Genesis

---

[6] I owe this insight as well to my former student Brian Verrett.

3:6, not Genesis 3:15. David is cast here not as the messianic seed, but as Eve, the sinner. The wrong note sounds loud and clear. David's fall brings disastrous consequences in the rest of 2 Samuel. Notice that this fall narrative features three words coming together and links Genesis 3, 6, and 2 Samuel 11:

- The woman "saw" that the tree was "good" (or "beautiful") for food . . . and she "took" of its fruit (Gen. 3:6). Judgment followed as Adam and Eve were cast out of the garden.
- The sons of God "saw" that the daughters of man were "attractive" (or "beautiful"). And they "took" as their wives any they chose (Gen. 6:2). Judgment follows as God brings a flood that destroys the earth with water.
- David "saw" from the roof a woman bathing; and she was very "beautiful." So David sent his messengers and "took" her (2 Sam. 11:2–4). We know based on the previous two examples that judgment is not far behind.

Judgment does not fall right away. David tries to hide his sin by getting Bathsheba's husband, Uriah, to come home so that they will sleep together, but Uriah is too righteous. His thoughts are set on his fellow brothers who are in harm's way on the battlefield. David has Uriah killed by sending a letter to the general and telling him to put Uriah on the front lines, where he is struck down and killed.

Yet all the while David refuses to own up to his sin. He refuses to call evil what God calls evil. A more literal translation will help us see the shocking word play. The king is supposed to adopt and enforce God's laws. Instead David says, "Don't let this thing be evil in your eyes" (2 Sam. 11:25, AT). The narrator says, "The thing that David had done was evil in Yahweh's eyes" (11:27, AT).

The prophet Nathan comes and God convicts David of his sin. David confesses, saying, "I have sinned" (2 Sam. 12:13). One is also struck by the fact that the narrator puts Saul's sin and David's sin in a similar framework, even though in substance they are quite different.

Rejecting or Despising the Word of the Lord

Saul: "Because you have rejected the word of the LORD, he has also rejected you from being king" (1 Sam. 15:30).

David: "Why have you despised the word of the LORD by doing evil in
His sight? . . . because you have despised me" (2 Sam. 12:9–10, NASB).

Confession of Sin

Saul: "I have sinned" (1 Sam. 15:24).
David: "I have sinned" (2 Sam. 12:13).

Difference of Pardon

Saul: "Now, therefore, please pardon my sin" (1 Sam. 15:25).
David: "The LORD also has put away your sin" (2 Sam. 12:13).

After seeing all the parallels, one wonders why only David's sin is
pardoned. Saul's kingdom was torn from him, but David continues as
king. Why?

Some assume that David's repentance is the reason why David is
forgiven. Certainly David's repentance is real, and there is no reason to
assume the authenticity of Saul's repentance. One cannot read Psalm 51
without feeling the depths of David's sorrow over his sin. But Paul tells
us that repentance is a gift (2 Tim. 2:24–26). This text assumes David's
repentance, but the narrative does not stress David's repentance. We
must look for an answer in the flow of the narrative.

It seems that a better understanding for why David is not removed from his kingly duties is that God made a covenant with him
(2 Samuel 7), and God does not break his promises! In other words,
David remains king because 2 Samuel 7 comes before 2 Samuel 11. The
story stresses God's faithfulness to his word, not David's faithfulness in
repenting.[7] Where is the royal son of David portrayed in 2 Samuel 7?

Solomon's Call and Fall

Solomon looks like the son of David who will fulfill the prophecy of
2 Samuel 7. He is humble and prays for wisdom (1 Kings 3:5–15). His
wisdom is on display in the next story (3:16–28). He has many officials, and Israel flourishes like the sand of the sea (1 Kings 4:20). His
kingdom spreads far (4:21), and reports of his wisdom spread even
wider (4:34). Solomon hears from the Lord and obediently builds the

---

[7] Once more I wish to thank my student and friend Brian Verrett. He made many excellent connections
in the Samuel narrative that helped me in this section.

temple (1 Kings 5–7). The ark comes into the temple (1 Kings 8). The Lord appears to Solomon again and answers his prayer (1 Kings 9). The Davidic promises are reaffirmed (1 Kings 9). The nations come to Israel as exemplified by the Queen of Sheba (1 Kings 10). Solomon is like the new Adam figure that will fulfill Adam's commission.

However, Solomon also has a fall narrative because he loves foreign wives and his heart turns away from God (1 Kings 11:1–8). The Lord brings judgment upon Solomon and promises to tear the kingdom from him. The kingdom divides in 1 Kings 12.

The Fall of Jerusalem

Jerusalem finally falls around 586 BC. Shockingly, it looks as though the false city has defeated the true city. Babylon, the city of the serpent, reemerges in the narrative and conquers the city of God (2 Kings 24–25). This defeat of the city of God is only a symbolic defeat. T. D. Alexander summarizes this history very clearly and crisply:

> When we read quickly through the continuous narrative that flows from Genesis to Kings we discover that in the time of King David, about 1000 BC, the footstool of God's throne, the ark of the covenant, is brought to Jerusalem. With this a special relationship is established between God and the city of Jerusalem. Jerusalem becomes the capital of God's kingdom on earth. In due course Jerusalem's status as God's special city is enhanced when Solomon builds a magnificent temple or divine palace. Although these historic events are clearly linked to God's creation plan, they are not perceived as being the fulfilment of all that God intended. They merely anticipate something greater to come in the future. As the book of Isaiah reveals, the less than perfect Old Testament Jerusalem will in the future be replaced by a radically-transformed, new Jerusalem.[8]

Ezra and Nehemiah show that the return of the Jews under Cyrus and the rebuilding of the temple fall short of the glorious return promised in the Prophets. Chronicles takes the reader back through the history of Israel with a focus on the Davidic line and ends with the call of Cyrus to return. The Gospels answer that call for a new return

---

[8]T. D. Alexander, *Genesis*, Biblical Theology for Christian Proclamation (Nashville: B&H, forthcoming).

from exile in the person of Jesus, the Son of God, the *amen* of all of God's promises.

8. THE TRUE KING

Jesus's Call Narrative

Jesus's birth is unlike any other birth in the history of the universe in that Jesus is born of a virgin (Luke 1:27). The power of the Spirit over-shadows Mary so that Jesus is conceived by the Holy Spirit, not male sperm. This miraculous conception highlights the uniqueness of Jesus in terms of what he will do (save his people from their sins—Matt. 1:23) and who he is (Immanuel: God with us—Matt. 1:25).

Luke links the birth of Jesus with his forerunner (John the Baptist). John was born to a barren woman (Luke 1:7), but Jesus is born to a virgin (1:27). An angel visited John's parents and said he would be great as one who prepares people for the Lord (1:15–17), but the same angel visits Jesus's parents and says that he will be great as Son of the Most High, whose kingdom will never end (1:32–33).

In the Gospel of Luke, Elizabeth finds great joy in being with Mary because she recognizes that Mary's child is none other than her Lord (Luke 1:41–44). Jesus is the "Savior, who is Christ the Lord" (Luke 2:11). Simeon is looking for "the Lord's Christ" (2:26), and he recognizes by the Spirit that Jesus is the Lord's Christ so that he can say, "my eyes have seen your salvation" (2:30).

Matthew's genealogy shows that Jesus is the son of Abraham and David. Luke traces Jesus's genealogy all the way back to Adam, the son of God. John traces Jesus's genealogy all the way back to his lineage to his heavenly Father. Jesus was the divine Word present in the beginning by whom all things were made.

No Fall Narrative: This Is the One We Have Waited For!

All of the Synoptic Gospels record what transpired at Jesus's baptism and temptation. They highlight that the Spirit came upon Jesus at his baptism (Matt. 3:16; Mark 1:10; Luke 3:22), and the voice of God the Father affirmed that Jesus is his beloved Son, in whom he is well pleased (Matt. 3:17; Mark 1:11; Luke 3:22). The Spirit then thrusts him into the wilderness in order to face the Devil and his temptations (Matt. 4:1;

Mark 1:11; Luke 4:1). The wilderness theme sounds off strongly here because Jesus is the new Israel. He is in the wilderness for forty days just as Israel was in the wilderness for forty years. His facing Satan as the tempter echoes the fact that Jesus is also the new Adam who must succeed where the first Adam failed.

Jesus overcomes all of Satan's temptations by citing Scripture as the authority for obeying God's word. Jesus even corrects Satan's Scripture twisting (Matt. 4:5–7; Luke 4:9–12). He quotes the very lesson that Moses said Israel should have learned in the wilderness (Deut. 8:4), but failed to take to heart: "Man does not live by bread alone" (Matt. 4:4a; Luke 4:4), "but by every word that comes from the mouth of God" (Matt. 4:4b). In fact, Moses said that what Israel experienced was God testing them to see if they would obey his commandments (Deut. 8:3). Jesus overcomes Satan's temptation and passes the test that God gave to Israel in the wilderness.

The Call of the Twelve

Jesus reconstitutes the nucleus of the new Israel by calling twelve disciples in the beginning of the Gospels. At the end of the story, he now commissions them to bring his purchase of redemption to all the families of the nations. The Gospels close with the promise to empower his disciples to fulfill this mission.

The Cross, Resurrection, and Ascension

Jesus's death, resurrection, and ascension represent the hinge of the whole story. All of the promises are blood-bought at the cross and find their *yes* of fulfillment in him. He defeats sin on the cross. He crushes death itself when he emerges from the grave. The victorious King ascends on high. In the books of Luke and Acts, the ascension of Jesus is the highest peak. Everything in Luke moves toward the ascension, and everything in Acts flows from the ascension.[9]

---

[9] Craig Blomberg postulates a chiasm for all of Luke-Acts that has the ascension at the center (Luke 24:1–53; Acts 1:1–11). This structural proposal would lend further support to my reading. See the overview in Craig L. Blomberg, *Jesus and the Gospels: An Introduction and Survey*, 2nd ed. (Nashville: B&H, 2009), 159–76.

9. THE TRUE CONQUEST

Acts

Jesus, the true King, is seated on the true throne of David in the true city, the heavenly Jerusalem. He empowers the Twelve by clothing them with power from on high. The day of Pentecost comes and the Holy Spirit falls upon them. Peter says that Jesus's pouring out of the Spirit is proof that he is ascended and reigning above (Acts 2:33). As noted in the last chapter, Acts is a new conquest narrative after the pattern of Joshua. The conquest extends from Jerusalem to Samaria (Acts 1–12). The call narrative of Saul (Acts 9) provides the impetus for the spread of the gospel to the ends of the earth (Acts 13–28).

Commentary on the Conquest: The Epistles

The apostolic commentary of the Epistles (Paul, James, Peter, John, and Jude) unpack the "already and not yet" nature of redemption. They highlight that Christ's first coming brought key aspects of redemption to bear that are already on display in the church. They also testify that the return of the King will bring the rest of redemption to fruition. They sharpen the focus of the church's mission as she lives in the overlap of the ages and stands in the gap between the first and the second comings.

10. THE RETURN OF THE KING AND THE FINAL CONQUEST

The Wrath of the Lamb

Revelation highlights the momentous victory of the Trinity (Father, Son, and Holy Spirit) as God decisively vanquishes the false trinity (Satan, Beast, and false prophet). Jesus's full glorious strength will be on display at the final judgment. He alone is worthy to open the scroll (Revelation 5). The seals and the bowls bring initial judgments as God's wrath is poured out upon the earth. The Bible calls this the wrath of the Lamb.

> Then the kings of the earth and the great ones and the generals and
> the rich and the powerful, and everyone, slave and free, hid them-
> selves in the caves and among the rocks of the mountains, calling to

the mountains and rocks, "Fall on us and hide us from the face of him who is seated on the throne, and from the wrath of the Lamb, for the great day of their wrath has come, and who can stand?" (Rev. 6:15–17)

The Resistance of Babylon

The archetypal anti-God city, Babylon, is back as part of a consolidated rebellion against the true city of God. The whole world hands over its power to the Beast, but God sovereignly reigns supreme over all of this rebellion. "God has put it into their hearts to carry out his purpose by being of one mind and handing over their royal power to the beast, until the words of God are fulfilled" (Rev. 17:17).

The Lamb Will Conquer

They will make war on the Lamb, but the outcome is certain: "The Lamb will conquer them, for he is Lord of lords and King of kings, and those with him are called and chosen and faithful" (Rev. 17:14). Babylon's fall is certain (Revelation 18). The Jerusalem above will triumph over Babylon. This victory is won with the Word as God's powerful weapon. This powerful weapon is Jesus. He "is clothed in a robe dipped in blood, and *the name by which he is called is the Word of God*" (Rev. 19:13). He will crush the enemies of God. He has the royal scepter like a rod of iron. He has the sharp sword of the word that comes "from his mouth." He will "tread the winepress of the fury of the wrath of God the Almighty" (19:15). He vanquishes the Beast and the false prophet and throws them into the lake of fire (19:20).

The nations deceived by Satan make one last-ditch effort at battle and try to siege the "beloved city," but fire falls from heaven and consumes them. Satan joins the other two members of the false trinity in the eternal torment of the lake of fire (Rev. 20:7–10). Jesus is the "bright morning star" that crushes all the enemies of God, as Numbers 24 foresaw (Rev. 22:16).

Earth and sky now pass away, and even death and hades are thrown into the lake of fire, along with anyone not found in the book of life (Rev. 20:11–15), which is elsewhere called the *Lamb's* book of life (Rev. 13:8; 21:27). It is finally time for the heavenly city to come in a glorious unveiling (Rev. 21:2, 9–27). The tree of life found in the beginning of the story in Genesis comes back into the picture at the end (Rev. 22:1–2). All the redeemed will finally see God face-to-face, and there will be no more cursing, crying, dying, or darkness (22:3–6).

CONCLUSION: BACK TO THE FUTURE

My favorite analogy for this reality comes from the movie *Back to the Future* 2. The villain (Biff—what a great name for a villain!) goes "back" to the future and finds a sports almanac. He becomes very wealthy betting on all the games because he knows all of the outcomes. When I was watching that movie as a kid, I thought he would be a major moron if he knew who was going to win and then tried to change his bet or started sweating when a game came down to the wire. He would be an idiot to change a bet.

But then it dawned on me. I have been an idiot more times than I care to count. I have the almanac in my hands! The Bible cuts through the fog of my doubts and confusion and reminds me of the clear view from above: God rules and reigns. The conflict and the casualties are real in the view from below. God sees all that we see, but he also sees more. Hearing his voice is the solution to cynicism. C. S. Lewis gives the solution:

> What is concrete but immaterial can be kept in view only by painful effort.[10]

> The real problem of the Christian life comes where people do not usually look for it. It comes the very moment you wake up each morning. All your wishes and hopes [and hurts and hates!] for the day rush at you like wild animals. And the first job each morning consists in shoving them all back; in listening to that other voice, taking that other point of view, letting that other larger, stronger, quieter life come flowing in. And so on, all day. . . .
>
> We can only do it for moments at first. But from those moments the new sort of life will be spreading through our system because now we are letting Him work at the right part of us.[11]

---

[10] C. S. Lewis, *Letters to Malcolm: Chiefly on Prayer* (New York: Harcourt, 1963), 114.
[11] C. S. Lewis, *Mere Christianity* (San Francisco: Harper & Row, 1980), 168–69.

It doesn't matter what the pain is or how much it hurts—it does not change the fact that we know the future. We have to shove all of our wild thoughts back and listen to the true voice of God's word. If we know the outcome, we would be fools to throw in the towel. We live in the gap between what we see in the word and what we see in the world. That calls for faith as we look and wait for all that God has promised. The hymn "It Is Well with My Soul," penned by Horatio Spafford, ends with a rousing confession that faith will one day be sight.

> And Lord, haste the day when my faith shall be sight,
> The clouds be rolled back as a scroll;
> The trump shall resound, and the Lord shall descend,
> Even so, it is well with my soul.

5

PARADIGM SHIFTS
OF STEWARDSHIP

Christ's glorious kingdom and the struggles of the unseen
world of spiritual reality must be as real and urgent to our
children and to us as the stories gossiped about at our family
reunions. The protagonists in the Bible narratives must be as
accessible to our minds and hearts as Grandma, Sister Sue,
and Uncle Bill.

Tedd Tripp

The previous chapter stressed that God will bring resolution to the
strained song of creation by bringing about a new creation through the
coming of the promised King and seed of the woman. The anticipated
note occurs in two comings of the King. He comes once as the very
incarnation of the Word of God (John 1:1) and then comes again as the
conquering One who is called "the Word of God" (Rev. 19:13).

God brings this work of redemption not through Jesus alone, but
through many stewards and heralds of his word over the course of
many years. The same word of God that brought the first creation into
existence will also bring the new creation into being. The word is the
same, but the process is different. This new creation does not come all
at once like the first creation. There is a period in which God entrusts
his life giving to many different stewards at many different times. They
declare the coming Son and his kingdom "at many times and in many
ways" (Heb. 1:1). This chapter will take a fresh look at this period of
the ministry of the word and the paradigm shifts of stewardship that
take place as the story progresses.

THE STEWARD PARADIGM

The Bible opens with a dazzling display of the life-giving power of the word of God. He said, "let there be" and as a result "it was so." God then called people to steward that life-giving word. This pattern is what I call the stewardship paradigm of Scripture. God at times speaks his word directly, but at other times he entrusts his word to others. These servants of the word are called to steward and herald the word.

One could also speak of the things that do not change concerning stewardship of the word by looking at the common denominator of stewardship. God reveals something to someone who is then called to deliver that *same* message to others. The following diagram is a pictorial representation of this process.

$$\text{God} \quad \rightarrow \quad \text{Servant of the word} \quad \rightarrow \quad \text{Audience}$$
$$\text{Message} \qquad\qquad\qquad \text{Same message}$$

PARADIGM SHIFTS IN THE STEWARDSHIP PATTERN

Stewardship of the word undergoes two major changes throughout the story. First, the entrusted message takes on a changing shape throughout redemptive history. Think of just some of the various descriptions: "the word of the Lord," "the law of God," "the decree," "the gospel of the kingdom," "the whole counsel of God," "Christ crucified," "sound doctrine," "the good deposit," "the apostles' teaching," "the faith once for all delivered to the saints." The description can be as simple as "the word" (2 Tim. 4:2).

Second, the specific identity of the servant of the word changes as well. Here one thinks of Abraham, Moses, Samuel, David, Elijah, Ezra, Isaiah, Jesus, the twelve apostles, Paul, Timothy, and Titus, among others. The specific titles change as well: mediator, servant, prophet, priest, scribe, apostle, elder/pastor, and so forth.

One's place in the Bible's story line determines the specifics of the steward's calling, not the basic job description. This common denominator stays constant throughout many different paradigm shifts. I have highlighted ten paradigm shifts, though one could get even more specific and further subdivide them.

Paradigm 1:   Stewardship of the covenant of creation
Paradigm 2:   Stewardship of the covenant of promise
Paradigm 3:   Stewardship of the covenant of law
Paradigm 4:   Stewardship of Joshua, the judges, and Samuel
Paradigm 5:   Stewardship of the covenant of kingship
Paradigm 6:   Stewardship of the prophets
Paradigm 7:   Stewardship of psalmists and scribes
Paradigm 8:   Stewardship of the Son
Paradigm 9:   Stewardship of the apostles
Paradigm 10: Stewardship of the pastor

Each stewardship paradigm has a counterfeit as part of the conflict of the two kingdoms in the view from below. Figure 4 lists some examples.

Figure 4. True stewards and their counterfeits

True		False
Adam	versus	Serpent
Abel	versus	Cain
Isaac	versus	Ishmael
Jacob	versus	Esau
Moses	versus	Pharaoh
Samuel	versus	Eli
David	versus	Saul
True kings	versus	False kings
Prophets	versus	False prophets
The wise	versus	The foolish
Modecai	versus	Haman
Nehemiah	versus	Sanballat and Tobiah
Jesus	versus	Pharisees and scribes
Apostles	versus	False apostles
Teachers	versus	False teachers

This struggle is our story; it is part of our family history. Thus, Ted Tripp makes the poignant observation that "the protagonists in the Bible narratives must be as accessible to our minds and hearts as [stories about] Grandma, Sister Sue, and Uncle Bill."[1]

The true stewards are a "cloud of witnesses" for us as we "run . . . the race set before us" (Heb. 12:1). The struggle took different twists and turns for all of them. Sometimes they looked like they won.

> What more shall I say? For time would fail me to tell of Gideon, Barak, Samson, Jephthah, of David and Samuel and the prophets— who through faith conquered kingdoms, enforced justice, obtained promises, stopped the mouths of lions, quenched the power of fire, escaped the edge of the sword, were made strong out of weakness, became mighty in war, put foreign armies to flight. Women received back their dead by resurrection. (Heb. 11:32–35a)

At other times, it looked like they lost.

> Some were tortured, refusing to accept release, so that they might rise again to a better life. Others suffered mocking and flogging, and even chains and imprisonment. They were stoned, they were sawn in two, they were killed with the sword. They went about in skins of sheep and goats, destitute, afflicted, mistreated—of whom the world was not worthy—wandering about in deserts and mountains, and in dens and caves of the earth. (Heb. 11:35b–38)

In the end, Hebrews emphasizes that both groups were victors. Hebrews highlights the word "faith" as the common denominator. The apostle John makes the same point: "This is the victory that has overcome the world—our faith" (1 John 5:4).

Therefore, in the next ten chapters we will attempt to drill down deeper into each of these paradigm shifts of stewardship. There is great benefit here for our faith. These chapters are not antiquarian history lectures with limited relevance for our lives. Knowing these stewards will strengthen our own stewardship today. The Bible commands this very sort of study. "Remember your leaders, those who spoke to you the word of God. Consider the outcome of their way of life, and imitate their faith" (Heb. 13:7).

As we "consider the outcome of their way of life" and "imitate

---

[1] Tedd and Margy Tripp, *Instructing a Child's Heart* (Wapwallopen, PA: Shepherd, 2008), 24–25.

their faith," we will be swept up into something massive and beautiful. Stewards throughout the ages join the symphony of praise. The song often called "Te Deum" gives voice to this heritage.

> The glorious company of the Apostles praise thee.
> The goodly fellowship of the Prophets praise thee.
> The noble army of Martyrs praise thee.
> The holy Church throughout all the world doth
>   acknowledge thee. . . .
> We therefore pray thee, help thy servants,
>   whom thou hast redeemed with thy precious blood.
> Make them to be numbered with thy Saints in glory everlasting.

WHICH WAY WILL YOU GO?

You have come to a fork in the road. Remember that the reader who enjoys big-picture reading could jump now to part three and then move on through the rest of the book. A reader who cares deeply about details and fundamental structures could read the book straight through as it stands.

If you choose to read part two, here is what you will find. Each chapter traces a different steward paradigm. I narrate the story and comment on important details along the way that will help modern-day stewards of the word. I pray that you come away with the feeling that you are surrounded by a great cloud of stewards and heralds to help cheer you on in your ministry of the word. Each chapter closes with some illustrations and applications.

PART TWO

A SURVEY OF PARADIGM SHIFTS IN THE MINISTRY OF THE WORD

6

THE STEWARDSHIP
OF THE COVENANT
OF CREATION

Paradigm 1

The world is charged with the grandeur of God.

Gerard Manley Hopkins

The first paradigm of stewardship covers the period from God's covenant with creation up until the covenant with Abraham. God calls various people to steward his word, while others prove that they are counterfeits and belong to the seed of Satan. Adam and Noah receive the most space in the narrative and thus stand out as the main stewards during this period.

CREATION, FALL, AND REDEMPTION: ADAM AND EVE

GOD'S CREATION OF THE WORLD BY THE WORD

Genesis 1 is like a treasure chest of God-centeredness. How sad it is that some do not see this treasure. Some miss it because they read Genesis 1 as if it were a stockpile of munitions to be mobilized in the war against evolution. Some miss it because they get excited about big "theological" concepts touching on salvation (e.g., justification) or God's sovereignty (e.g., election). Many miss the theological saturation here because few people think of *speaking* as an essential and exciting theological term. This attitude is a mistake. We should not minimize the jaw-dropping fact that God is a speaking God. The implications are enormous. The author of the Pentateuch also seems to be fixated on God's speech. Forms of the word "say" occur nine times in rhythmic repetition (Gen. 1:3, 6, 9, 11, 14, 20, 26, 28, 29). God is the subject of *all of them.*

It is no accident that he is also the subject of every use of the words "create" (Gen. 1:1, 21, 27 [3x]) and "make" (1:7, 16, 25, 26, 31). Think of the implications for a moment. God creates by speaking. The rest of Scripture stresses the importance of this relationship between speaking and creating. Consider the poetic commentary of Psalm 33:6:

> By the *word of the* LORD the heavens were *made,*
>   and by *the breath of his mouth* all their host.

Genesis 2 is like the zoom feature found in Google maps. The reader sees the creation of all things at a glance in Genesis 1, and now the author zooms in for a more intimate look. The zoom feature provides readers with surprising suspense. God calls his creation "good" (1:10, 12, 18, 21, 25) and even "very good" (1:31). The suspense of chapter 2 is the revelation that there is something that is "not good" (2:18). What is not good? The man God made is alone, which is not good.

We see the man working in chapter 2. Is that also not good? Contrary to the way some people feel about work *today,* work was not a negative thing in *that day* prior to the fall. In fact, we find the man doing good things that are much like the good things that God does in chapter 2. Even though they do similar things, the author narrates them in a way that highlights Adam's dependence in and derivative authority from God. The man can call and name the animals that God has made, but he does not create them with his words.[1] In fact, the man speaks for the first time as a climax to God's creation, not man's creation. Adam speaks in climactic celebration when God creates the woman. God decisively deals with the deficit of being alone by giving the man a suitable helper; so the man gives her a suitable name. He calls her "woman" because she is taken from man (Gen. 2:23).

---

[1] God speaks something into existence (Gen. 1:3, 6, 9, 11, 14, 20, 26, 28, 29) and then calls (1:5 [2x], 8, 10 [2x]) it a name, while the man calls (Gen. 2:19 [2x], 20, 23) and names (2:19, 20) the things God created.

FAILED STEWARDSHIP AND THE FALL

Chapter 3 describes a shocking development. A speaking serpent is certainly a big surprise. The shock factor grows even bigger when it uses its ability to speak in order to question what God spoke (Gen. 3:1). The woman's first recorded speech is an attempt at stewarding the word in response to the serpent's challenge (3:2–3). The serpent's first act of speaking *challenges* God's word; his second speech *contradicts* God's word (3:4–5). The woman and the man fail to steward God's word because they fail to believe God's word. Shockingly, they put their trust in the serpent's words instead (3:6). The next two verses describe the disastrous effects of this disobedience and Adam and Eve's pitiful patchwork attempt to fix the problem and evade God (3:7–8).

This episode deserves a sustained spotlight owing to its prominent place at the beginning of Scripture and the clarity that it brings to the rest of the story of Scripture and the struggle to steward God's word that follows. This story represents Scripture's first example of someone relaying a message from God, both explicitly and implicitly. First, Eve explicitly "instructs" the serpent concerning God's word, even though in the end she is deceived by the serpent. (Note the importance of this fact for later revelation, such as 2 Cor. 11:3 and 1 Tim. 2:4.) Second, the narrative implicitly demonstrates that Adam informed Eve about God's word given to him in Genesis 2:16–17. In other words, the narrative of Genesis 3 shows that Eve knows something that God spoke directly to Adam alone in Genesis 2. The required assumption is that Adam shared this word from God with Eve.

In the interplay between Eve and the serpent, the serpent strikes at the core of humanity's existence: their relationship with God through the word of God. The implications are already on display in Genesis 2:16. God speaks and warns that if his life-sustaining words are not followed, death is inevitable. Satan knows that if he can cut off their connection with God's words of life, death will surely follow.

Therefore, it is interesting to note that Satan questions not the goodness of God's works, but the goodness of God's word when he asks, "Did God actually *say*?" (Gen. 3:1). Satan deceptively reduces God's word to a blanket prohibition: "You shall not eat of any tree in the garden" (3:1). In shocking contrast to all of Genesis 1–2, Satan dares to insinuate that God's word is not good. This moment of confrontation calls for Eve to steward God's word in the face of Satan's attack. Eve must correct Satan's twisting of Genesis 2:16–17, which says, "And the LORD God commanded the man, saying, 'You may surely eat of every tree of the garden, but of the tree of the knowledge of good and evil you shall not eat, for in the day that you eat of it you shall surely die.'"

How does Eve respond? "And the woman said to the serpent, 'We may eat of the fruit of the trees in the garden, but God said, "You shall not eat of the fruit of the tree that is in the midst of the garden, neither shall you touch it, lest you die"'" (Gen. 3:2–3).

God's words in Genesis 2 are full of provision and protection. God has given humanity a bounty: they may eat of "every tree of the garden" except the tree of the knowledge of good and evil. The stress of Genesis 2:16 is upon "every tree" with only one exception. Satan's tactic effectively turns this provision on its head by focusing solely on the prohibition. Eating from "every tree" except one in Genesis 2 becomes, in Satan's summary, *not* eating of "any tree" in Genesis 3:1.

There is some debate as to whether or not Eve accurately represented God's original words. She correctly notes that they may eat of the fruit of the trees in the garden except for the tree of the knowledge of good and evil, which is "in the midst of the garden" (Gen. 3:3). Eve adds a comment not found in Genesis 2: they shall not "touch" the fruit. God's words prohibited eating, while Eve adds touching to the list of what is forbidden.

What is clear is that Satan moves from subterfuge and sneak-attack mode to full-frontal assault when he contradicts God's word and offers a correction: "But the serpent said to the woman, 'You will not surely die. For God knows that when you eat of it your eyes will be opened, and you will be like God, knowing good and evil'" (Gen. 3:4–5).

Something inside of a steward of God's word should snap at this point. We instinctively bristle inwardly and know that Adam and Eve should spring into action and crush this uprising against God's word. We groan with the knowledge of what happens next with the tragic turn of events in the rest of the story. Adam, who was there with Eve (Gen. 3:7), does not beat down Satan's uprising. Adam fails in his commission to "keep" or guard the garden (Gen. 2:15), and Eve does not hold firmly to the truth of God's word. She eats and gives the fruit to Adam, who eats as well.

Adam and Eve do not stop the rebellion against God's word; sadly, they join it. They even heighten the rebellion as they use their words to drive a further wedge between one another by shifting the blame for their own sin (Gen. 3:12–13). But God's word cannot be mocked. God's word enters the picture forcefully once more—this time as words of judgment when he enacts a curse upon the serpent, the woman, and the man (3:14–19).

STEWARDING THE WORD OF REDEMPTION

Significantly, God's curse upon the serpent also contains a messianic promise of deliverance and redemption (Gen. 3:15). Adam seems to respond with faith in this promise. He names his wife "Eve" because he sees that she will be the "mother of all the living" (3:20). God's promise of life leaves its unmistakable mark by bringing light into the darkness once more. In the face of the curse and the death that come from forsaking God's word of life, Adam places the emphasis back on life by naming the woman "mother of all *living*."

Furthermore, in contrast to their hopeless attempt to cover their nakedness, God makes suitable garments to cover their nakedness and shame (Gen. 3:21). God's justice is on display as he drives them from the garden and establishes a guard to prevent their return. Many also rightly interpret this act as a demonstration of God's mercy. This act represents God's provision to prevent them from eating the tree of life and thus becoming unchangeably confirmed in their current state of sin.[2]

APPLICATION: LIFE AND DEATH AS POWERS OF THE WORD

The preceding summary of Genesis 1–3 highlights some significant points for creating conceptual categories for preaching. First, God's word is bursting at the seams with life-giving power and man's word is not. Second, sin and rebellion stem from a failure to steward God's word. Third, God's word is a word of blessing when followed and a curse-bearing word of judgment when broken. Fourth, even after

---

[2] See W. J. Dumbrell, *Covenant and Creation: A Theology of the Old Testament Covenants*, 2nd ed., Biblical and Theological Classics Library 12 (Milton Keynes, UK: Paternoster, 2002).

God's word is broken, it provides the promise of redemption with the announcement of a coming deliverer. Fifth, redemption results from hearing and trusting God's work of redemption promised by his word.

Of these points of application, I will focus on the second. Adam and Eve fail to steward the word. They do not trust God's trustworthy word, and thus they fail to correct and silence the serpent when he contradicts it. We could draw out the principle that says stewarding the word means rebuking Satanic contradictions of the word. Does this theme ever come up again?

It is easy to fault Adam and Eve for their failure and think that things would have been different had we been there. We sometimes miss the fact that Titus 1:9 says *we are there*. The elder as God's steward "must hold firm to the trustworthy word as taught, so that he may be able to give instruction in sound doctrine and also to rebuke those who contradict it." This verse calls for rebuking those who contradict the word. Paul says that the source of this rebellion against the word is still satanic: "Now the Spirit expressly says that in later times some will depart from the faith by devoting themselves to deceitful spirits and teachings of demons" (1 Tim. 4:1).

Therefore, there can be no smugness in faulting Adam and Eve for their failure. We are now forced to reflect upon our own calling to crush the uprisings that contradict God's word today. May God give scriptural clarity and Spirit-wrought courage to rebuke those who contradict the word and to take it seriously as spiritual warfare.

PRE-NOAH

The time between Adam and Noah stresses the stewardship of Abel, Cain, and Enoch. Apostolic commentary highlights the faith of both Abel and Enoch (Heb. 11:4–6). This stress on faith reinforces the link once more between faith in God and faithfulness to his entrusted word. Apostolic commentary also addresses the false stewardship of Cain (1 John 3:10, 12).

ABEL AND ENOCH

Hebrews stresses that Abel offered a sacrifice by faith (Heb. 11:4). God commended Abel because of his faith. His faith in God allows Abel still to speak today, even long after death (11:4). Enoch appears next in the list as someone who pleased God by faith (11:5), which Hebrews reiterates is the only way to please God (11:6).

CAIN

Shortly after the promise that the woman's seed would crush the head of the serpent, a son is born. Eve names him Cain, which sounds like the word for "gotten." Could this son be the child of promise? Cain quickly shows that he is not the hoped-for seed of the woman—he is a seed of the serpent. God entrusts Cain with his word, saying that sin lies crouching at his door ready to strike (reminiscent of the serpent of Genesis 3). Cain fails to overcome the assault of sin and Cain rises up and strikes Abel. Cain is clearly the seed of the serpent striking at the seed of the woman. Abel's blood cries out against Cain, and God brings judgment to bear upon him as he is cast out to be a wanderer on the face of the earth. Cain once again defies the entrusted word that he is to be a wanderer. He becomes a settler and resides in a land east of Eden.

CAIN'S ANTI-GENEALOGY

Genesis 4:17–24 is a genealogy for the seed of the serpent, which is really an anti-genealogy. The line of curse consolidates in rebellion against God by building cities. Cain builds a city and names it after his son, Enoch. The genealogy ends with poetry. Poetry is a good created structure that can be turned in a Godward or godless direction. Lamech turns it in a godless direction as he glories in his anti-God rebellion. As Stephen Dempster says, "It begins with Cain, the brother-killer, and ends with the child-killer, Lamech, the seventh from Adam."[3] The downward spiral of sin that starts with an attempt to deny murder (Cain) now descends into celebrating murder (Lamech).

Apostolic commentary in 1 John also stresses that Cain was a counterfeit steward because he was a seed of the serpent (1 John 3:12). Cain's actions are contrasted with the actions of the true seed of the woman, Jesus. We should not love like Cain, because he killed his brother. His

---

[3] Stephen G. Dempster, *Dominion and Dynasty: A Biblical Theology of the Hebrew Bible*, New Studies in Biblical Theology (Downers Grove, IL: InterVarsity, 2003), 70.

"love" was the taking of life. Jesus, by contrast, laid down his life. His love was the giving of life (1 John 3:16). We should follow in Jesus's footsteps and lay down our lives for our brothers through self-sacrificial, practical acts of love (not just word or tongue) (1 John 3:16–17).

NOAH

Noah, the tenth from Adam, has a name that sounds like the word meaning "rest," because he is cast as a savior providing rest from the curse. The Genesis narrative describes Noah as a man who has found favor in God's sight, a man righteous and blameless who walked with God (Gen. 6:8–9). God speaks directly to Noah concerning God's future plans to judge the whole world (6:13, 17) and deliver both Noah's family (6:18) and the animals (6:19–20). God also provides a detailed description of how to build the ark as a means of deliverance (6:14–16). The rest of the world has broken God's life-giving words of blessing, and thus his word comes bearing the curse of judgment. The narrator, however, stresses that Noah does everything that the Lord has commanded him to do (6:22; 7:5). Therefore, even in the darkest circumstances, keeping God's words of life brings life to humanity.

NOAH'S CALL NARRATIVE

Noah's call narrative comes in Genesis 6:8–9:17. Finding "favor" in God's eyes, Noah is called to make an ark, and he does exactly as God says. The Lord judges the earth and destroys every living thing with water, but he preserves Noah and the ark and then reestablishes the covenant with creation. God also gives Noah a calling of blessing, saying, "Be fruitful and multiply and fill the earth" (Gen. 9:1). This time the human race may eat not only the plants, but also the animals (9:2–3). As we saw earlier, fallen humanity still possesses the image of God (9:6), and thus the original calling to be fruitful and multiply remains (9:7). God also puts his weapon (his "bow") away in the clouds, promising never to destroy the earth with water again (9:8–17).

NOAH'S FALL NARRATIVE

Noah, the new Adam, has a fall narrative as well. The narrator takes us back to Genesis 3. Noah plants a vineyard and then sins with the fruit of the vine as Adam sinned with the fruit of the tree. "[Noah] drank of the wine and became drunk and lay uncovered in his tent" (Gen. 9:21). The fall is once again followed by a curse, though the curse is pronounced on only one of Noah's descendants.

APOSTOLIC COMMENTARY ON NOAH'S STEWARDSHIP

As mentioned above, Hebrews highlights Noah's faith in God's word. "By faith Noah, being warned by God concerning events as yet unseen, in reverent fear constructed an ark for the saving of his household. By this he condemned the world and became an heir of the righteousness that comes by faith" (Heb. 11:7).

Another New Testament comment on Noah's life presents him as a "herald of righteousness" (2 Pet. 2:5). A fascinating connection is made here in these two texts because Noah is both a "herald of righteousness" (2:5) and an "heir of . . . righteousness" (Heb. 11:7). This twofold focus brings believing and speaking together. Noah received God's word by faith and thus was not ashamed to herald God's promise.

Some may wonder if it is legitimate to make the word of the Lord the focus of the narrative as I have done here. Second Peter 3 serves as evidence that this focus is entirely fitting because Peter focuses his comments on the word of God, which remains constant in all three verses as part of the parallel structure in 2 Peter 3:5–7. Peter says that God formed the world by means of water and the word of God (3:5); destroyed the world by means of water and the word of God (3:6), and will destroy the world in the future by means of fire and the word of God (3:7). Peter stresses that the word that once created and destroyed the world is the "same word" that keeps the heavens and the earth moment by moment until the final judgment (3:7).[4]

LIFE LESSONS FROM NOAH, REVERENT AND FEARLESS

Noah stands out as a righteous and reverent steward. First, Genesis characterizes Noah as a righteous and blameless man who walked with God (Gen. 6:8–9). These verses go a long way toward establishing the

---

[4] I am taking the plural "by means of these" as referring to water and the word, as do most commentators. See, for example, Richard J. Bauckham, *Jude, 2 Peter*, Word Biblical Commentary 50 (Dallas: Word, 2002), 298.

character requirements of a steward of God's word. This same emphasis on a faithful, godly character becomes a prominent feature for stewards that appear later in the story as described in the Pastoral Epistles.

Second, Noah also challenges us as a fearless steward of the word because he feared God. Noah received the warning from God "by faith" and obeyed "in reverent fear" (Heb. 11:7). This fearless action itself proclaimed condemnation on the world: "By this he condemned the world" as an heir of righteousness looking for another world (11:7).

The covenant of creation celebrates the wonder of all that God has made. The word of God reveals even greater wonders. Isaac Watts caught sight of this majesty in his hymn, "The Heavens Declare Thy Glory, Lord." The first and the last stanzas remind us of the wonder of the word.

> The heav'ns declare your glory, Lord;
> In ev'ry star your wisdom shines;
> But when our eyes behold your Word,
> We read your Name in fairer lines.
>
> Your noblest wonders here we view
> In souls renewed, and sins forgiv'n:
> Lord, cleanse my sins, my soul renew,
> And make your Word my guide to heav'n.

7

THE STEWARDSHIP OF THE COVENANT OF PROMISE

Paradigm 2

These all died in faith, not having received the things promised, but having seen them and greeted them from afar, and having acknowledged that they were strangers and exiles on the earth.

Hebrews 11:13

The patriarchs possess no real estate in the book of Genesis. They dwell in tents. "By faith [Abraham] went to live in the land of promise, as in a foreign land, living in tents with Isaac and Jacob, heirs with him of the same promise" (Heb. 11:9). They lived like sojourners, not settlers, because they were desiring "a better country, that is, a heavenly one" (11:16a). And "God is not ashamed to be called their God, for he has prepared for them a city" (11:16b). God proclaims that he is the "God of Abraham, Isaac, and Jacob" (Ex. 3:15). Jesus testifies that God is the God of the living and not the dead. Therefore, when he is not ashamed to be called their God, it means that he is always their God and thus they live today (Matt. 22:32). They are armed with the promise, "I will be with you" (see Gen. 17:4; 26:3; 28:15; 31:3).

ABRAHAM

Abraham is the first person to be called a prophet in the book of Genesis (Gen. 20:7). He is a prophet of the promise. We will look at his calling (and falling), stewarding, and heralding, and the effects they had.

ABRAM'S CALL AND FALL

The narrator introduces Abram in Genesis 11 as the husband of a barren wife and the son of Terah. Genesis 12 opens with God's call to Abram:

> Now the LORD said to Abram, "Go from your country and your kindred and your father's house to the land that I will show you. And I will make of you a great nation, and I will bless you and make your name great, so that you will be a blessing. I will bless those who bless you, and him who dishonors you I will curse, and in you all the families of the earth shall be blessed." (12:1–3)

The author of Hebrews reminds us that Abraham's faith in God's word is on display here: "By faith Abraham obeyed when he was called to go out to a place that he was to receive as an inheritance. And he went out, not knowing where he was going" (Heb. 11:8).

As I stated above, it is important that Abram is a sojourner throughout the narrative and never a settler. Hebrews tells us that he lived by faith in the Land of Promise "as in a foreign land" (Heb. 11:9). That is, Abraham did not build a city or own part of the Promised Land; he lived in tents with Isaac and Jacob. He saw that the promise pointed toward a city that God would build (Heb. 11:10).

God calls Abram not only to "go to a land," but also to steward the promises of Genesis 12:1–3, which have sometimes been called the "quad-promise." The Lord promises land, seed, blessing, and protection. The rest of the Bible plays out the fulfillment of these promises.

Notice that the calling already highlights what will flow from this promise to Abram. In a word, it is "blessing." In contrast to the five uses of "curse" up to this point in Genesis 1–11, Genesis 12:2–3 uses the word "bless" five times as a reversal of the curse. Through Abram, all the families of the earth shall be blessed (12:3). In contrast to the conduct of the citizens of Genesis 11 (they tried to make a name for themselves), God himself is going to make Abram's name great. The

Lord also promises to protect Abram. God will bless those who bless Abram, but he will curse those who curse Abram.

The divine narration in Genesis makes it clear that Abram has a fall narrative. Abram leaves the Land of Promise and fails to trust God's promise of protection while in Egypt. Abram fears the Egyptians, and thus he pawns his wife off as his sister for his own protection and so it will go well for him. His plan seems to work: Pharaoh takes Sarai into his house, and the text says that for her sake Pharaoh "dealt well with Abram" (Gen. 12:15–16). Abram receives both flocks and servants. He thus fails to believe God's promise to bless those he blesses and curse those who curse him. The promise of seed seems to be threatened as Sarai is in Pharaoh's harem, but God preserves the promise himself by afflicting Pharaoh with plagues. Therefore, Pharaoh tells Abram to "go." This fall narrative is essentially replayed again in Genesis 20:1–18.

Genesis 16 is another dark spot in the life of Abram and Sarai as they try to fulfill the seed promise in their own strength (the Hagar episode—16:1–16). Abram and Sarai put the seed promise in jeopardy with an Egyptian once again (cf. Gen. 12:10–20), but God brings his promise to pass so that a baby is born to them in God's strength.

ABRAHAM'S STEWARDING AND HERALDING

Abraham faithfully stewards the word as a prophet of the promise. There are many other opportunities for Abraham to carry out this calling. God tells Abraham to call his wife Sarah instead of Sarai (Gen. 17:15). We can safely assume that Abraham explained this change to Sarah; he probably did not just start calling her a different name without further comment! Abraham also carries out God's command to circumcise his household "as God had said to him" (17:23). We can once again imagine that Abraham would have provided some explanation for the men in his household concerning this painful act of obedience. Genesis 18 includes the account of the Lord's announcing the conception and birth of a son to aged Abraham and Sarah. God speaks to Abraham, but Sarah overhears the conversation and takes part in it (Gen. 18:10–15).

Abraham is the first individual in Genesis described as a "prophet" (Gen. 20:7). God's words to him bring blessing to others as he prays for Pharaoh so that he "will live" and not fall under God's word of judgment (20:7). Genesis 22:8 shows Abraham delivering the message to Isaac that "God will provide for himself the lamb for a burnt offering." Genesis 23:6 reveals the Hittites' assessment of Abraham as a "prince of God."

Genesis 24 goes to great lengths to highlight the way Abraham stewards the promises of God entrusted to him by ensuring that the word of promise will be carried over to the next generation. Abraham makes his servant swear by the Lord that he will find a wife for Isaac among Abraham's people. He tells the servant, "The LORD, the God of heaven, who took me from my father's house and from the land of my kindred, and who spoke to me and swore to me, 'To your offspring I will give this land,' he will send his angel before you, and you shall take a wife for my son from there" (24:7).

The servant shares this message with Rebekah (Gen. 24:27) and her household (24:33–41). They all attribute the situation to the Lord and order that the arrangement be carried out "as the LORD has spoken [*davar*]" (24:51).

ABRAHAM'S EFFECTS

Many effects flow from Abraham's faith-filled stewardship of the word. He and Sarah receive Isaac as a miracle baby; then they get him back after Abraham passes the test of faith. God sovereignly brings about what he promised to Abraham, but God also chooses the means to this end by his very choice of Abraham as a servant of his word. Abraham is also instrumental in ensuring that Isaac will continue the legacy of faith in God's promise. God's electing call to Abraham involves Abraham's commission not only to keep the way of righteousness, but also to instruct others in the way of righteousness: "For I have chosen him, that he may command his children and his household after him to keep the way of the LORD by doing righteousness and justice, so that the LORD may bring to Abraham what he has promised him" (Gen. 18:19).

APPLICATION: FAITH IN THE WORD OF GOD

The depiction of Abraham's faith in Genesis and later apostolic commentary deserve a much more detailed look. Abraham was a man of faith in God's word. We have already seen in Hebrews an assessment of Abraham's faith described in Genesis 12. Genesis 15 is another notable example. God promises Abraham that his descendants will be as numerous as the stars of the sky. The next verse says that Abraham "believed the LORD, and he counted it to him as righteousness" (15:6). This verse informs the reader of Abraham's faith in God and his promise and the result of this faith: Abraham is considered righteous in God's sight.

Apostolic commentary makes it clear that Abraham believed God's word, especially the life-giving, resurrecting power of God through his word. Genesis says that the object of Abraham's faith was "the LORD" (Gen. 15:6). One must not make the mistake of thinking that this faith was in God as an abstract philosophical construct. Paul observes that the object of Abraham's faith was God as he revealed himself *through his word*. Romans 4:20–21 offers inspired commentary on the substance of Abraham's faith. "No unbelief made him waver concerning *the promise of God*, but he grew strong in his faith as he gave glory to God, fully convinced that God was able to do *what he had promised*."

Did you catch the substance of Abraham's faith? He believed that God was able to do *what he had said*. The focus remains squarely on the power of God contained in the word of God. His words are trustworthy because he is almighty. He is able to do what he says he will do. Abraham looked away from the inability that glared back at him like an ugly reflection in the mirror. He looked at his life and saw a dead body and a wife with a dead womb and then he looked at God.

C. S. Lewis saw this same dynamic.[1] He postulated an intricate connection between an action and the object that produces the action. Everything hinges upon keeping your eyes fixed on the object. Figure 5 presents some examples.

Figure 5. Sample human actions and their divine objects

Human Action	Divine Object
Love	the God of love (we love because he first loved)
Faith	the God who is faithful to do what he says

---

[1] C. S. Lewis, *Surprised by Joy: The Shape of My Early Life* (New York: Houghton Mifflin Harcourt, 1995).

Human Action	Divine Object
Endurance	the God of endurance
Hope	the God of hope

If one's gaze remains fixed in the right place (object), the action will follow. Almost the minute one's gaze turns to consider the action, both the action and object vanish together. Abraham did not allow his gaze to stay fixed upon the absurdity that his dead body and Sarah's dead womb were to produce an incalculable output of descendants. He had learned something about the life-giving power of God. He found a living hope as he looked away from his hopeless inability and fixed his focus firmly on God's almighty ability. In fact, the life-giving power of God through the word of God is on display here again according to Paul. The apostle informs us that Abraham believed specifically in the God "who *gives life to the dead* and *calls into existence the things that do not exist*" (Rom. 4:17). This God, as Genesis 1–2 so powerfully has shown, has the power of life and death in his word.

Despite the unbelief of Abraham and Sarah, the Lord will fulfill his promise of seed. The reader cannot miss the cause-and-effect nature of the pronouncement of fulfillment in Genesis 18: "The Lord said, 'I will surely return to you about this time next year [cause], and Sarah your wife shall have a son [effect]'" (18:10). Sarah responds with incredulous laughter (18:12). The Lord's rebuke is striking in form. He frontloads the promise with a focus on the almighty power of God and the result that follows: "Is anything too hard for the Lord? At the appointed time I will return to you [cause], about this time next year, and Sarah shall have a son [effect]" (18:14).

Later commentary on this story reveals that Sarah must have responded well to this rebuke because the author of Hebrews highlights her faith in the trustworthy nature of God and his word: "By faith Sarah herself received power to conceive, even when she was past the age, *since she considered him faithful who had promised*" (Heb. 11:11).

The Lord fulfills his promise exactly according to his word in Genesis 21:1. The stress falls on the reliability of God's word: "The Lord visited Sarah *as he had said*, and the Lord did to Sarah *as he had promised*.

And Sarah conceived and bore Abraham a son in his old age *at the time of which God had spoken to him*" (21:1–2).

Genesis 21 also reveals that the Lord will carry out his promise through Isaac because "through Isaac shall your offspring be named" (21:12). Thus, it is all the more dramatic when God calls Abraham to sacrifice his son in the next chapter. Abraham believes the seed promise so much by this point that he is willing to obey the Lord's command to sacrifice his son. Listen to the author of Hebrews again:

> By faith Abraham, when he was tested, offered up Isaac, and he who had received the promises was in the act of offering up his only son, of whom it was said, "Through Isaac shall your offspring be named." He considered that God was able even to raise him from the dead, from which, figuratively speaking, he did receive him back. (Heb. 11:17–19)

Did you catch the focus on the Creator's life-giving power again? Where did Abraham learn this resurrection kind of faith? A comparison of Paul and Hebrews is instructive at this point concerning the faith of Abraham (fig. 6).

Figure 6. Abraham's resurrection faith according to Paul and Hebrews

Abraham's Faith (Paul)	Abraham's Faith (Hebrews)
"God . . . gives life to the dead and *calls into existence the things that do not exist*" (Rom. 4:17).	"God was able even to raise him from the dead" (Heb. 11:19).

Where did Abraham's life-out-of-death type of faith develop? Abraham simply applied the lesson he learned from the birth of Isaac in Genesis 21 to the call to put Isaac to death in Genesis 22. If God showed that he can give life to dead bodies and wombs and call the not-being into being as he did in Genesis 21, then surely he could do it again in Genesis 22. Abraham had put the seed promise in jeopardy many times on his own, and yet God proved faithful to preserve it. This time it looked like God was putting the seed promise in jeopardy, but Abraham had come to trust the faithfulness of God and the trustworthy nature of his promises. Abraham's faith was in the life-giving power of God, the Creator of all things. This life-from-the-dead faith stands in significant parallel to the light-out-of-darkness reality on display in Genesis 1. The Creator that gives life through his word and calls the not-being into being was able to raise Isaac from the dead.

Therefore, do not miss the link between Abraham as a man of faith *in God's word* and Abraham as a steward *of God's word*. Abraham is like Noah. He believes God's entrusted word, and thus he heralds God's entrusted word to others.

THE FAMILY OF ABRAHAM

CHILDREN OF THE FLESH AND CHILDREN OF THE PROMISE

The patriarchal narratives help the reader distinguish between the seed of the serpent and the seed of the woman. Ishmael and Esau are sons of Abraham, but still the seed of the serpent. Isaac and Jacob are true stewards of the promise of seed.

Hebrews 11 mentions that Isaac and Jacob were "heirs with him [i.e., Abraham] of the same promise" (11:9). Genesis 26 shows that faith in God's word of promise remained firm in the family of Abraham, which even outsiders to the promise came to acknowledge. The Philistines recognized that Abraham's son Isaac had a special relationship with the Lord, and so they urged Isaac to make a covenant with them (26:28–29). Isaac speaks a prophetic blessing over his sons Jacob (Gen. 27:27–29) and Esau (27:39–40). The author of Hebrews highlights Isaac's faith at work in this activity: "by faith Isaac invoked future blessings on Jacob and Esau" (Heb. 11:20). This statement is likely a commentary on Isaac's faith in the word of blessing as recorded in Genesis. Isaac asks Esau who the person was that came in his place and received the blessing (Gen. 27:33). He even adds an emphatic statement of faith in the effectual nature of the blessing: "Yes, and he shall be blessed" (27:33).

Stewardship of the word continues as a theme in the rest of the Jacob narrative. Jacob speaks to his wives concerning God's hand at work to protect and preserve him (Gen. 31:5–13). His wives respond by saying, "Whatever God has said to you, do" (31:16). Laban also relays a message from God to Jacob: "But the God of your father spoke to me last night, saying, 'Be careful not to say anything to Jacob, either good or bad'" (31:29). Jacob and Laban make a covenant and call on the Lord to be a witness and judge between them (31:49–50, 53). God speaks to Jacob, instructing him to build an altar to the Lord (Gen. 35:1) and then Jacob conveys the message to his household (35:2–3).

Apostolic commentary highlights God's sovereignty in creating children of the promise (Rom. 9:6–9). Man has the power to create children of the flesh, but only God can create children that are born in the line of promise. In fact, Paul says that the word of promise itself creates children like Isaac (9:9).

In the same way, God makes a distinction between the sons of Isaac. We are surprised to find that the older child, Esau, is rejected in favor of the younger, Jacob. Apostolic commentary once again highlights God's choice. Someone could argue that God chose Jacob because he knew beforehand that Esau would despise his birthright and marry foreign wives. Paul eliminates that possibility by stressing that Rebekah was told while they "were not yet born and had done nothing either good or bad" that "the older will serve the younger" (Rom. 9:11–12). Apostolic commentary makes it clear that God made this decision "in order that God's purpose of election might continue, not because of works but because of him who calls" (9:11). Prophetic commentary on the narrative confirms this same point: "Jacob I loved, but Esau I hated" (Mal. 1:2, 3; cited in Rom. 9:13). The word of promise creates children in the line of promise. God sovereignly appoints Isaac and Jacob as "seed." Isaac and Jacob are true seed and true stewards, but their fall narratives show that they are not *the* promised seed.

FALL NARRATIVES OF ISAAC AND JACOB

Isaac and Jacob are part of the line of promise, but they are not the promised seed that will crush the serpent, as their fall narratives make plain. Isaac repeats the fall narrative of Abraham by making Abimelech think that Rebekah is his sister (Gen. 26:6–11). Jacob lives up to the meaning of his name (he cheats or grasps the heel). Esau says it well: "Is he not rightly named Jacob? For he has cheated me these two times. He took away my birthright, and behold, now he has taken away my blessing" (Gen. 27:36). Jacob and his relative Laban take turns tricking each other in the narrative that follows (Genesis 28–31).

ESAU

Esau is an example of a false steward of the promise to Abraham. The author of Genesis documents how Esau comes to lament that Jacob stole both his birthright and his blessing (Gen. 27:36). What Esau fails to note in this accusation is that he "despised his birthright" long before this point because he sold it to Jacob for a bowl of soup (Gen. 25:33–34). He also did not show any remorse after selling his birthright. Rather, he "ate and drank and rose and went his way. Thus Esau *despised* his birthright" (25:34).

The author of Hebrews goes further in warning his readers about false stewards like Esau. The writer warns that without holiness no one will see the Lord (Heb. 12:14). Esau proves the truth of this warning as a negative test case. He is a fearful example of someone "sexually immoral and unholy": "See to it . . . that no one is sexually immoral or unholy like Esau, who sold his birthright for a single meal. For you know that afterward, when he desired to inherit the blessing, he was rejected, for he found no chance to repent, though he sought it with tears" (12:15–17).

The author of Hebrews is commenting on the Genesis narrative. Esau sold his birthright for a bowl of soup (Gen. 25:33), but he later showed a desire to have Isaac speak a blessing over him (Gen. 27:34). Jacob and Rebekah tricked Isaac so that Jacob received the blessing, echoing the Abrahamic promise,

> Cursed be everyone who curses you,
>   and blessed be everyone who blesses you! (27:29)

When Esau realized Jacob had tricked him, he "sought it [i.e., the blessing] with tears" (Heb. 12:17). This phrase from Hebrews 12 is commentary on these words from Genesis 27:

> As soon as Esau heard the words of his father, *he cried out with an exceedingly great and bitter cry* and said to his father, "Bless me, even me also, O my father!" (27:34)

> Esau said to his father, "Have you but one blessing, my father? Bless me, even me also, O my father." And Esau *lifted up his voice and wept.* (27:38)

Isaac commands Esau to take a wife from the daughters of Laban and reiterates the Abrahamic blessing over his life (Gen. 28:1–4). Esau shows contempt for the Abrahamic line of promise by marrying foreign wives, even from the family of Ishmael (28:8–9), when he sees that it would grieve his parents. Two families of false stewardship (Ishmael and Esau) become fused together.

JUDAH'S FALL NARRATIVE

Genesis 38 makes it plain that Judah is not the promised one, but it does highlight God's sovereignty in overcoming threats to the seed promise. Judah fails to give Tamar one of his sons after the first two die. Tamar resorts to deceit, tricking Judah into thinking that she is a prostitute. He sleeps with her and (unknowingly) provides a replacement seed for the line of promise. When Tamar reveals that Judah has actually slept with her, he confesses that she is more righteous than he. Tamar actually believes more in the seed promise than Judah does. God, however, overcomes this threat to the seed promise. Genesis 49 shows that the promised one will come from the line of Judah.

THE PROPHECY OF THE PROMISE

Genesis 48–49 offers the most sustained prophetic message in the book of Genesis. Jacob first blesses Joseph's two sons (Gen. 48:15–20) and his own twelve sons (Gen. 49:1–27). The author of Hebrews once again highlights the faith of Jacob in this prophetic stewarding and heralding: "By faith Jacob, when dying, blessed each of the sons of Joseph, bowing in worship over the head of his staff" (Heb. 11:21). Jacob demonstrates faith not only in the Abrahamic promise of Genesis 12, but also in the prior promise of Genesis 3:15 because Judah will have his hand on the "neck of his enemies" (Gen. 49:8). The content of this prophetic blessing has an unmistakably messianic component because of the reference to the lionlike (49:9) figure from the tribe of Judah. "The scepter shall not depart from Judah, nor the ruler's staff from between his feet, until tribute comes to him; and to him shall be the obedience of the peoples" (49:10).

THE STEWARDSHIP OF JOSEPH

Joseph features prominently as an interpreter of dreams and visions from God. He shares his dreams with his brothers (Gen. 37:5–7, 9). Outsiders of the promise continue to recognize God's hand upon the line of promise. Potiphar realizes that the Lord is with Joseph (Gen. 39:3), and this captain of the guard makes Joseph an overseer in charge of his household (39:4–6). The Lord also reveals to Joseph the correct interpretation of dreams for the cupbearer (Gen. 40:9–15), the baker (40:16–19), and Pharaoh (Gen. 41:25–36). As a result, Pharaoh too realizes that the Lord is with Joseph, and so he sets Joseph over all of Egypt (41:37–45). Joseph reveals the outworking of God's plan and purpose (Gen. 45:7–9; 50:19–21).

The narrator stresses the life-sustaining impact of stewarding and obeying God's word. God reveals the seven years of abundance and seven years of famine, and Pharaoh believes Joseph's stewarded words. Pharaoh's plan to make Joseph steward over Egypt leads to the sustaining of life for both Israel and Egypt (Gen. 42:2; 45:5) through Joseph's obeying God's life-giving word. Joseph remains a faithful steward of God's promise to Abraham even at the end of his life. The author of Hebrews once again highlights his faith as a steward and herald: "By faith Joseph, at the end of his life, made mention of the exodus of the Israelites and gave directions concerning his bones" (Heb. 11:22; cf. Ex. 13:19).

CONCLUSION

A good summary of the faith of every believer with respect to God's word appears in the commentary on the faith of the patriarchs found in Hebrews 11:13. The author of Hebrews stresses once again that the patriarchs did not experience the fullness of the things promised to them in their day (those things remain unseen at least in part). But the patriarchs did see them in part (from a distance) and welcome them. "These all died in faith, not having received the things promised, but having *seen* them and *greeted* them from afar, and having acknowledged that they were strangers and exiles on the earth" (11:13).

Did you note the beautiful picture of seeing and welcoming the unseen? We all live in the gap between what was promised and what we see. God has to bridge the gap. We cling to what God says even when we do not see it. Faith opens up the door of our hearts and says to God's word, "Welcome, please come and stay." Your experience of the word can grow if you see the promises and welcome them into your heart while refusing to fixate on the gap between what you read in the word and what you see in your world. Anxiety comes from comparing your situation with your abilities; faith comes from comparing your situation with God's abilities.

8

THE STEWARDSHIP
OF THE COVENANT
OF LAW

Paradigm 3

> Now when all the people saw the thunder and the flashes
> of lightning and the sound of the trumpet and the moun-
> tain smoking, the people were afraid and trembled, and they
> stood far off and said to Moses, "You speak to us, and we will
> listen; but do not let God speak to us, lest we die."
>
> *Exodus 20:18–19*

Calling the Mosaic covenant a covenant of "law" is not a slur against it.
It is not a legalistic covenant. The apostle Paul even considers it one of
the covenants of the promise (Eph. 2:12). Calling it a covenant of "law"
merely shows what a large shadow Sinai casts over Exodus through
Deuteronomy.

Moses is undoubtedly the steward and herald who receives the
most attention in the Pentateuch, and we will turn to him in the
next section as the central paradigm in the Pentateuch. However, the
prominence given to Moses should not overshadow other examples
of stewards and heralds in Exodus through Deuteronomy. In what
follows, we will focus on Aaron, the Levites, and Moses as true stewards. Balaam appears as the most prominent false steward in the book
of Numbers.

AARON, THE LEVITES, AND BALAAM

AARON'S CALL

God calls Aaron as Moses's helper in stewarding the word of God: "You [Moses] shall speak to him [Aaron] and put the words in his mouth, and I will be with your mouth and with his mouth and will teach you both what to do. He shall speak for you to the people, and he shall be your mouth, and you shall be as God to him" (Ex. 4:15–16; cf. 7:1–2).

The Lord will speak to Moses and then Moses will pass the word on to Aaron, who will then deliver the message to the Israelites or others like Pharaoh. Exodus 4:27–30 is a good example of this dynamic:

> The LORD said to Aaron, "Go into the wilderness to meet Moses." So he went and met him at the mountain of God and kissed him. And Moses told Aaron all the words of the LORD with which he had sent him to speak, and all the signs that he had commanded him to do. Then Moses and Aaron went and gathered together all the elders of the people of Israel. Aaron spoke all the words that the LORD had spoken to Moses and did the signs in the sight of the people.

God also allows Aaron to come up on the mountain with Moses, and he beholds the Lord along with the seventy elders (Ex. 24:1, 9–11). God also gives Aaron and his sons detailed instructions for ministering before the Lord as priests (Ex. 27:21–30:38).

Aaron sometimes succeeds in his commission as a steward of the word, and Israel responds appropriately, as in Exodus 4:31: "And the people believed; and when they heard that the LORD had visited the people of Israel and that he had seen their affliction, they bowed their heads and worshiped." At other times, the people grumble against both Aaron and Moses (e.g., Ex. 16:2; Num. 14:1–4) and rebel against the word of the Lord (Num. 14:10; 16:1–3). Some of the Levites (sons of Korah) decide to rebel against the special role that God has given Moses and Aaron (Num. 16:1–3), but they are destroyed (Numbers 16).

AARON'S FALL

Snapshots of Aaron would be incomplete if we did not note the times he fails miserably in his calling as a steward and herald of God's word, as in the story of the golden calf (Exodus 32). He goes along with the Israelites' rebellion in their request to fashion gods for them to lead them through the wilderness. Aaron tells the people to bring him gold, and he fashions a golden calf, which the people proclaim to be their god (32:2–4). Aaron goes on to lead the rebellion as he makes an altar, proclaims a feast, and sacrifices to this false god (32:5–6).

Aaron also has the dubious distinction of coming up with the lamest excuse in all of Scripture. He first blames his sin on the people (Ex. 32:22–23), and when he gets to his part, he doctors the part of the story in which he actively fashioned the calf. He makes it sound as if it magically popped out of the fire as a calf without any help from him! "So I said to them, 'Let any who have gold take it off.' So they gave it to me, and I threw it into the fire, *and out came this calf*" (32:24).

Aaron also takes part in a rebellion against Moses in Numbers 12. Both of these times, Moses must make intercession for the Lord to spare Aaron.

THE PRIESTS AND LEVITES[1]

The Pentateuch stresses God's choice of the priests and the Levites to serve as his ministers. Numbers 18:3–7 summarizes their ministry in a nutshell. They are the guardians of covenant worship, which is a gift to the covenant people.

> They shall keep *guard* over you and over the whole tent, but shall not come near to the vessels of the sanctuary or to the altar lest they, and you, die. They shall join you and keep *guard* over the tent of meeting for all the service of the tent, and no outsider shall come near you. And you shall keep *guard* over the sanctuary and over the altar, that there may never again be wrath on the people of Israel. And behold, I have taken your brothers the Levites from among the people of Israel. They are a *gift to you, given to the Lord*, to do the service of the tent of meeting. And you and your sons with you shall *guard* your priesthood for all that concerns the altar and that is within the veil; and you shall

---

[1] I want to thank my friend and Old Testament scholar Jason S. DeRouchie for an instructive Power-Point presentation on the role of the priests and Levites in Israel. Much of this section comes from that presentation.

serve. *I give your priesthood as a gift*, and any outsider who comes near shall be put to death. (18:3–7)

This divine calling enables the Levites to have a mediatorial role between the Lord and the Israelites because the Levite "ministers in the name of the Lord his God" (Deut. 18:7) and "bless in his name" (Deut. 10:8) according to God's choice (Deut. 18:5). The nearest parallel to this ministry today in the church is that of the worship pastor.

Therefore, the priests and Levites serve in the tabernacle and guard against future apostasy and divine wrath (Num. 18:4–5, 7; Deut. 17:8–9, 18; 21:5; 24:8; 27:14; 31:9–10, 24–26; 33:10). As covenant guardians, their very presence reminds Israel of God's holiness and their proneness to sin.

Furthermore, as guardians of God's instruction and worship, the tribe of Levi is a picture of what the nation is to be on a global scale— mediators of God's blessing to the nations. Up until the end of Old Testament history, God's prophets declare the failure of the tribe of Levi to perform their role and, with that, the failure of the nation to give proper witness to God's greatness.

Malachi 2:4–9 offers the clearest indictment of the tribe of Levi. Notice that its ministry focused not only on content, but also on reverence. Notice too that as "messenger[s] of the Lord of hosts" they gave instruction and guarded knowledge so that they might turn people from iniquity. Their failure had the opposite effect; their false stewardship caused many to stumble.

> So shall you know that I have sent this command to you, that my covenant with Levi may stand, says the Lord of hosts. My covenant with him was one of life and peace, and I gave them to him. It was a covenant of fear, *and he feared me. He stood in awe of my name. True instruction* was in his mouth, and no wrong was found on his lips. He walked with me in peace and uprightness, and *he turned many from iniquity. For the lips of a priest should guard knowledge, and people should seek instruction from his mouth, for he is the messenger of the Lord of hosts.* But you have turned aside from the way. *You have caused many to stumble by your instruction.* You have corrupted the covenant of Levi, says the Lord of hosts, and so I make you despised and abased before all the people, inasmuch as you do not keep my ways but show partiality in your instruction. (2:4–9)

APPLICATION

Today's stewards can learn much from the function of the Levites within Israel and their failure. I desire to practice stewardship according to the picture of Malachi 2. They were faithful *stewards*, guarding knowledge (2:7) and having no wrong found on their lips (2:6). They were also called to be fearless and reverent *heralds*: fearing God and standing in awe of his name (2:5), having true instruction in their mouths (2:6), and speaking as messengers of the Lord of hosts (2:7). Levi's ministry of the word should have the *effect* of turning many from iniquity (2:6). But Levi's corrupt stewardship "caused many to stumble" (2:8).

Paul functioned in this role in giving authoritative guidance for worship in the churches (cf. 1 Cor. 14:26–40). He later gave Timothy instructions concerning "how one ought to behave in the household of God" (1 Tim. 3:15). Paul passes on his role as a guardian of new covenant worship to pastoral shepherds.

FALSE STEWARD: BALAAM

Balaam appears as a prophet for hire in Numbers 22–24. Balak, the king of Moab, enlists him to curse Israel. The Lord intervenes and uses Balaam to bless Israel. Balaam even speaks a word of promise concerning the coming Messiah (Num. 24:15–17).

Numbers 25 is the reason why Balaam appears in the rest of the Bible as an enemy of God even though he spoke truth in the previous chapter. Numbers 31:16 charges Balaam with guilt in the seduction and apostasy at Baal Peor (see Num. 25:1–18). God refuses to hear him (Deut. 23:5; Josh. 24:10). As one of the enemies of Israel he is killed (Num. 31:8; Josh. 13:22). Balaam becomes a pattern for future false teachers who gain influence in the Christian community and encourage immorality (2 Pet. 2:15–16; Jude 11; Rev. 2:14).

The New Testament presents Balaam as a false steward not so much because he spoke what was false, but because he loved what was false ("gain from wrongdoing"). His false living proved that he was a false prophet. His false stewardship would have the effect of causing people to stumble.

Forsaking the right way, they have gone astray. They have followed the way of Balaam, the son of Beor, *who loved gain from wrongdoing*, but was rebuked for his own transgression; a speechless donkey spoke with human voice and restrained the prophet's madness. (2 Pet. 2:15–16)

But I have a few things against you: you have some there who hold the teaching of Balaam, who taught Balak *to put a stumbling block* before the sons of Israel, so that they might eat food sacrificed to idols and practice sexual immorality. (Rev. 2:14)

MOSES

God's choice of Moses as a servant of his word brings the stewardship theme into even clearer focus in the rest of the Pentateuch. Moses serves as the paradigm for preaching in the Pentateuch as a servant of God's word in his role as mediator in the covenant between God and Israel.

This point in the narrative brings us to a pattern that will carry us through the rest of the study. The pattern involves (1) God's calling of the steward, (2) the activity of stewarding and heralding, and (3) the effects of encountering God through his word. We will provide snapshots of all three aspects.

MOSES'S CALL

The call of Moses deserves closer scrutiny because it serves as a paradigm for future stewards of the word. The author of Hebrews says that faith was operative even from the outset of Moses's story because his parents did not fear the king's edict. "By faith Moses, when he was born, was hidden for three months by his parents, because they saw that the child was beautiful, and they were not afraid of the king's edict" (Heb. 11:23).

Moses's first attempt at deliverance failed after he struck down an Egyptian. He thought the Israelites would know that he was trying to deliver them (Acts 7:25). The author of Hebrews sees faith at work even in the early phase of Moses's life.

By faith Moses, when he was grown up, refused to be called the son of Pharaoh's daughter, choosing rather to be mistreated with the people of God than to enjoy the fleeting pleasures of sin. He considered the reproach of Christ greater wealth than the treasures of Egypt, for he was looking to the reward. By faith he left Egypt, not being afraid of the anger of the king, for he endured as seeing him who is invisible. (Heb. 11:24–27)

In other words, Moses continues to focus on the things unseen, not the things that are seen. He gives up the life of ease he sees as the son of Pharaoh's daughter and risks receiving the harsh treatment he sees the people of God receiving. This decision shows that he chooses not to enjoy the pleasures and treasures of Egypt that are seen. Moses regards these pleasures and treasures as fleeting and so he places greater value on the "reproach of Christ" and the future reward. He leaves Egypt not fearing the anger of Pharaoh, because he trusts in the unseen and invisible God (11:27).[2]

Second, the calling of Moses itself stresses that God does not call Moses because of Moses's ability. God does not call the equipped; he equips the called. He calls Moses and stresses that he, God, would enable Moses to fulfill that call. Third, even after Moses fails to believe in God's ability, God graciously condescends to Moses's weakness by giving him Aaron as his mouthpiece.

Israel believes the signs God entrusts to Moses and believes that God will deliver them from Egypt, but this faith quickly turns to unbelief in the wilderness. Israel's continual failure to follow God's word is a common feature of the rest of the Pentateuch. Israel's sinful, rebellious, and stiff-necked condition makes it necessary for Moses to serve as a mediator. God's calling of Moses is confirmed by the request of the people. God's unmediated holiness is so terrifying that they urge Moses to be their mediator.

---

[2] I am aware that some take Moses's leaving Egypt as part of the exodus (Exodus 14), but I am taking this as a description of Moses's first departure as documented in Ex. 2:14–15. Some see a reference to the exodus itself because Hebrews says Moses was not afraid of the king's anger (Heb. 11:27), while Ex. 2:14 explicitly says that Moses was afraid and so he left. One can certainly understand this way of reading the text, but there are a couple of problems. First, this reading would make the exodus from Egypt (Exodus 13) come before the Passover (Exodus 12). Furthermore, the words about the king's anger would not make as much sense as a reference to the exodus of chapter 13, because Pharaoh finally consented to let the people go. What about the reference to Moses's fear in Ex. 2:14 and the reference to Moses's lack of fear in Heb. 11:27? In my reading, Hebrews is probably commenting on how Moses overcame his fear mentioned in Ex. 2:14–15: by looking to the invisible God. For a similar reading, see William Lane, *Hebrews 9–13*, Word Biblical Commentary (Dallas: Word, 2002), 375.

> Now when all the people saw the thunder and the flashes of lightning and the sound of the trumpet and the mountain smoking, the people were afraid and trembled, and they stood far off and said to Moses, "You speak to us, and we will listen; but do not let God speak to us, lest we die." (Ex. 20:18–19; cf. Heb. 12:18–21)

As covenantal mediator, Moses is called by God to deliver messages from the Lord for the people. We turn to this aspect of Moses's life in the next section.

STEWARDING AND HERALDING GOD'S WORD

Moses takes on this mediatorial role from his call in Exodus 3 onward, long before the people request that he take on this role permanently and exclusively in Exodus 19. The author of Hebrews continues to comment on how Moses's belief in God's word caused him to be an effective steward of it in leading the people to keep the Passover and to cross through the Red Sea. "By faith he kept the Passover and sprinkled the blood, so that the Destroyer of the firstborn might not touch them. By faith the people crossed the Red Sea as on dry land, but the Egyptians, when they attempted to do the same, were drowned" (Heb. 11:28–29).

Other examples abound concerning this stewarding role of Moses both before Exodus 19 (Ex. 12:1–20; 13:1–2; 14:1–4; 16:12; etc.) and henceforth (Ex. 19:20–23:33). Perhaps the clearest description of Moses's ministry as a steward of God's word comes in a context where Aaron and Miriam question Moses's ministry. They claim that the Lord has also spoken to them, not just to Moses (Num. 12:1–2). God comes and sets the record straight:

> And he said, "Hear my words: If there is a prophet among you, I the Lord make myself known to him in a vision; I speak with him in a dream. Not so with my servant Moses. He is faithful in all my house. With him I speak mouth to mouth, clearly, and not in riddles, and he beholds the form of the Lord. Why then were you not afraid to speak against my servant Moses?" (Num. 12:6–8)

The narrator often includes the precise content of what the Lord says to Moses or what Moses says to the people. At other times, the narrator gives an abbreviated summary of Moses relaying the messages to the people and summaries of the people's response. Moses is the mediator of the covenant between God and Israel in Exodus 19:20–24:8. Exodus 19:20–23:33 provides a detailed account of the specific words that God entrusts to Moses, while Exodus 24:3 gives a very short summary of what Moses says and how the people respond: "Moses came and told the people all the words of the LORD and all the rules. And all the people answered with one voice and said, 'All the words that the LORD has spoken we will do'" (24:3).

It is interesting to note that these examples are expressed in general terms for speaking, not with a specialized vocabulary for preaching. It is also vitally important to see that Moses not only speaks these words from God; he also records them so that they become the written word of God, Scripture: "And Moses wrote down all the words of the LORD" (Ex. 24:4).

These written words serve as the words of the covenant. Moses reads them aloud and the people respond:

> Then he took the Book of the Covenant and read it in the hearing of the people. And they said, "All that the LORD has spoken we will do, and we will be obedient." And Moses took the blood and threw it on the people and said, "Behold the blood of the covenant that the LORD has made with you in accordance with all these words." (Ex. 24:7–8)

The narrator puts frequent stress on the fact that God remains faithful to the covenant but the people do not. Part of Moses's role as mediator is to make intercession for the people so that God will not wipe them off the face of the earth for their sin. After another lengthy description of what God spoke to Moses on the mountain (Ex. 25:1–31:18), the reader catches a glimpse of Israel's stiff-necked spiritual disposition (Ex. 32:1–6). Moses intercedes for them (32:11–14), and the text says that the Lord "relented" from the judgment that he had spoken of concerning Israel. Moses comes down from the mountain and shows a burning resolve to deal swiftly with Israel's covenant breaking (32:19–29). He then returns to the Lord's presence to make intercession for the people (32:31–34). He simply will not accept the possibility that God's presence will not go with them; the presence of

God defines their very identity (Ex. 33:3). Moses continues to intercede until the Lord promises to go with them (33:14). Moses goes so far as to say that he would rather stay in the barren wasteland of the wilderness and enjoy God's presence than have the promised rest of the Promised Land *without* God's presence. Other examples of this intercessory role abound (Num. 14:13–19).

Moses must deliver the message accurately, but God also requires him to herald it humbly and reverently. Moses's attitude toward the Lord is a vital part of the message. Moses is called "very meek, more than all people who were on the face of the earth" (Num. 12:3). He has a fearless meekness even in the face of opposition from his family members (12:1–2).

Moses fails only once in respect to reverence. As a result, he must go up on a mountain and see the Promised Land only from a distance before his death. This judgment comes upon him for "failing to uphold me as holy at the waters before their eyes" (Num. 27:14).

THE EFFECTS

When we read Israel's story, it is important to identify the link between belief/unbelief and blessing/curse. Israel's faith or lack of faith in God's word dictates the effects, for good or ill. Belief and unbelief are the upstream source of the downstream effects of blessing and curse. Before we canvass some of the downstream effects of faith or unbelief, recall the fourfold problem, promise, sign, and faith paradigm that pops up in Exodus through Deuteronomy:

Exodus 4:31

> Problem: Moses is worried the people won't believe him (4:1).
> Promise: God promises that the people will believe the signs (4:8).
> Sign: The staff becomes a snake; the hand becomes leprous (4:8).
> Faith: The Israelites believe (4:31).

Exodus 14:31

> Problem: Egyptian army is at the heels of the Israelites (14:1–12).
> Promise: The Lord will fight for the Israelites (14:13).
> Sign: The Red Sea is parted with the staff (14:16, 21).

Faith: "The people feared the LORD, and they believed in the LORD and in his servant Moses" (14:31).

Numbers 14:11

Problem: People are grumbling against their leaders (14:1–4).
Promise: The Lord will bring them into the land (14:6–9).
Sign: The Lord has performed signs among them (14:11).
Faith: The people fail to believe in the Lord and all his signs (14:11).

Numbers 20:12

Problem: People gather against leaders because of a lack of water (20:2–5).
Promise: Moses will bring water from the rock (20:7–8).
Sign: Moses strikes the rock with his staff (20:11).
Faith: Moses and Aaron did not believe (20:12).

So Israel receives a divine calling and begins with faith (Exodus 4; 14; Heb. 11:29), but then falls into unbelief (Numbers 14; 20). Israel's fall narrative in Exodus 32 already has set the stage for these subsequent failures. Israel's "redemption" from Egypt has done nothing to deal with her stiff-necked nature. The rest of the Pentateuch keeps referencing how the people are stiff-necked, rebellious, and unbelieving. The first generation fails to enter the Promised Land because of unbelief. God responds in judgment of their unbelief and rebellion and forces them to wander in the wilderness until all of them die. As noted above in Numbers 20, even Moses and Aaron fail to believe and die outside of the Promised Land.

By the end of the Pentateuch, the reader has more than enough evidence to agree with Moses's assessment of Israel as stiff-necked, rebellious, and unbelieving.

Know, therefore, that the LORD your God is not giving you this good land to possess because of your righteousness, for you are a stubborn people. Remember and do not forget how you provoked the LORD your God to wrath in the wilderness. *From the day you came out of the land of Egypt until you came to this place, you have been rebellious against the LORD.* Even at Horeb you provoked the LORD to wrath, and the LORD was so angry with you that he was ready to destroy you. (Deut. 9:6–8)

Moses understands that the Lord has not given the people hearts to trust and obey (Deut. 29:1). Moses even recognizes that their rebellion will be even worse after his death. "For I know how rebellious and stubborn you are. Behold, even today while I am yet alive with you, you have been rebellious against the LORD. How much more after my death!" (Deut. 31:27).

Israel as a whole is physically circumcised, but spiritually un-circumcised (Deut. 10:16). Their hard hearts have effectively made Moses's command to internalize the law an impossibility. Even as Israel stands on the outskirts of the Promised Land on the plains of Moab, Deuteronomy stresses that the unthinkable is inevitable: Israel's sinful rebellion will continue even after they possess the land that God has given them, and thus God will forcefully remove them from the Land of Promise just as he cast Adam and Eve out of the garden of Eden.

Despite God's judgment upon Israel (both present and future), God grants the promise of future restoration. Even if internalizing the law is impossible for sinful man, the Pentateuch eloquently testifies that nothing is impossible with God. He will circumcise the people's hearts and cause them and their offspring to obey him. In the future, God will create the faithfulness for which he calls. "And the LORD your God will circumcise your heart and the heart of your offspring, so that you will love the LORD your God with all your heart and with all your soul, that you may live" (Deut. 30:6).

The end of the story in Deuteronomy helpfully clarifies the relationship between God, the word of God, and the people of God. Moses points out that "the word" is very near to them (Deut. 30:14), and so he stirringly reminds them that "life and good, death and evil" hang in the balance depending upon their obedience to that word (30:15–16). He can even call "heaven and earth to witness against them" that he has set before them "life and death, blessing and curse" (30:19). Therefore, he urges them, "Choose life, that you and your offspring may live" (30:19).[3]

Two statements further clarify the identity of this "life." First,

---

[3] See the excellent exposition of this theme in J. G. Millar, *Now Choose Life: Theology and Ethics in Deuteronomy*, New Studies in Biblical Theology (Downers Grove, IL: InterVarsity, 2000).

Deuteronomy 30:20 says that choosing life means "loving the Lord your God, obeying his voice and holding fast to him, *for he is your life and length of days*, that you may dwell in the land that the Lord swore to your fathers, to Abraham, to Isaac, and to Jacob, to give them." In other words, God is their life.

Second, Deuteronomy 32 adds that God's words are their very life:

> And when Moses had finished speaking all these words to all Israel, he said to them, "Take to heart all the words by which I am warning you today, that you may command them to your children, that they may be careful to do all the words of this law. For it is no empty word for you, *but your very life*, and by this word you shall live long in the land that you are going over the Jordan to possess." (32:45–47)

Therefore, one should not create any false dichotomies between God and his word. God is Israel's "life" (Deut. 30:20) and that life is mediated by his word, which is their "very life" (Deut. 32:47).

A PROPHET LIKE MOSES?

The Pentateuch also stresses that a prophet like Moses will arise. The announcement of this future prophet comes on the heels of God's warning to the Israelites not to follow the abominable practices of the nations they are dispossessing. Special stress is placed upon the fact that they "listen to fortune-tellers and to diviners" (Deut. 18:14). By way of contrast with this abomination, God's word will be entrusted to a future prophet, and the spiritual state of the people will hinge on their response to him. These verses establish a paradigm for prophets to come, but also for *the* prophet to come. We will analyze this text according to our threefold pattern.

CALLING

> The Lord your God will raise up for you a prophet like me from among you, from your brothers. (Deut. 18:15)

> And the Lord said to me, "They are right in what they have spoken. I will raise up for them a prophet like you from among their brothers." (18:17–18)

STEWARDING AND HERALDING

The True Steward and Herald

> And I will put my words in his mouth, and he shall speak to them all that I command him. (Deut. 18:18)

The False Steward and Herald

> But the prophet who presumes to speak a word in my name that I have not commanded him to speak, or who speaks in the name of other gods, that same prophet shall die. (Deut. 18:20)

Criteria for Distinguishing a True Steward and Herald from a False One

> And if you say in your heart, "How may we know the word that the LORD has not spoken?"—when a prophet speaks in the name of the LORD, if the word does not come to pass or come true, that is a word that the LORD has not spoken; the prophet has spoken it presumptuously. You need not be afraid of him. (Deut. 18:21–22)

THE EFFECTS OF ENCOUNTERING
GOD THROUGH HIS WORD

> It is to him you shall listen—just as you desired of the LORD your God at Horeb on the day of the assembly, when you said, "Let me not hear again the voice of the LORD my God or see this great fire any more, lest I die." (Deut. 18:15–16)

> And whoever will not listen to my words that he shall speak in my name, I myself will require it of him. (18:19)

Again, these verses establish a paradigm for prophets to come (see the next chapter), but they point primarily to *the* prophet to come, as the New Testament narrative makes clear:

> Repent therefore, and turn back, that your sins may be blotted out, that times of refreshing may come from the presence of the Lord, and that he may send the Christ appointed for you, Jesus, whom heaven must receive until the time for restoring all the things about which God spoke by the mouth of his holy prophets long ago. *Moses said, "The Lord God will raise up for you a prophet like me from your brothers. You shall listen to him in whatever he tells you. And it shall be that every soul who does not listen to that prophet shall be destroyed from the people."* (Acts 3:19–23)

CONCLUSION

Moses's words at the end of Deuteronomy foreshadow the problems that future stewards will have in leading Israel: "For I know how rebellious and stubborn you are. Behold, even today while I am yet alive with you, you have been rebellious against the LORD. How much more after my death!" (Deut. 31:27).

The blessing and the curse will again mark Israel's history in the story of the stewardship of Joshua, the judges, and Samuel.

9

THE STEWARDSHIP OF JOSHUA, THE JUDGES, AND SAMUEL

Paradigm 4

> Only be strong and very courageous, being careful to do according to all the law that Moses my servant commanded you. Do not turn from it to the right hand or to the left, that you may have good success wherever you go. This Book of the Law shall not depart from your mouth, but you shall meditate on it day and night, so that you may be careful to do according to all that is written in it.
>
> *Joshua 1:7–8*

The following short survey of the stewardship of Joshua, the judges, and Samuel will once again focus on three aspects: (1) calling, (2) stewarding and heralding God's word, and (3) the effects. I will give more space to tracing the narrative of Israel's downward spiral of sin.

JOSHUA

JOSHUA'S CALL

God calls Joshua to lead Israel after the death of Moses (Josh. 1:1–2). This calling to lead God's people has three points of continuity with the leadership of Moses: (1) continuity of God's presence ("just as I was with Moses, so I will be with you"—1:5; cf. 1:9), (2) continued stewardship of the same word ("all the law that Moses my servant commanded you"—1:7), and (3) the same promises of blessing for stewarding the word. The dynamic relationship between stewarding and blessing is clear in Joshua 1:7–8 (fig. 7).

Figure 7. Stewarding and blessing of the word in Joshua 1:7–8

Stewarding the Word of God	Blessing from God
. . . being careful to do according to all the law that Moses my servant commanded you.	
Do not turn from it to the right hand or to the left . . .	that you may have good success wherever you go.
This Book of the Law shall not depart from your mouth, but you shall meditate on it day and night, so that you may be careful to do according to all that is written in it.	For then you will make your way prosperous, and then you will have good success.

Notice as well that Israel recognizes God's call upon Joshua. The people confess their allegiance to Joshua as part of their overall commitment to follow the word of the Lord while remembering the consequences of failing to heed God's word. The word of the Lord and the words of his steward Joshua become intertwined in all of the second-person-singular uses of "you" and "your" in the following verses:

> All that you have commanded us we will do, and wherever you send us we will go. Just as we obeyed Moses in all things, so we will obey you. Only may the Lord your God be with you, as he was with Moses! Whoever rebels against your commandment and disobeys your words, whatever you command him, shall be put to death. Only be strong and courageous. (Josh. 1:16–18)

JOSHUA'S STEWARDING AND HERALDING

Joshua proves to be a faithful, fearless, and reverent minister of the word. He gives authoritative commands based on the words of Moses and brings them to bear upon the people and the situation at the appropriate times (e.g., Josh. 1:13–15). Perhaps the clearest example of

Joshua stewarding the written word of God in the Law of Moses comes in Joshua 8:32–35:

> And there, in the presence of the people of Israel, he wrote on the stones a copy of the law of Moses, which he had written. . . . And afterward he read all the words of the law, the blessing and the curse, according to all that is written in the Book of the Law. There was not a word of all that Moses commanded that Joshua did not read before all the assembly of Israel, and the women, and the little ones, and the sojourners who lived among them. (8:32, 34–35)

Joshua also stewards words that God spoke directly to him. This dynamic is on full display in Joshua 3. The Lord first speaks his words to Joshua:

> The LORD said to Joshua, "Today I will begin to exalt you in the sight of all Israel, that they may know that, as I was with Moses, so I will be with you. And as for you, command the priests who bear the ark of the covenant, 'When you come to the brink of the waters of the Jordan, you shall stand still in the Jordan.'" (3:7–8)

And then Joshua delivers this word to the people. "And Joshua said to the people of Israel, 'Come here and listen to the words of the LORD your God'" (3:9). He not only accurately conveys the message, but also insists upon reverence and consecration because of God's presence: "Then Joshua said to the people, 'Consecrate yourselves, for tomorrow the LORD will do wonders among you'" (3:5).

Joshua also worshipfully responds to God's revelation when the commander of the Lord's army appears. He removes his sandals like Moses before him (Ex. 3:5) because of the holy ground on which he stands (Josh. 5:14–15). The author of Hebrews also stresses the faith of Joshua and the people in God's word at the destruction of Jericho: "By faith the walls of Jericho fell down after they had been encircled for seven days" (Heb. 11:30).

Examples like these could be multiplied as the Lord speaks to Joshua about the need for circumcision (Josh. 5:2), the details of battle instructions (6:1–5; 8:1–2, 18), or how the land should be apportioned. Joshua's belief in God's word makes him effective not only in stewarding and heralding God's words to the people, but also in carrying out the Lord's instructions (7:10–15) when people do not obey his word (7:16–26).

THE EFFECTS

The book of Joshua follows the pattern of the Pentateuch in high-lighting the consequences that flow from stewarding or failing to steward God's life-giving word. The rest of the book brings this dual focus to bear. Conquest flows from obedience to God's word, not from the Israelites' military might (at Jericho); defeat comes hard on the heels of failing to heed God's word (at Ai following the disobedience of Achan).

Many summary statements throughout the book of Joshua read like a stunning success story of God accomplishing his word of promise. For example:

> Thus the LORD gave to Israel all the land that he swore to give to their fathers. And they took possession of it, and they settled there. And the LORD gave them rest on every side just as he had sworn to their fathers. Not one of all their enemies had withstood them, for the LORD had given all their enemies into their hands. Not one word of all the good promises that the LORD had made to the house of Israel had failed; all came to pass. (Josh. 21:43–45)

The end of Joshua comes full circle back to the beginning of the book with the same themes of being strong and courageous, God's presence, no man standing against them, and stewarding the word. The difference is that Joshua now passes along his calling to all of Israel, including this specific call to steward the word: "Therefore, be very strong to keep and to do all that is written in the Book of the Law of Moses, turning aside from it neither to the right hand nor to the left" (Josh. 23:6; cf. Josh. 1:7–8).

The fact that God entrusts Joshua's calling to all of Israel and does not appoint a specific individual as his successor does not bode well for Israel. The nation will fail in the stewardship of the word, and so the book sounds an ominous note that paves the way for the rest of Israel's history of rebelliousness against God's word:

But Joshua said to the people, "You are not able to serve the LORD, for he is a holy God. He is a jealous God; he will not forgive your transgressions or your sins. If you forsake the LORD and serve foreign gods, then he will turn and do you harm and consume you, after having done you good." (Josh. 24:19–20; cf. Deut. 29:1)

Despite this warning concerning their spiritual infidelity, the people once again reaffirm their covenantal commitment to the Lord at Shechem (Josh. 24:21, 24–25). Just as Moses wrote down God's word and provided a song as a witness against Israel, Joshua writes down God's word and sets up a stone as a witness against Israel.

And Joshua wrote these words in the Book of the Law of God. And he took a large stone and set it up there under the terebinth that was by the sanctuary of the LORD. And Joshua said to all the people, "Behold, this stone shall be a witness against us, for it has heard all the words of the LORD that he spoke to us. Therefore it shall be a witness against you, lest you deal falsely with your God." (24:26–27)

JUDGES: THE WORD OF DELIVERANCE

The book of Judges picks up the narrative where the book of Joshua left off: with the mention of Joshua's death (Josh. 24:29; Judg. 1:1; 2:8). Thereafter, things begin to unravel quickly as a generation that does not know the Lord comes on the scene (Judg. 2:10). The Lord's word of judgment for Israel becomes a centerpiece of the Former Prophets from this point forward, as made clear by the angel of the Lord:

Now the angel of the LORD went up from Gilgal to Bochim. And he said, "I brought you up from Egypt and brought you into the land that I swore to give to your fathers. I said, 'I will never break my covenant with you, and you shall make no covenant with the inhabitants of this land; you shall break down their altars.' But you have not obeyed my voice. What is this you have done? So now I say, I will not drive them out before you, but they shall become thorns in your sides, and their gods shall be a snare to you." (2:1–3)

The rest of the narrative unveils a tragic tale of how the Israelites progressively become like the nations they have dispossessed because they fail to steward God's word of life and blessing. In fact, God leaves the nations in their midst as a test to see whether his people will rightly steward his word. "They were for the testing of Israel, to know whether Israel would obey the commandments of the LORD, which he commanded their fathers by the hand of Moses" (Judg. 3:4).

The people do not steward the word but begin to do what is right in their own eyes, which the Lord already warned against in the Pentateuch. Compare the following verses, with my emphasis added:

> The LORD said to Moses, "Speak to the people of Israel, and tell them to make tassels on the corners of their garments throughout their generations, and to put a cord of blue on the tassel of each corner. And it shall be a tassel for you to look at and remember all the commandments of the LORD, to do them, not to follow after your own heart and *your own eyes*, which you are inclined to whore after. So you shall remember and do all my commandments, and be holy to your God. (Num. 15:37–40)

> "You shall not do according to all that we are doing here today, everyone doing *whatever is right in his own eyes*, for you have not as yet come to the rest and to the inheritance that the LORD your God is giving you. (Deut. 12:8–9)

> In those days there was no king in Israel. Everyone did *what was right in his own eyes*. (Judg. 17:6)

> In those days there was no king in Israel. Everyone did *what was right in his own eyes*. (Judg. 21:25)

In their disobedience to the word of God (e.g., Judg. 2:1–3), God delivers them over to their enemies and they are enslaved (2:10–15). At this point, what happened in a large scale in the book of Exodus takes place many times on a much smaller scale. The Israelites call out to God in their bondage, and God hears their cry for deliverance and raises up deliverers, called judges (2:16).

We will briefly survey the stewards and heralds among the judges, following our threefold grid of calling, stewarding and heralding, and the effects of encountering God through his word.

THE JUDGES' CALL

Judges 2:16 says that the Lord raised up all of the judges, and it is striking to note how frequently the book of Judges makes this point explicit with examples such as Othniel (3:9), Ehud (3:15), Gideon (6:11–14), and Samson (13:1–25). Gideon and Samson deserve more focus here because they have somewhat lengthy call narratives that resemble the earlier callings of Moses and Joshua.

The calling of Gideon is preceded by the Lord's calling an unnamed prophet to come and speak to Israel (Judg. 6:8–10). The angel of the Lord comes and speaks to Gideon, describing his call and his commissioning to send Gideon (6:12, 14, 16). Gideon responds like Moses before him in a way that emphasizes his own weakness and uncertainty (6:13, 15), even to the degree that he asks for signs so that he can be certain (6:17–21, 36–40). Gideon comes to understand that he has encountered the angel of the Lord himself, and yet Gideon does not die (6:22–23).

The calling of Samson is even lengthier and features a birth narrative like that of Moses before or Samuel later. The angel of the Lord appears to Manoah and his barren wife at separate times describing the upcoming birth of this deliverer whom they will name Samson (Judg. 13:1–20). They both come to realize that the angel is the angel of the Lord, and they marvel that they see God and live (13:21–23).

In other words, the calling narratives of Moses, Gideon, and Samson (his parents) are all similar in that all three meet the angel of the Lord (Ex. 3:2; Judg. 6:11–23; 13:1–23), while Moses and Gideon are similar in further ways because of their reticence to answer the call and God's gift of helpers (Aaron for Moses [Ex. 4:14] and Purah for Gideon [Judg. 7:10]).

THE JUDGES' STEWARDING AND HERALDING

The judges are entrusted with instruction from the Lord (Judg. 4:6–7, 14; 6:25–26; 7:2, 4–5, 7, 9–11), sometimes including ongoing revelation concerning the details of battle. Although they have a word-based ministry in receiving instruction from the Lord, the aspect of military action dominates the narrative. Sometimes the "message from God" is a literal sword (Judg. 3:16–22)!

The narrative in Judges stresses one other consistent thing concerning these judges: the presence of the Lord through his Spirit empowering them in their work (Judg. 3:10; 6:34; 11:29; 13:25; 14:6, 19; 15:14). In other words, the Lord's grace is evident from first to last in the lives of these stewards and heralds because he has raised them up and then empowered them so their work will succeed.

The author of Hebrews mentions four of the judges as examples of faith (Gideon, Barak, Samson, Jephthah—Heb. 11:32), even if the narrative of Judges also points out their moments of weakness and unbelief.

THE EFFECTS

The whole of Judges stresses the cycle of blessings or curses that flow from obeying or disobeying God's word. Disaster follows when everyone does what is right in his own eyes instead of what is right according to God's word. Judges 2:17–19 summarizes this cycle:

> Yet they did not listen to their judges, for they whored after other gods and bowed down to them. They soon turned aside from the way in which their fathers had walked, who had obeyed the commandments of the LORD, and they did not do so. Whenever the LORD raised up judges for them, the LORD was with the judge, and he saved them from the hand of their enemies all the days of the judge. For the LORD was moved to pity by their groaning because of those who afflicted and oppressed them. But whenever the judge died, they turned back and were more corrupt than their fathers, going after other gods, serving them and bowing down to them. They did not drop any of their practices or their stubborn ways.

The last section of the book (Judges 17–21) contains two powerful pointers to the downward spiral that flows from Israel's failure to steward God's word. The story of Samson is not only a painful narrative of an individual's failure; it is also a mirror image of Israel's failure. Stephen Dempster gives us this summary:

> Samson, the supernaturally born Israelite, was set apart as a Nazirite with a distinctive vocation. He constantly breaks his religious vows, is enamoured of Philistine women, loses his identity and physical strength through these encounters, becomes a slave and has his eyes

gouged out by the enemy. He represents his own people, who had a supernatural origin, were set apart from among the nations with a distinctive vocation, broke their vows and were enamoured of foreign idols, until finally they lost their identity and spiritual power and became the blind slaves of their oppressors in exile.[1]

Judges sounds a terrifying note of judgment near the end of the book, in Judges 19. The Israelites do not risk spending the night at a Canaanite city (Jebus or Jerusalem). They decide instead to seek shelter in the Israelite city of Gibeah. The Israelite city proves to be worse than the pagan city as one of the sojourners is gang-raped and then murdered. The point of this gruesome story is to provide a telling link between the depravity of Sodom and the depravity of the Israelites (Gen. 19:4–9; Judg. 19:22–25). If God judged the former group, then certainly the destruction of Israel is not far behind. Dempster makes this point explicit: "Israel has become Sodom! 'A holy war must be conducted on the people of God' (Judg. 20–21)."[2]

The end of Judges provides a link with the book of Samuel via the theme of kingship. The last line of Judges reminds us again that "in those days there was no king in Israel. Everyone did what was right in his own eyes" (Judg. 21:25). The book of Samuel will introduce the emergence of the monarchy. Maybe a godly king will lead people back to God's word so that they will do what is right according to it.

The ministry of the word enters a transitional phase with the arrival of Samuel as one who fulfills functions like prophet, priest, and judge. Samuel is a transitional figure between the monarchy and the prophets because as prophet and judge he prophesies and rules, whereas those roles are later reassigned to prophets and kings. The relationship between God's prophets and kings will show up several times throughout this survey. God calls the prophets to appoint kings in his kingdom. The kings are also called to steward God's word. The kings who steward God's word well are invariably identified as the kings who rule well and bring blessing to Israel; those who don't, bring the curse.

---

[1] Stephen G. Dempster, *Dominion and Dynasty: A Biblical Theology of the Hebrew Bible*, New Studies in Biblical Theology (Downers Grove, IL: InterVarsity, 2003), 132.
[2] Ibid., 130.

The prophets come back into the picture at this point of failure to steward God's word. When his words are not heeded, God calls prophets as servants of his word to rebuke Israel and her rulers (e.g., Samuel with Saul, Nathan with David, Elijah with Ahab). We will begin with Samuel as both judge and prophet, and then move to the kings and the prophets that appear alongside them.

SAMUEL

SAMUEL'S CALL

The fact that the prophet Samuel has a birth narrative shows his importance in the story line of Scripture. The opening of the book of Samuel also paves the way for the distinction between Eli and his sons as false stewards and Samuel as a true steward of God's word.

Hannah, the wife of Elkanah, prays in agony to the Lord because she is barren. Eli the priest observes her praying, but thinks she is drunk (1 Sam. 1:13–14). The irony is that he falsely rebukes Hannah, but he fails to rebuke his own sons who truly need it.

Eli's sons are false stewards because they do not know the Lord: they are greedy, are sexually immoral, and do not follow the Lord's instructions (1 Sam. 2:12–17, 22–25; 3:13–14). Eli also proves to be a false steward of God's word because he fails to rebuke his sons, and thus he honors them above the Lord. Failing to uphold the Lord's word accurately, he thus fails to carry out his calling with reverence for the Lord's honor. Consider the following texts:

> Why then do you scorn my sacrifices and my offerings that I commanded . . . , and honor your sons above me by fattening yourselves on the choicest parts of every offering of my people Israel? Therefore the Lord, the God of Israel, declares: "I promised that your house and the house of your father should go in and out before me forever," but now the Lord declares: "Far be it from me, for those who honor me I will honor, and those who despise me shall be lightly esteemed." (1 Sam. 2:29–30)

> And I declare to him that I am about to punish his house forever, for the iniquity that he knew, because his sons were blaspheming God, and he did not restrain them. (1 Sam. 3:13)

Hannah bears a son, names him Samuel (1 Sam. 1:20), and devotes him to the Lord's service (1:22–28). Samuel serves alongside Eli for a time, but the Lord raises up a man of God to speak his words of rebuke to Eli (1 Sam. 2:27–36), which includes the announcement that Eli's ministry is coming to an end. This announcement is fulfilled in the calling of Samuel (1 Sam. 3:1–18), the death of Eli's sons (1 Sam. 4:11), and the death of Eli himself (4:18).

SAMUEL'S STEWARDING AND HERALDING

Samuel as a prophet is a true steward and herald of God's word, as the description in 1 Samuel 3:19–21 makes clear. The Lord is with Samuel so that his words do not fall to the ground, all Israel confirms his call, and the word of the Lord continually comes to him.

> And Samuel grew, and the LORD was with him and let none of his words fall to the ground. And all Israel from Dan to Beersheba knew that Samuel was established as a prophet of the LORD. And the LORD appeared again at Shiloh, for the LORD revealed himself to Samuel at Shiloh by the word of the LORD. (3:19–21)

It is hard to overstate the importance of this summary. Notice the link again between the Lord and his word. "The LORD revealed *himself* . . . by the word of the LORD" (1 Sam. 3:21). Samuel stewards and heralds the word of the Lord boldly, without the fear of man, because he is a man of faith in God and his word (Heb. 11:32). Samuel is grieved by Israel's sin (e.g., 1 Sam. 8:6), and both he and the people of Israel testify of his integrity (1 Sam. 12:1–5). This picture of fidelity to God is not passed on to his sons, who prove to be false stewards: "Yet his sons did not walk in his ways but turned aside after gain. They took bribes and perverted justice" (1 Sam. 8:3).

EFFECTS

Samuel stewards the word in a way that causes the people to return to the Lord (1 Sam. 7:3–4). He intercedes for them and the Lord answers, giving them victory over their enemies (7:7–11, 13–15). When the people see that Samuel's sons would not be good judges like Samuel, they ask for a king. The Lord tells Samuel to listen to the people, even in their rejection of the Lord, which has been the scarlet thread of Israel's spiritual condition since Egypt (1 Sam. 8:7–8). Israel's motive in asking for a king shows the nation's true condition. They refuse to hear Samuel's warnings about what the monarchy will be like. Even if it means that the Lord will not answer them, they still want to have a king, like the nations, because Israel has in fact become like the nations (8:18–20).

Therefore, Samuel listens to the Lord and appoints Saul as king over Israel (1 Sam. 9:17; 10:1). Samuel speaks as a witness against Israel in showing them how great their sin is in choosing a king when God is their king (1 Sam. 12:16–19). Despite this great sin, the Lord shows them that if they and the king properly steward God's life-giving word, blessing will follow.

> If you will fear the LORD and serve him and obey his voice and not rebel against the commandment of the LORD, and if both you and the king who reigns over you will follow the LORD your God, it will be well. But if you will not obey the voice of the LORD, but rebel against the commandment of the LORD, then the hand of the LORD will be against you and your king. (12:14–15)

The test is clear: will the king and the people properly steward the word? The reader does not have to wait long to know the futility that comes from their lack of faithfulness. One thing we see for sure is that God's word will be fulfilled.

APPLICATION: GOD'S WORD DOES NOT RETURN VOID

One event links Joshua to the time of the monarchy in the next chapter. The curse predicted by Joshua concerning Jericho becomes a reality: "In his days Hiel of Bethel built Jericho. He laid its foundation at the cost of Abiram his firstborn, and set up its gates at the cost of his youngest son Segub, according to the word of the LORD, which he spoke by Joshua the son of Nun" (1 Kings 16:34).

We are once again reminded of the sufficiency and power of God's word. A story from the ministry of Puritan John Flavel exemplifies this point. Michael Boland, in his 1963 introduction to Flavel's *Mystery of Providence*, tells the story in a nutshell:

Luke Short was a farmer in New England who attained his hundredth year in exceptional vigour though without having sought peace with God. One day as he sat in his fields reflecting upon his long life, he recalled a sermon he had heard in Dartmouth [England] as a boy before he sailed to America. The horror of dying under the curse of God was impressed upon him as he meditated on the words he had heard so long ago and he was converted to Christ—eighty-five years after hearing John Flavel preach.[3]

As Isaiah 55:10–11 says, God's word does not return to him empty. It will accomplish the purpose for which he sent it. Many will not have to wait eighty-five years, but other works of God may not be seen until they are viewed in the bright light of heaven.

Blessed is the man who believes in the unfailing reliability and unsurpassed power of God's word. Those who take their stand on the word of God in this way can testify with the words of the old hymn "Standing on the Promises" by R. Kelso Carter:

> Standing on the promises that cannot fail,
> When the howling storms of doubt and fear assail,
> By the living Word of God I shall prevail,
> Standing on the promises of God.

---

[3] Michael Boland, "Publisher's Introduction" to John Flavel, *The Mystery of Providence* (London: Banner of Truth, 1963), 11.

10

THE STEWARDSHIP OF THE COVENANT OF KINGSHIP

Paradigm 5

> You have spoken also of your servant's house for a great while to come, and this is instruction for mankind, O Lord God! And what more can David say to you? For you know your servant, O Lord God! Because of your promise, and according to your own heart, you have brought about all this greatness, to make your servant know it. Therefore you are great, O Lord God. For there is none like you, and there is no God besides you, according to all that we have heard with our ears.
>
> *2 Samuel 7:19–22*

SAUL

SAUL'S CALL

The monarchy of Israel does not get off to a good start. King Saul has a call narrative that looks impressive at first glance. The Spirit rushes on Saul twice in the space of two chapters. First, Saul is anointed by Samuel and has the Spirit rush upon him so that he prophesies and the people say, "Is Saul also among the prophets?" (1 Sam. 10:11). This auspicious beginning proves to be a false hope. Though Saul is a head taller than others in Israel, he is found hiding among the baggage when it comes time to be presented as king (10:20–23).

Second, the Spirit of the Lord rushes upon him again as he leads Israel against the Ammonites (1 Samuel 11). The Ammonites loom large in the narrative of Samuel. The king of the Ammonites is an ominous figure because his name, Nahash, is the Hebrew word for "serpent." Saul defeats the serpent king and arouses hope that he may be the promised king.

SAUL'S FALL

Any hopes that he is the Messiah are quickly dashed when he makes an unlawful sacrifice, thus rejecting the word of the Lord, and the Lord rejects him as king (1 Samuel 13). Samuel says to Saul, "You have not kept the command of the LORD your God, with which he commanded you" (13:13), and his kingdom will not endure (13:14). Saul makes rash vows (1 Samuel 14) and does not follow the instructions of the Lord concerning the Amalekites. The Lord sends Samuel with a message of rebuke for Saul:

> Because you have *rejected the word of the* LORD,
>   he has also rejected you from being king. (1 Sam. 15:23)

This interplay between Samuel and Saul anticipates the rocky relationship that will exist between the kings and prophets in the rest of the Old Testament. Saul's fall prepares for the rise of another.

DAVID

David has an amazing rise to rule over Israel. He is anointed king in 1 Samuel 16, but is not recognized as such until much later. The next chapter features David crushing the skull of a Philistine giant and thus evoking the imagery of Genesis 3:15. David's rise as king culminates in his defeating the king of the Ammonites, identified as the son of Nahash. The parallels are striking in that both Saul and David conquer the Ammonite "serpent."

1 Samuel 11: Saul conquers Nahash (serpent)
2 Samuel 10: David conquers the seed (son) of Nahash (serpent)

Could David be the one Israel has waited for? We will look at his ministry of the word through our three lenses of calling, stewarding, and effects.

DAVID'S CALL

David's calling comes in 1 Samuel 16:1–13. David is an unlikely candidate for king as the youngest of Jesse's sons, but the Lord directs Samuel to anoint David (16:12). The Spirit comes to empower David's kingship: "And the Spirit of the LORD rushed upon David from that day forward" (16:13).

DAVID'S STEWARDING AND HERALDING

David shows courageous zeal for the honor of the Lord, as the battle with Goliath shows. David is incredulous that Israel would allow an uncircumcised Philistine to "defy the armies of the living God" (1 Sam. 17:26), and he defeats Goliath "in the name of the LORD of hosts" (17:45) so that all assembled may know that "the battle is the LORD's" (17:47).

David frequently inquires of the Lord concerning his decisions, and the Lord speaks to him and directs his steps in fighting the Lord's enemies (e.g., 2 Sam. 5:22–25). David shows integrity and concern for the Lord's anointed and will not strike down Saul or take matters into his own hands (1 Samuel 24, 26).

Another prophet comes on the scene in 2 Samuel 7. Nathan the prophet brings an extravagant promise from the Lord to build a dynasty for David. The Lord will raise up a king from David's offspring and will "establish the throne of his kingdom forever" (7:13). David shows great concern to steward this word with grateful praise (7:18–29).

DAVID'S FALL

Any hopes that David is the Messiah will soon be decisively dashed. David's reign of righteousness is about to turn into a reign of terror. As mentioned earlier, the author wants to take us back to Genesis 3, but we arrive at 3:6, not 3:15. David is cast here not as the messianic seed, but as Eve, the sinner.

The wrong note sounds loud and clear in 2 Samuel 11. David's fall brings disastrous consequences in the rest of 2 Samuel. Notice that this "fall" narrative features three words coming together, which happens three times in biblical fall narratives:

- The woman "saw" that the tree was "good" (or "beautiful") for food . . . and she "took" of its fruit (Gen. 3:6). Judgment followed as Adam and Eve were cast out of the garden.
- The sons of God "saw" that the daughters of man were "attractive" (or "beautiful"). And they "took" as their wives any they chose (Gen. 6:2). Judgment follows as God brings a flood that destroys the earth with water.
- David "saw" from the roof a woman bathing; and she was very "beautiful." So David sent his messengers and "took" her (2 Sam. 11:2–4).

David commits adultery with Bathsheba and finds later that she is pregnant. Sin continues to pick up a head of steam as David tries to hide his sin. It builds as David hatches a new plan to cover up his sin. He tries to trick Uriah, but Uriah's righteousness and concern for his fellow soldiers stands in stark contrast with David's unrighteousness and lack of concern for the soldiers in harm's way.

This hurricane makes landfall upon Uriah and brings Joab into the torrent along with the death of other soldiers. They even fear David's former commitment to limit the risk of human death and hatch a plan of their own concerning how to break the news to David. Yet David passes judgment on all of it as good. A more literal translation will help us see the shocking word play. Though the king is supposed to adopt and enforce God's laws, David says, "Don't let this thing be evil in your eyes" (1 Sam. 11:25, AT). The narrator adds, "The thing that David had done was evil in Yahweh's eyes" (11:27, AT).

As I made clear back in chapter 4, David remains king because God is faithful to his covenantal promises. God's promise in 2 Samuel 7 comes before David's sin in 2 Samuel 11.

Nathan comes and brings the word of the Lord forcefully to bear upon David as the king's sin is described in a similar manner to that of Saul:

Why have you *despised the word of the Lord,* to do what is evil in his sight? You have struck down Uriah the Hittite with the sword and have taken his wife to be your wife and have killed him with the sword of the

> Ammonites. Now therefore the sword shall never depart from your house, because you have *despised me* and have taken the wife of Uriah the Hittite to be your wife. (2 Sam. 12:9–10)

Note the parallel description here: despising the word of the Lord (12:9) is tantamount to despising the Lord himself (12:10). David demonstrates the true difference between himself and Saul through full repentance and restoration. Despite David's return to the Lord, his failure concerning stewarding the word brings severe consequences.

EFFECTS

David's military triumphs are frequently highlighted and celebrated throughout Samuel (e.g., 2 Samuel 8, 10), but David's disobedience also brings the sword of the Lord (2 Sam. 12:10) upon himself and all of Israel through a series of judgments that unfold in shocking fashion in the chapters that follow (2 Sam. 12:15–19:8). David's sin in numbering Israel and its disastrous effects comes in the last chapter of 2 Samuel. Hope must now turn to David's offspring. Who will fulfill the promise of 2 Samuel 7? Solomon looks like the son of David who will fulfill this prophecy.

SOLOMON

SOLOMON'S CALL

David's son Solomon also has an auspicious beginning to his reign. He is anointed king of Israel (1 Kings 1:28–48), and David charges him to be a steward of the word:

> Keep the charge of the LORD your God, *walking in his ways and keeping his statutes, his commandments, his rules, and his testimonies, as it is written in the Law of Moses,* that you may prosper in all that you do and wherever you turn, that the LORD may establish his word that he spoke concerning me, saying, "If your sons pay close attention to their way, to walk before me in faithfulness with all their heart and with all their soul, you shall not lack a man on the throne of Israel." (1 Kings 2:3–4)

The narrator tells us that Solomon loves the Lord and walks in the statutes of David (1 Kings 3:3). It looks like Solomon will succeed

in his task because he shows great concern for properly stewarding the word when he asks the Lord for wisdom: "'Give your servant therefore an understanding mind to govern your people, that
I may discern between good and evil, for who is able to govern this
your great people?' It pleased the Lord that Solomon had asked this"
(1 Kings 3:9–10).

STEWARDING AND HERALDING

Having humbly prayed for wisdom (1 Kings 3:5–15), Solomon displays
wisdom in the next story (3:16–28). He has many officials, Israel flourishes like the sand of the sea (1 Kings 4:20), his kingdom spreads far
(4:21), and reports of his wisdom spread even wider (4:34). Solomon
hears from the Lord and obediently builds the temple (1 Kings 5–7).
The ark comes into the temple (1 Kings 8), and the Lord appears to
Solomon again, answering his prayer (1 Kings 9). The Davidic promises
are reaffirmed (1 Kings 9), the nations come to Israel (as exemplified by
the Queen of Sheba—1 Kings 10), and he is like the new Adam figure
that will fulfill Adam's commission.

SOLOMON'S FALL

1 Kings 3:3 says that Solomon loved the Lord and walked in the statutes
of David, but 1 Kings 11:1–8 documents a reversal of chilling proportions: "For when Solomon was old his wives turned away his heart
after other gods, and his heart was not wholly true to the Lord his
God, as was the heart of David his father" (11:4). With Solomon's love
for many foreign wives who turn him away from the Lord and the
ways of David, the departure from 1 Kings 3:3 is complete. The Lord
brings judgment upon Solomon and promises to tear the kingdom
from him. The kingdom divides in 1 Kings 12.

EFFECTS

Solomon's successful stewardship of the word unleashes a flood of
prosperity and peace into the narrative (1 Kings 4–10), while his failure as a steward of the word brings disaster and division (1 Kings
11:9–16:24).

THE DIVIDED KINGDOM

FALSE STEWARDS

Sadly, the history of the divided monarchy on the whole reads like a list of failed stewardship. Jeroboam's actions highlight Israel's continued rebellion as he builds not one, but two golden calves (1 Kings 12:25–33). Like Solomon, many of the kings have a summary statement saying that the king "did what was evil in the sight of the Lord" (1 Kings 11:6; 15:26, 34; 16:19, 25, 30; 2 Kings 3:2, 8:18, 27; 13:2, 11; 14:24; 15:9, 18, 24, 28; 17:2, 17; 21:2, 6, 20; 23:32, 37; 24:9, 19). It is striking how many times these descriptions are immediately followed by the effect that this failed stewardship had on the rest of the people so that the king's sin "made Israel to sin" (1 Kings 15:26, 34; 16:19, 26; 22:52; 2 Kings 3:3; 13:2, 11; 14:24; 15:9, 18, 24, 28; cf. 21:16). In fact, sometimes the singular "he did what was evil in the sight of the Lord" gives way to the plural for the people as a whole: "they did what was evil in the sight of the Lord" (1 Kings 14:22; 2 Kings 17:17; 21:15–16).

Prophets like Jehu occasionally come on the scene to pronounce the Lord's decree of judgment upon the kings (1 Kings 16:1), but a downward spiral of rebellion continues to plague the people of God. While Judah enjoys the good reign of King Asa, Israel suffers under the wicked rule of King Omri, who does more evil than all who were before him (16:25). Omri's son, King Ahab, outdoes even his father so that he does more evil and provokes the Lord to wrath more than all who were before him (16:30, 33; 21:25).

The focus next switches from the prophets to the kings. Israel goes into exile because the people and their kings do what is evil in the sight of the Lord. What is the basis of assessment for doing evil in the sight of the Lord? Fidelity to the law of the Lord (e.g., 2 Kings 10:31). Second Kings 17 may contain the fullest and clearest depiction of this dynamic. Siege and exile come upon the people because, the text says, they "feared other gods" (17:7) and "walked in the customs of the nations whom the Lord drove out" (17:8), which the "kings of Israel had practiced" (17:8). They do wicked things that the Lord has told them not to do (17:12), and so the Lord sends prophets to warn them, saying:

"Turn from your evil ways and *keep my commandments and my statutes, in accordance with all the Law that I commanded your fathers, and that I sent to you by my servants the prophets.*"

But they would not listen, but were stubborn, as their fathers had been, who did not believe in the LORD their God. *They despised his statutes and his covenant that he made with their fathers and the warnings that he gave them.* They went after false idols and became false, and they followed the nations that were around them, concerning whom the LORD had commanded them that they should not do like them. *And they abandoned all the commandments of the Lord their God*, and made for themselves metal images of two calves; and they made an Asherah and worshiped all the host of heaven and served Baal. (2 Kings 17:13–16)

Did you catch in verse 15 the chilling assessment in terms of the effects of this failed stewardship upon the people? "They went after false idols and became false." Israel and her kings did not steward God's words of life (cf. 18:12). They went after what was false and became false because of failed stewardship and false stewards of the word.

Some kings in Judah did what was good in the sight of God, but still failed in some respects. For example, Amaziah "did what was right in the eyes of the Lord," but not like David because Amaziah did not remove the high places (2 Kings 14:3–4) or conduct his rule on a specific matter "according to what is written in the Book of the Law of Moses, where the LORD commanded" (14:6).

GOOD STEWARDS: HEZEKIAH AND JOSIAH

Failing to remove the high places is a serious flaw for stewards of the law of Moses because the high places serve as centers of Israelite disobedience against the word of the Lord. However, a few of the kings shine as effective stewards of the word. We will focus attention on Hezekiah and Josiah.

Hezekiah is a shining light among the kings of Judah. The summary of his reign is full of evidence of effective stewardship of the word:

And he did what was right in the eyes of the LORD, according to all that David his father had done. He removed the high places and broke the pillars and cut down the Asherah. And he broke in pieces the bronze serpent that Moses had made, for until those days the people

of Israel had made offerings to it (it was called Nehushtan). He trusted
in the LORD, the God of Israel, so that there was none like him among
all the kings of Judah after him, nor among those who were before
him. For he held fast to the LORD. *He did not depart from following him,*
but kept the commandments that the LORD commanded Moses. And the LORD
was with him; wherever he went out, he prospered. He rebelled against the
king of Assyria and would not serve him. (2 Kings 18:3–7)

Second Kings 19 puts Hezekiah's trust in the Lord on display in
partnership with the prophet Isaiah. The word of the Lord proves
to be more powerful than the Assyrians (2 Kings 18:30–19:37). The
word through the prophet Isaiah also proves to be life-giving again as
the Lord adds fifteen years to Hezekiah's life (2 Kings 20:1–11). However, the shadow of exile in Babylon is already present even here in
the story (20:12–18).

Josiah has a startling summary statement compared with the other
kings: "And he did what was right in the eyes of the LORD and walked
in all the way of David his father, and he did not turn aside to the right
or to the left" (2 Kings 22:2). What makes Josiah's reign different? The
high priest Hilkiah rediscovers the law of Moses (22:8), and Josiah
stewards it well. When word reaches King Josiah, he gives a statement
that could stand as a summary of all of Kings:

Go, inquire of the LORD for me, and for the people, and for all Judah,
concerning the words of this book that has been found. For great is
the wrath of the LORD that is kindled against us, *because our fathers*
have not obeyed the words of this book, to do according to all that is written
concerning us. (22:13)

Josiah immediately shows what a serious steward of the word he
is. He gathers all the people, reads all the words of the book of the covenant (2 Kings 23:1–2), and leads the response by making a covenant
before the Lord "to walk after the LORD and to keep his commandments and his testimonies and his statutes with all his heart and all
his soul, to perform the words of this covenant that were written in
this book" (23:3).

The effect follows immediately: "And all the people joined in the
covenant" (2 Kings 23:3). Having heard the truth according to God's

word, Josiah immediately sets about to systematically remove all practices that contradict this truth (23:4–20). He even reinstitutes the Passover celebration according to the book of the covenant (23:21–23). Josiah removes everything contrary to God's word so that "he might establish the words of the law that were written in the book that Hilkiah the priest found in the house of the Lord" (23:24). As if to tighten the screw on this description one more turn, the narrator adds: "Before him there was no king like him, who turned to the Lord with all his heart and with all his soul and with all his might, according to all the Law of Moses, nor did any like him arise after him" (23:25).

Yet even this valiant attempt to steward the word accurately and reverently cannot erase all the former provocations of the people, because the Lord decreed judgment upon the southern kingdom (2 Kings 23:26–27), as was already prophesied back in Hezekiah's time (20:12–18). With both Israel and Judah languishing in exile, the focus moves once again to the ministry of the prophets—this time in the books of the Latter Prophets. Here we move from the narrative back to prophetic commentary.

APPLICATION: FLEE SEXUAL TEMPTATION (DAVID AND SOLOMON)

I wish the application "flee sexual temptation" were not necessary. I would pass up mention of it if I thought it was not an occupational hazard in ministry. Both David and Solomon left the path of fidelity to God and were snared by sexual temptation. The contrast between 1 Kings 3:3 ("Solomon loved the Lord") and 1 Kings 11:1 ("Now King Solomon loved many foreign women") is jarring. Solomon's heart turned away from the Lord and toward other gods (11:4). David committed adultery and then committed murder to cover it up.

The opening note struck in David's fall is that he was in the wrong place at the wrong time. David in a sense was just asking for trouble. At the time "when kings go to war," David sent others but stayed behind. He was by himself, separated from accountability, and alone with his sin. One cannot read 2 Samuel 11 without hearing the haunting notes of a horror movie like *Jaws*. When you hear the notes, you know the shark is close.

We learn here that sometimes the first step toward victory over sin is the step away from it. Remove yourself from the situation. Don't surf the Web or turn on the TV without accountability. Don't walk by that section of the store that has the magazines. Don't put yourself in situations that tempt you toward small compromises. Those small steps are like the start of the haunting notes that anticipate the fuller horror to come.

The second thing we see in David's fall is the destructiveness of sin. Unchecked, unconfessed breezes of sin will build into a full-blown hurricane. Refuse to believe the lie that sin will shrink over time if left alone. Sin is one of the only things that grows by keeping it in the dark and dies by bringing it into the light.

Refuse to believe the lie that our sinful choices really do not impact other people. We do not sin in a vacuum. Our hurricane of sin will blow into the path of others and wreak havoc. The leaven principle applies to homes and churches: a little bit of leaven will work through the whole lump. Do not make peace with sin. Refuse to believe the lie that sin is serious only if we get caught. Part of being a moral fool is believing the lie that sin can be hidden.

I know far too many who have fallen to sexual sin. Some observers are saying that the millennials have come to the point where they tolerate sexual sin because it is so pervasive. Please, if you are reading these words, do not think that you are above it. Few things can ruin someone's life so quickly and decisively. "Flee from sexual immorality" (1 Cor. 6:18). Ultimately, the way to flee all forms of sexual immorality is to flee to Christ. In the hymn "Before the Throne," Charitie Bancroft reminds us to look to Christ as our "perfect spotless righteousness." We will see that our true life is to be found not in sex, but in heaven, hidden with Christ on high.

> Behold Him there the risen Lamb,
> My perfect spotless righteousness,
> The great unchangeable I AM,
> The King of glory and of grace,
> One in Himself I cannot die.
> My soul is purchased by His blood,
> My life is hid with Christ on high,
> With Christ my Savior and my God!

11

THE STEWARDSHIP
OF THE PROPHETS

Paradigm 6

The goodly fellowship of the Prophets praise thee.

"Te Deum" or "Ambrosian Hymn"

Apostolic commentary on the prophets highlights prophecy's divine origin. Second Peter 1:19–21 affirms three things: (1) men spoke, (2) they were carried along by the Spirit, and thus (3) they spoke *from God*. Prophetic speech moves in two directions: forthtelling and foretelling. First, the prophets are forthtelling covenant lawsuit preachers promising judgment on the basis of Israel's breaking of the Mosaic covenant. Second, they also foretell the advent of a new age with the coming of the Messiah.

First Peter 1:10–12 stresses the prophetic labors in searching out this coming salvation. The prophets understood that these labors would serve a future generation, not merely their own.

> Concerning this salvation, the prophets who prophesied about the grace that was to be yours searched and inquired carefully, inquiring what person or time the Spirit of Christ in them was indicating when he predicted the sufferings of Christ and the subsequent glories. It was revealed to them that they were serving not themselves but you, in the things that have now been announced to you through those who preached the good news to you by the Holy Spirit sent from heaven, things into which angels long to look.

The prophets serve as examples of long-suffering patience as they minister for the sake of a future generation while facing their own hard-hearted generation. Apostolic commentary makes the same point: "As an example of suffering and patience, brothers, take the prophets who spoke in the name of the Lord" (James 5:10). Jesus himself pointed out that this suffering and patience often led to martyrdom.

> Therefore also the Wisdom of God said, "I will send them prophets and apostles, some of whom they will kill and persecute," so that the blood of all the prophets, shed from the foundation of the world, may be charged against this generation, from the blood of Abel to the blood of Zechariah, who perished between the altar and the sanctuary. (Luke 11:49–51)

The first two prophets in this survey, Elijah and Elisha, focus on Israel's covenant breaking, while the books of the prophets contain both emphases (forthtelling and foretelling). All of the prophets exercise their ministry in the context of affliction and patience as they look forward to the future work of God.

THE PROPHETS IN THE BOOKS OF THE FORMER PROPHETS

ELIJAH

During these dark days, the word of the Lord continues to speak with power. The word of the Lord spoken by Joshua concerning Jericho becomes a reality in 1 Kings 16:34, and in the very next two verses the word of the Lord comes on the scene as God confronts Ahab through a new prophet: Elijah the Tishbite (1 Kings 17:1–2). Elijah proves to be a great steward of the word. The word of the Lord comes to him (17:2–4, 8–9), and immediately he performs his task according to it (17:5–6, 10). The Lord listens to the voice of Elijah, multiplying food for the widow of Zarephath (17:14–16) and bringing her son back to life (17:22). The Gentile widow recognized the truth of the word of the God of Israel: "Now I know that you are a man of God, and that the word of the LORD in your mouth is truth" (17:24). It is a bitter stroke of irony that a Gentile widow sees and confesses what the people of God blindly reject. They have become worse than the nations.

First Kings 18 features a conversation between the true prophets

Obadiah and Elijah. Obadiah must go and tell Ahab to come and meet Elijah. Obadiah fears the Lord and obeys even though Jezebel has already murdered many of the prophets and Obadiah's life is in great risk (18:7–16). Ahab comes to meet Elijah, who arranges a test to determine the identity of the true God and his prophets. The story that follows is one of the great moments in the history of stewarding God's word.

Elijah stands alone against the 450 prophets of Baal on Mount Carmel, but he stands against them with extreme courage—even to the point of mocking them and their "god" (1 Kings 18:27). Baal is not the true God because he cannot answer by fire. When Elijah's turn comes, he makes the test even more difficult as he takes twelve stones, representing the twelve tribes of Israel, and uses them to construct an altar. He then orders twelve jars of water to be poured over the wood and the sacrifice. Elijah prays that the Lord will answer to show that he is the true God and Elijah is God's true prophet and that all transpires according to his word (18:36–37). God answers with fire that consumes the sacrifice, the wood, the stones, and all the water (18:38). The people recognize that God is the true God and Elijah is his true prophet. Elijah slaughters all the false prophets of Baal (18:40), and rain falls according to the word of the Lord (18:45).

Jezebel sends a death threat to Elijah, who flees to the wilderness and comes to Mount Sinai after receiving supernatural provision from the angel of the Lord (1 Kings 19:1–8). The Lord asks Elijah what he is doing at Mount Sinai, and Elijah shares the narrative of despairing events that have transpired. The Lord reveals himself to Elijah as he did to Moses. The Lord's presence is not in the wind, earthquake, or fire, but in a small whisper (19:11–12).

This demonstration shows that the Lord is still present and still in control by the power of his word. The narrative proceeds with displays of the power of God's word. First, God immediately sends Elijah to anoint Hazael as king over Syria, Jehu as king over Israel, and Elisha as a prophet in Elijah's place (1 Kings 19:15–16). The Lord is still in control over his kings and prophets. He also remains in control over his people as he has preserved a remnant of seven thousand that have not bowed the knee to Baal (19:18). Elijah obeys and Elisha follows him (19:19–21).

Second, chapter 20 also demonstrates the power of the word of the

Lord over the king of Syria. The Lord brings two unnamed prophets to Ahab (1 Kings 20:13, 22, 28) in the next chapter and reveals himself as the one true God again over the Syrians (20:13, 28). Ahab, however, disobeys the Lord by letting the king of Syria go free (20:33–34). The next few verses show the disastrous consequences of failing to obey the word of the Lord—whether the disobedient one is a prophet (20:36) or a king (20:42).

Third, chapter 22 has all of the prophets affirm that Ahab should go forth to battle, but Micaiah, a true prophet, speaks the truth and refuses to say what the king wants to hear. In fact, the Lord has put a lying spirit in the mouths of the other prophets because he has decreed disaster for the king (1 Kings 22:5–23), which comes to pass (22:38) despite all attempts to evade it.

Fourth, God's word triumphs over king Ahaziah (2 Kings 1:4, 17), who foolishly inquires not of the Lord, but of Baal-zebub, the god of Ekron. Elijah's words call down fire upon two captains and a hundred soldiers in the process (1:1–17).

ELISHA

Elijah is then taken up to heaven in 2 Kings 2, and God gives a double portion of his spirit to Elisha. Elisha also performs miracles that display the power of the word of the Lord (2:14, 21–22). He even calls down curses upon those who mock him, and as a result forty-two young mockers meet their end by the paws of two she-bears (2:23–24). Elisha's words also triumph over the nations like the Moabites (2 Kings 3:10–27) and the Syrians (2 Kings 6–7; 13:15–17).

As with Elijah before him, the word of the Lord has power to sustain life through food miracles (2 Kings 4:38–44) or to give life, as in the birth of a son to a Shunnamite woman. The life-giving power of the word is powerfully displayed again after the child is raised back to life in a way similar to God's miraculous work through Elijah (4:16–37; cf. 1 Kings 17:17–22). Even the pronouncement Elijah made upon Jezebel comes back into the picture (2 Kings 10:25–37).

Second Kings 5 also features the word of the Lord coming to the Gentiles once more. This time God extends mercy to a Gentile military leader, Naaman the Syrian, who has to humble himself to accept the word of the Lord (5:1–14). Elisha demonstrates that he is a true steward of the word and not a lover of money as he refuses Naaman's gift, but his servant Gehazi fails this test (5:15–27).

THE PROFILE OF A TRUE PROPHET IN THE LATTER PROPHETS

The paradigm of calling, stewardship, and effects appears again and again in the Latter Prophets. Rather than giving extended examples, let us look briefly at a profile sketch of a true prophet contrasted with a false prophet and the effects that flow from each. In a recurring pattern among true prophets, (1) God calls and sends them, (2) they steward and speak his words, and (3) their "thus says the LORD" is shown to be true as their words come to pass.

TRUE CALLING AND SENDING

First, an extended calling narrative is a striking feature of the three major writing prophets: Jeremiah (1:1–10), Ezekiel (2:1–3:13), and Isaiah (6:8–13). Later I will briefly describe their callings and highlight the similarities.

The Lord reveals himself to Jeremiah through his word: "the word of the LORD came" (Jer. 1:2, 4). The Lord stresses that Jeremiah's consecration and appointment as a prophet came while he was still in his mother's womb (1:5). Jeremiah hesitates because of his youth, but the Lord reaffirms the scope of his call: Jeremiah will go where he is sent and say what he is commanded to say (1:7). The Lord's hand touches Jeremiah's mouth and puts his words in Jeremiah's mouth (1:9). The effect of these words is on display immediately:

> See, I have set you this day over nations and over kingdoms,
> to pluck up and to break down,
> to destroy and to overthrow,
> to build and to plant. (1:10)

Ezekiel sees a stunning theophany of the glory of the Lord. The prophet sees wind, fire, powerful living creatures, and even a throne and a highly metaphorical description of the appearance of God upon the throne (Ezek. 1:4–28). The Lord speaks to him and the Spirit enters him (2:1–2). The Lord explains that Ezekiel's commission is to

Israel as a rebellious and stubborn people (2:3–7). The Lord also puts his words inside Ezekiel as God calls him to eat the scroll of his word (3:1–3), which is sweet like honey. Ezekiel then speaks the word of the Lord (3:4ff.).

Isaiah too sees a riveting vision of God's glory as creation shakes and winged creatures loudly testify to the holiness of God (Isa. 6:1–4). Significantly, the prophet who pronounces "woe" upon the nations comes to pronounce a "woe" upon himself in light of God's holiness and his own sin (6:5). Notice that the sin focuses on the lips of Isaiah and the nation (6:5), but the Lord provides atonement as a burning coal from the altar touches the lips of Isaiah (6:6–7). Isaiah then hears God's call to go and he answers (6:8). Many sermons on Isaiah 6 stop at verse 8, because verses 9–13 do not present a pretty picture as to where God is calling Isaiah to go. Israel is spiritually dead—the people have ears that do not hear, eyes that do not see, and hearts that do not respond (6:9–10). The word will bring judgment (6:11–12), but a remnant remains (6:13).

These callings emphasize God's initiative in bringing his word to the prophets. All three callings also stress the rebellious nature of the people to whom God has called them. The Book of the Twelve also focuses on God's judgment upon those who rebel against his word.

Though the Book of the Twelve does not have extended calling narratives, each book opens with a word, vision, or oracle from the Lord (Hos. 1:1; Joel 1:1; Amos 1:1; Obad. 1:1; Jonah 1:1; Mic. 1:1; Nah. 1:1; Hab. 1:1; Zeph. 1:1; Hag. 1:1; Zech. 1:1; Mal. 1:1). In each case the next verse proclaims the beginning of the word or oracle or vision (Hos. 1:2; Joel 1:2; Amos 1:2; Obad. 1:2; Jonah 1:2; Mic. 1:2; Nah. 1:2; Hab. 1:2; Zeph. 1:2; Hag. 1:2; Zech. 1:2; Mal. 1:2).

TRUE STEWARDING AND HERALDING

The issue of stewarding the word is important all the way through the ministries of the prophets as the word of the Lord comes to them repeatedly. Consider, for example, how prominent the phrase "the word of the LORD came" (or similar wording) is in the books of Jeremiah (1:2, 4, 11, 13; 2:1; 13:3, 8; 14:1; 16:1; 18:5; 21:1; 24:4; 26:1; 27:1; 28:12; 29:30; 32:1, 6, 8, 26; 33:1, 19, 23; 34:1, 8, 12; 35:1, 12; 36:1, 27; 37:6; 39:15; 40:1;

42:7; 43:8; 46:1; 47:1; 49:34) and Ezekiel (1:3; 3:16; 6:1; 7:1; 11:14; 12:1, 8, 17, 21, 26; 13:1; 14:2, 12; 15:1; 16:1; 17:1, 11; 18:1; 20:2, 45; 21:1, 8, 18; 22:1, 17, 23; 23:1; 24:1, 15, 20; 25:1; 26:1; 27:1; 28:1, 11, 20; 29:1, 17; 30:20; 31:1; 32:1, 17; 33:1, 23; 34:1; 35:1; 36:16; 37:15; 38:1).

There are many other distinguishing features concerning the relationship between the prophet and the word of God. The word is a consuming internal influence:

> If I say, "I will not mention him,
>   or speak any more in his name,"
> there is in my heart as it were a burning fire
>   shut up in my bones,
> and I am weary with holding it in,
>   and I cannot. (Jer. 20:9)

God's word is a weight or burden that continues to rest upon the prophets (Zech. 9:1; 12:1) and that they cannot shake. True prophets speak by the Spirit of God (Ezek. 2:2; 3:12, 14, 24; 8:3; 11:1, 5, 24; 37:1; 43:5; Mic. 3:8; Zech. 7:12), while false prophets "follow their own spirit, and have seen nothing" (Ezek. 13:3). The link between the Lord's word and the Lord's Spirit should come as no surprise, given how they come together in parallel descriptions of the Lord's work:

> For the mouth of the LORD has commanded,
>   and his Spirit has gathered them. (Isa. 34:16)

TRUE OBEDIENCE

True prophets do not just speak the word; they obey the word. They do not speak with false motives or for false gain. They fear God more than man, and so they speak the truth even when it is unpopular—sometimes at great risk and great harm.

The command not to fear man comes up in all of the calling narratives of Jeremiah, Ezekiel, and Isaiah, and there are plenty of opportunities for them to put their call into practice. For example, the priests and prophets declare that Jeremiah deserves to die for prophesying against Jerusalem (Jer. 26:8, 11). Jeremiah can say, "But as for me, behold, I am in your hands. Do with me as seems good and right to you"

(26:14). He continues to claim that the Lord has truly sent him and spoken through him, and thus the people will bring innocent blood upon themselves and the city if they kill him (26:15). Examples of this boldness could be multiplied.

EFFECTS

The earlier discussion concerning the line of responsibility for speaker and hearer remains true in the Latter Prophets. Recall in our discussion from chapter 1 that I referenced Ezekiel 3 as an example:

> If I say to the wicked, "You shall surely die," and you give him no warning, nor speak to warn the wicked from his wicked way, in order to save his life, that wicked person shall die for his iniquity, but his blood I will require at your hand. But if you warn the wicked, and he does not turn from his wickedness, or from his wicked way, he shall die for his iniquity, but you will have delivered your soul. Again, if a righteous person turns from his righteousness and commits injustice, and I lay a stumbling block before him, he shall die. Because you have not warned him, he shall die for his sin, and his righteous deeds that he has done shall not be remembered, but his blood I will require at your hand. But if you warn the righteous person not to sin, and he does not sin, he shall surely live, because he took warning, and you will have delivered your soul. (Ezek. 3:18–21; cf. 33:7–9)

When the true prophet truly stewards and heralds God's word, the baton of stewardship passes from prophet to hearer. Sadly, Israel practices poor stewardship in her calling as a servant of the word. Various descriptions of Israel create a composite picture of tragic proportions: Israel is spiritually blind, deaf, stiff-necked, and hard-hearted. Consider Isaiah 42 as an example. Israel is God's servant whom God has sent, but the people have not stewarded the word rightly.

> Who is blind but my servant,
>   or deaf as my messenger whom I send?
> Who is blind as my dedicated one,
>   or blind as the servant of the LORD?
> He sees many things, but does not observe them;
>   his ears are open, but he does not hear. (Isa. 42:19–20)

Even those within Israel who were charged with stewarding the word (priests, shepherds, prophets, elders, kings, and scribes) have failed miserably.

> The *priests* did not say, "Where is the LORD?"
>   Those who handle the law did not know me;
> the *shepherds* transgressed against me;
>   the *prophets* prophesied by Baal
>   and went after things that do not profit. (Jer. 2:8)

> Disaster comes upon disaster; rumor follows rumor. They seek a vision from the *prophet*, while the law perishes from the *priest* and counsel from the *elders*. The *king* mourns, the *prince* is wrapped in despair, and the hands of the people of the land are paralyzed by terror. According to their way I will do to them, and according to their judgments I will judge them, and they shall know that I am the LORD. (Ezek. 7:26–27)

> Even the stork in the heavens
>   knows her times,
> and the turtledove, swallow, and crane
>   keep the time of their coming,
> but my people know not
>   the rules of the LORD.

> How can you say, "We are wise,
>   and the law of the LORD is with us"?
> But behold, the lying pen of the *scribes*
>   has made it into a lie.
> The *wise men* shall be put to shame;
>   they shall be dismayed and taken;
> behold, they have rejected the word of the LORD,
>   so what wisdom is in them? (Jer. 8:7–9)

> Son of man, prophesy against the *shepherds of Israel*; prophesy, and say to them, even to the shepherds, Thus says the Lord GOD: Ah, shepherds of Israel who have been feeding yourselves! Should not shepherds feed the sheep? (Ezek. 34:2)

> Thus says the Lord GOD, Behold, I am against the shepherds, and I will require my sheep at their hand and put a stop to their feeding the sheep.

No longer shall the shepherds feed themselves. I will rescue my sheep from their mouths, that they may not be food for them. (Ezek. 34:10)

The LORD will enter into judgment
    with the *elders* and princes of his people:
"It is you who have devoured the vineyard,
    the spoil of the poor is in your houses.
What do you mean by crushing my people,
    by grinding the face of the poor?"
        declares the Lord GOD of hosts. (Isa. 3:14–15)

The Mosaic covenant continues to be a source of judgment. Even though the Lord wills "to magnify his law" (Isa. 42:21), Israel refuses to obey his law (42:24). Therefore, he pours out his wrath on Israel, but Israel still does not take it to heart (42:25). Israel's disobedience to the word is like a scarlet thread in the Prophets as they point to both past and present failures to obey God's word (Jer. 23:38–40; 42:21–22; 43:1–4; Ezek. 2:3–4; 14:1–11; 16:1–63; 20:1–39).

For example, Jeremiah 7 shows that the people are placing a vain trust in the temple as a talisman against God's wrath (7:4). They must face the facts that God continually has sent prophets, but Israel perpetually has remained in rebellion. That rebellion will even persist in the future.

From the day that your fathers came out of the land of Egypt to this day, I have persistently sent all my servants the prophets to them, day after day. Yet they did not listen to me or incline their ear, but stiffened their neck. They did worse than their fathers.
    So . . . you shall call to them, but they will not answer. (7:25–27)

Zechariah shares the same message with priests and the people who remain in the land after the exile: "Were not these the words that the LORD proclaimed by the former prophets, when Jerusalem was inhabited and prosperous" (Zech. 7:7), but "they refused to pay attention and turned a stubborn shoulder and stopped their ears that they might not hear" (7:11). Note the true Spirit-empowered stewardship of the prophets, contrasted with the hardened response of the people and the effect of judgment that follows:

> They made their hearts diamond-hard lest they should hear the law and the words that the LORD of hosts had sent by his Spirit through the former prophets. Therefore great anger came from the LORD of hosts. . . . and I scattered them with a whirlwind among all the nations that they had not known. Thus the land they left was desolate, so that no one went to and fro, and the pleasant land was made desolate. (Zech. 7:12, 14)

Judgment is not the final word among the prophets. They also speak words of overflowing comfort through the picture of restoration that takes on cosmic proportions. A group within Israel continues to cling to God's word and thus constitutes a remnant within Israel (Isa. 10:20–22; 11:11, 16; 28:5; 37:31–32). The prophets even provide personal pictures of blessing for obedience. Israel at times obeys the Lord and the prophet whom he sent, and experiences blessing (Hag. 1:12–13).

At times, God even makes a distinction between a small number of those who obey during widespread disobedience. For example, Jeremiah 35 highlights the divine sending of the prophets: "I have sent to you all my servants the prophets, sending them persistently" (35:15). The majority of the people do not listen or obey (35:15), but the "sons of Jonadab" keep the command of the Lord (35:16). Therefore, the Lord brings disaster upon the people of Judah, but those who obey are blessed (35:18–19).

People know that prophets are truly sent by God and truly speak the word of God when the word of the prophet comes to pass (Deut. 18:22; Jer. 28:9). The *effect* of the word proves the *source* of the word and the *sending* of the prophet. The Lord continually announces that his word has now come to pass or will come to pass (Isa. 2:2; 37:26; 42:9; 46:11; 48:3; Jer. 12:16; 30:8; 32:24; Ezek. 24:14). Indeed the Lord's ability to speak and declare things in advance is one of the things that proves he is the true God, in contrast to idols.

> I declared them to you from of old,
>   before they came to pass I announced them to you,
> lest you should say, "My idol did them,
>   my carved image and my metal image commanded them."
>   (Isa. 48:5)

This ability explains the constant refrain in the Prophets: God speaks and then it comes to pass so that people "will know that I am the Lord" (Isa. 49:23, 26; Ezek. 6:14; 7:4, 9; 20:38; 24:24; 25:5, 7, 11, 17; 26:6; 28:23, 24, 26; 29:6, 9, 16, 21; 30:8, 19, 25, 26; 32:15; 33:29; 35:9, 15; 36:11, 36, 38; 37:14, 28; 38:23; 39:28). Divine activity also shows divine sending: "And you shall know that the LORD of hosts has sent me to you" (Zech. 6:15; cf. 2:9, 11; 4:9).

The power of the word receives sustained emphasis in the Latter Prophets, especially in the sections of the books describing God's promised restoration. All know that God is the true God because he alone can bring his word to pass. The word of God endures forever (Isa. 40:8) and always accomplishes the purpose for which he sent it (Isa. 55:11).

The power of the word underscores why prophets must be faithful to the word. "Let the prophet who has a dream tell the dream, but let him who has my word speak my word faithfully. What has straw in common with wheat? declares the LORD. Is not my word like fire, declares the LORD, and like a hammer that breaks the rock in pieces?" (Jer. 23:28–29).

We move now to consider those who do not steward the word rightly. We will simply sketch the profile of a false prophet and his relation to the spiritual condition of the people.

PROFILE OF A FALSE PROPHET

FALSE CALLING

The calling narrative that is so prominent among the prophets sets them apart from false prophets. Virtually every description of a false prophet in the book of Jeremiah stresses that God never sent them (Jer. 14:14, 15; 23:21, 32; 27:15; 28:15; 29:9, 31; cf. Ezek. 13:6). The prominence of this theme is easy to understand once one sees the link between a fake calling and false stewarding and heralding: if the calling does not come from God, then neither do the words.

FALSE STEWARDING AND HERALDING

Because God does not call or send the false prophets, their stewarding and heralding is "false" (Ezek. 13:6, 7, 9, 23; 21:29; 22:28; Zech. 10:2), and they speak "lies" (Jer. 14:14; 23:32; 27:10, 14, 16; 28:15; 29:9, 21, 23, 31; Ezek. 13:6, 7, 8, 9). They speak false prophecies from their own imaginations (Jer. 23:16) and "pervert" the word of God (23:36). They prophesy from "their own hearts," yet claim that it comes from the Lord ("Hear the word of the LORD"—Ezek. 13:2–3). They "follow their own spirit, and have seen nothing" (13:3). All of this blindness is part of the Lord's judgment upon them:

> For the LORD has poured out upon you
>> a spirit of deep sleep,
> and has closed your eyes (the prophets),
>> and covered your heads (the seers). (Isa. 29:10)

FALSE LIVING

The false words of the prophets correspond to their false living. They do not fear God, know God, or obey God. Therefore, they do not live godly lives. They commit adultery (Jer. 23:14; 29:23) and speak falsehood (23:14) with false motives for false gain. Jeremiah 8:10 says as much in a sweeping and shocking way:

> From the least to the greatest
>> everyone is greedy for unjust gain;
> from prophet to priest,
>> everyone deals falsely.

DISASTROUS EFFECTS

False prophets bring harm upon both themselves and the people. They fill people with "vain hopes" (Jer. 23:16) by preaching "peace," when there is no peace, and thus they put a mere Band-Aid on the wound of Israel (Jer. 8:11). If the false prophets were to stand in the Lord's council and speak his words, they would turn people from evil (Jer. 23:22), but instead they speak lies that lead people astray. All three pieces of the puzzle are on display in Jeremiah 23:32 (fig. 8).

Figure 8. False calling, stewarding and heralding, and their effects

False Calling	False Stewarding and Heralding	Bad Effects
"I did not send them or charge them."	". . . who prophesy lying dreams."	". . . lead my people astray." ". . . do not profit this people at all."

In fact, they do not turn the people from evil; they live evil lives and actually strengthen the cause of evil:

> But in the prophets of Jerusalem
>   I have seen a horrible thing:
> they commit adultery and walk in lies;
>   they strengthen the hands of evildoers,
>   so that no one turns from his evil;
> all of them have become like Sodom to me,
>   and its inhabitants like Gomorrah. (Jer. 23:14)

Calling them "Sodom" and "Gomorrah" evokes the fearful anticipation of judgment. God's people have become like the places he destroyed with fire and brimstone.

Isaiah depicts the prophets of Israel as false, but also the people of Israel as false. In other words, the wound of Israel goes deeper than just believing false prophesy; the people actually *want* false prophesy because they do not want to hear true words from the living God.

> For they are a rebellious people,
>   lying children,
> children unwilling to hear
>   the instruction of the LORD;
> who say to the seers, "Do not see,"
>   and to the prophets, "Do not prophesy to us what is right;
> speak to us smooth things,
>   prophesy illusions,
> leave the way, turn aside from the path,
>   let us hear no more about the Holy One of Israel."
>   (Isa. 30:9–11)

False prophets speak what is false to people who are false. Consider Jeremiah 23:17: "They say continually *to those who despise the word of the LORD*, 'It shall be well with you'; and *to everyone who stubbornly follows his own heart*, they say, 'No disaster shall come upon you.'" But the Lord will not allow his word and his servants of the word to be perpetually mocked. The truth of his word will powerfully overcome false prophecy.

THE FUTURE HOPE

Of the many examples in the Prophets, let us focus on Ezekiel 12. God decrees that his effectual word will put an end to a false proverb that states, "The days grow long, and every vision comes to nothing" (12:22). The Lord will decisively bring his word to pass, as the following verses make plain:

> For there shall be no more any false vision or flattering divination within the house of Israel. For I am the LORD; I will speak the word that I will speak, and it will be performed. It will no longer be delayed, but in your days, O rebellious house, I will speak the word and perform it, declares the Lord GOD.
>
> . . . Therefore say to them, Thus says the Lord GOD: None of my words will be delayed any longer, but the word that I speak will be performed, declares the Lord GOD. (12:24–25; 28)

We will not rehearse all the judgment texts again, but can move to consider some faithful stewards of God's word among the people of Israel and then focus upon the Messiah as the preeminent steward of God's word. Given the stiff-necked and hard-hearted history of Israel, one wonders how these promises of restoration could ever become a reality. The answer is a spectacular new act of grace that comes with the arrival of the Messiah and brings a new covenant, a new return from exile, and even a new creation.

NEW COVENANT

God is going to ensure the faithfulness of his covenant partner in a stunning work of grace through the Messiah and the new covenant that he will bring. One may wonder what is "new" about the new covenant. The contrast is clear in Jeremiah 31 with the emphasis on "not like" and "no longer." The new covenant is "not like" the former covenant that was broken (31:32), because the new cannot be broken. The people will "no longer" teach, saying "know the LORD" because now everyone in the covenant will know the Lord and he will remember their sin "no more" (31:34).

One should not denigrate the Mosaic covenant and treat it as a legalistic covenant. It in fact commanded the right things (e.g., a circumcised heart—Deut. 10:16). The problem was not legalism; the problem was that the covenant lacked the power to effect the good things for which it called. The new covenant promise is that God will intervene himself and accomplish the work of grace he calls for. It is a thrilling thing to read the "I wills" of the new covenant as God intervenes and changes the heart.

Ezekiel 36:26 highlights God saying "*I will*" give Israel a "new heart" and a "new spirit." Ezekiel further clarifies this promised "newness" by contrasting the old heart with the new one that will replace it. He says, "*I will* remove your heart of stone and give you a heart of flesh." The description of the two hearts highlights the difference in grace in the new covenant. The old heart is hard like a rock, while the new heart of the new covenant is soft like flesh. God again says, "*I will* put my Spirit within you, and *cause* you to walk in my statutes and be careful to obey my rules" (36:27).

Jeremiah 31–32 also contrasts the new covenant with the Mosaic covenant. Unlike the old covenant that Israel broke, the grace of the new covenant will overcome Israel's rebellion. The old covenant remained an external work of grace. The law came to Israel through Moses as mediator, and the Israelites were to take that external grace and internalize it: "These words I am commanding you today shall be upon your heart" (Deut. 6:6). This outside-to-inside work failed because the old covenant could not overcome Israel's hard heart and effect the internalization of the law. New covenant grace works from the inside out as God writes the law on the heart. The grace of the new covenant changes the heart, forgives sin, and causes all in the covenant to know the Lord.

> For this is the covenant that *I will* make with the house of Israel after those days, declares the LORD: *I will* put my law within them, and *I will* write it on their hearts. And *I will* be their God, and they shall be my people. And no longer shall each one teach his neighbor and each his brother, saying, "Know the LORD," for they shall all know me, from the least of them to the greatest, declares the LORD. For *I will* forgive their iniquity, and *I will* remember their sin no more. (Jer. 31:33–34)

Jeremiah 32 develops this contrast between the covenants further. The problem with the old covenant is that the people did not obey God. They broke the covenant and thus were broken by the curses of the covenant: "But they did not obey your voice or walk in your law. They did nothing of all you commanded them to do. Therefore you have made all this disaster come upon them" (Jer. 32:23). The announcement of the new covenant a few verses later says that God's future work will reverse this history of hardness and disobedience:

> *I will* give them one heart and one way, that they may fear me forever, for their own good and the good of their children after them. *I will* make with them an everlasting covenant, that *I will* not turn away from doing good to them. And *I will* put the fear of me in their hearts, that they may not turn from me. *I will* rejoice in doing them good, and *I will* plant them in this land in faithfulness, with all my heart and all my soul. (32:39–41)

Notice that every single description highlights the cause-and-effect relationship of what God does (i.e., changes the heart) and then what the people do in response (i.e., obey God).

The Mosaic covenant featured a stunning display of grace in a paradigmatic deliverance: the exodus from Egypt. The Mosaic covenant as a broken covenant also brought a paradigmatic judgment: the exile from the Promised Land. The prophets foresee a time coming with the new covenant that will feature a new paradigmatic act of deliverance (a new exodus) and a greater reversal of God's judgment in the exile (a return from exile).

NEW EXODUS AND RETURN FROM EXILE

> Was it not you who dried up the sea,
> > the waters of the great deep,
> who made the depths of the sea a way
> > for the redeemed to pass over?
> And the ransomed of the LORD shall return
> > and come to Zion with singing;
> everlasting joy shall be upon their heads;
> > they shall obtain gladness and joy,
> > and sorrow and sighing shall flee away. (Isa. 51:10–11)

NEW CREATION

> "For behold, I create new heavens
>   and a new earth,
> and the former things shall not be remembered
>   or come into mind.
> But be glad and rejoice forever
>   in that which I create;
> for behold, I create Jerusalem to be a joy,
>   and her people to be a gladness. . . .
> The wolf and the lamb shall graze together;
>   the lion shall eat straw like the ox
>   and dust shall be the serpent's food.
> They shall not hurt or destroy
>   in all my holy mountain,"
>   says the LORD. (Isa. 65:17–18, 25)

> For as the new heavens and the new earth
>   that I make
> shall remain before me, says the LORD,
>   so shall your offspring and your name remain. (Isa. 66:22)

The prophets tie this future work of grace in the new covenant, new exodus, and new creation to the Messiah's coming, which we will consider now.

THE MESSIAH AS HERALD, PROPHET, SERVANT, SHEPHERD, KING, AND RIGHTEOUSNESS

The remnant takes the future promises of restoration to heart and waits for the coming of the Messiah to bring it to pass.

> Then I will gather the remnant of my flock out of all the countries where I have driven them, and I will bring them back to their fold, and they shall be fruitful and multiply. I will set shepherds over them who will care for them, and they shall fear no more, nor be dismayed, neither shall any be missing, declares the LORD.
>
> Behold, the days are coming, declares the LORD, when I will raise up for David a righteous Branch, and he shall reign as king and deal wisely, and shall execute justice and righteousness in the land. In his days Judah will be saved, and Israel will dwell securely. And this is

the name by which he will be called: "The LORD is our righteousness." (Jer. 23:3–6)

The Prophets present the Messiah as the true King, prophet, shepherd, and herald over against all the flawed or false predecessors. Second Samuel 7 presents the Messiah as David's Son who will rule forever. He will be the true King that will not fail where other kings faltered. He is the true end-time shepherd of Ezekiel, who will be different from Israel's false shepherds (Ezekiel 34).

He is the true herald who is unlike all false heralds because he is truly sent by God and speaks the true word of God: the good news of God's reign (Isa. 52:7). He is the servant who stewards God's word and brings it to its culmination and climax. The word-based, Spirit-empowered preaching of this Messiah is striking in the vision of the Latter Prophets.

> Behold my servant, whom I uphold,
>> my chosen, in whom my soul delights;
> I have put my Spirit upon him;
>> he will bring forth justice to the nations. (Isa. 42:1)

> And the Spirit of the LORD shall rest upon him,
>> the Spirit of wisdom and understanding,
>> the Spirit of counsel and might,
>> the Spirit of knowledge and the fear of the LORD.
>>> (Isa. 11:2; cf. 48:16)

> The Spirit of the Lord GOD is upon me,
>> because the LORD has anointed me
> to bring good news to the poor;
>> he has sent me to bind up the brokenhearted,
> to proclaim liberty to the captives,
>> and the opening of the prison to those who are bound;
> to proclaim the year of the LORD's favor,
>> and the day of vengeance of our God;
>> to comfort all who mourn. (Isa. 61:1–2)

The Messiah's ministry brings knowledge of the Torah and the covenant to the nations (Isa. 42:4–6). Because he is supremely anointed with the Spirit, his coming will also result in the Spirit's being poured out on others as part of the new covenant.

> And I will give you a new heart, and a new spirit I will put within you. And I will remove the heart of stone from your flesh and give you a heart of flesh. And I will put my Spirit within you, and cause you to walk in my statutes and be careful to obey my rules. (Ezek. 36:26–27)

> And I will put my Spirit within you, and you shall live, and I will place you in your own land. Then you shall know that I am the LORD; I have spoken, and I will do it, declares the LORD. (Ezek. 37:14)

> And I will not hide my face anymore from them, when I pour out my Spirit upon the house of Israel, declares the Lord GOD. (Ezek. 39:29)

> For I will pour water on the thirsty land,
>   and streams on the dry ground;
> I will pour my Spirit upon your offspring,
>   and my blessing on your descendants. (Isa. 44:3)

> "And as for me, this is my covenant with them," says the LORD: "My Spirit that is upon you, and my words that I have put in your mouth, shall not depart out of your mouth, or out of the mouth of your offspring, or out of the mouth of your children's offspring," says the LORD, "from this time forth and forevermore." (Isa. 59:21)

> And it shall come to pass afterward,
>   that I will pour out my Spirit on all flesh;
> your sons and your daughters shall prophesy,
>   your old men shall dream dreams,
>   and your young men shall see visions.
> Even on the male and female servants
>   in those days I will pour out my Spirit. (Joel 2:28–29)

The Messiah is both servant of the word and a suffering servant who bears the punishment for others' not obeying the word. He fulfills the covenant requirements, makes substitutionary atonement for the sins of the people (Isa. 53:5–6, 11), and establishes an everlasting covenant with all who accept his free offer to partake of his covenant meal (Isa. 55:1–2).[1]

Isaiah 50 provides a holistic perspective in seeing that the servant of the Lord is both a servant of the word and a suffering servant who suffers at the hands of those who refuse to hear the word:

> The Lord God has given me
> > the tongue of those who are taught,
> that I may know how to sustain with a word
> > him who is weary.
> Morning by morning he awakens;
> > he awakens my ear
> > to hear as those who are taught. (50:4)

> The Lord God has opened my ear,
> > and I was not rebellious;
> > I turned not backward.
> I gave my back to those who strike,
> > and my cheeks to those who pull out the beard;
> I hid not my face from
> > disgrace and spitting.

> But the Lord God helps me;
> > therefore I have not been disgraced;
> therefore I have set my face like a flint,
> > and I know that I shall not be put to shame. (50:5–7)

The Messiah will serve as the herald of this coming restoration (Isa. 40:9; 41:27; 52:7; 60:6; 61:1–2; Nah. 1:15).

> Go on up to a high mountain,
> > O Zion, herald of good news;
> lift up your voice with strength,
> > O Jerusalem, herald of good news;
> > lift it up, fear not;
> say to the cities of Judah,
> > "Behold your God!" (Isa. 40:9)

---

[1] Stephen G. Dempster, *Dominion and Dynasty: A Biblical Theology of the Hebrew Bible*, New Studies in Biblical Theology (Downers Grove, IL: InterVarsity, 2003), 180–81.

How beautiful upon the mountains
  are the feet of him who brings good news,
who publishes peace, who brings good news of happiness,
  who publishes salvation,
  who says to Zion, "Your God reigns." (Isa. 52:7)

The Spirit of the Lord God is upon me,
  because the Lord has anointed me
to bring good news to the poor;
  he has sent me to bind up the brokenhearted,
to proclaim liberty to the captives,
  and the opening of the prison to those who are bound;
to proclaim the year of the Lord's favor,
  and the day of vengeance of our God;
  to comfort all who mourn. (Isa. 61:1–2)

APPLICATION: THE "I WILLS" OF SCRIPTURE

C. H. Spurgeon says that he rejoices in the "I wills" of Scripture:

> How greatly I prize a portion of Scripture which is filled with God's
> shalls and wills. Every thing he says is precious, but His, "I wills," are
> peculiarly precious. . . . When we come to the "I wills" of God, then
> we get among the precious things, the deep things, the things which
> minister comfort and strength to the people of God![2]

How encouraging it is to look at the powerful grace of the new age. It
is a grace in which God creates that for which he calls. This grace is so
great that it causes poetry to swell up in the heart as in the following:

> To run and work the law commands,
> Yet gives me neither feet nor hands;
> But better news the gospel brings,
> It bids me fly and gives me wings.[3]

The minister of the word must have a solid grasp of these "I wills"
in order to preach with passionate conviction. Confidence in the word

---

[2] C. H. Spurgeon, "Two 'I Wills' in Isaiah 41," Metropolitan Tabernacle Pulpit, Sermon #2270, accessed June 9, 2013, http://www.spurgeongems.org/vols37-39/chs2270.pdf. The sermon was preached on March 16, 1890.
[3] Quoted in F. F. Bruce, Romans, Tyndale New Testament Commentary, rev. ed. (Grand Rapids: Eerdmans, 1985), 154.

leads to preaching with conviction. Great truths create great preachers, and not the other way around. We must celebrate the "I wills" and the "I'll nevers" of Scripture. The hymn, "How Firm a Foundation," rousingly reminds us of these promises.

> How firm a foundation, ye saints of the Lord,
> Is laid for your faith in His excellent Word!
> What more can He say than to you He hath said,
> You, who unto Jesus for refuge have fled?
>
> Fear not, I am with thee, O be not dismayed,
> For I am thy God and will still give thee aid;
> I'll strengthen and help thee, and cause thee to stand
> Upheld by My righteous, omnipotent hand.
>
> The soul that on Jesus has leaned for repose,
> I will not, I will not desert to its foes;
> That soul, though all hell should endeavor to shake,
> I'll never, no never, no never forsake.

12

THE STEWARDSHIP OF
PSALMISTS AND SCRIBES

Paradigm 7

Open my eyes, that I may behold
wondrous things out of your law. . . .
My soul clings to the dust;
give me life according to your word! . . .
Remember your word to your servant,
in which you have made me hope.
This is my comfort in my affliction,
that your promise gives me life. . . .
If your law had not been my delight,
I would have perished in my affliction. . . .
Oh how I love your law!
It is my meditation all the day. . . .
How sweet are your words to my taste,
sweeter than honey to my mouth! . . .
My soul longs for your salvation;
I hope in your word.
My eyes long for your promise;
I ask, "When will you comfort me?"

Psalm 119:18, 25, 49–50, 92, 97, 103, 81–82

The Writings consist of two parts: poetry (Psalms to Lamentations) and
narrative (Daniel to Chronicles). The Writings open with the narrative
of Ruth. In effect, Ruth provides a bridge between the Latter Prophets
and the Writings so that the sequence is commentary (Latter Prophets),

narrative (Ruth), poetry (Psalms through Lamentations), and then narrative (Daniel to Chronicles). Some break up the Writings into Former (Ruth to Lamentations) and Latter (Daniel to Chronicles) Writings, just like the Former and Latter Prophets. The concepts of stewarding and heralding are present in the Writings. There are numerous examples of stewards and heralds and plenty of evidence for what follows when that stewardship succeeds or fails.

We can summarize this period of stewardship in terms of *psalmists who celebrate, scribes who study and give the sense, and sufferers who wrestle with the word of God*. Some books, like Psalms and Proverbs, offer a picture of engagement through hearing, celebrating, and doing God's word. Both of those books also show the path of the fool, who ignores God's voice and thus heads for irreparable harm. Other books aptly describe people in deep anguish who may be "wrestling with God's word" (Psalms, Job, Ecclesiastes, and Lamentations). Other books have positive examples of stewards in narrative form (e.g., Daniel, Ezra, and David), but the entirety of the Writings points beyond these stewards to the messianic hope. There is a sense in which the Writings manifest a singular concern to steward God's word of promise to David for a royal descendant who would rule forever.

RUTH

The book of Ruth dates chronologically to the period of the judges, but canonically it follows the commentary of the Latter Prophets. The book awakens fresh hope in the coming of a king like David. The reader cannot help but notice that the narrative begins in Bethlehem. This time the threat to the seed promise is not barren women, but dead husbands.[1]

The family has left Bethlehem and traveled to Moab only to experience death. Naomi's husband and two sons die, leaving her and her two daughters-in-law (Ruth and Orpah) as widows. Naomi hears that prospects have improved in Israel, and so she decides to return. She tells Ruth and Orpah to stay behind and take husbands from among the Moabites. Orpah leaves, but Ruth clings movingly to Naomi and con-

---

[1] Stephen G. Dempster, *Dominion and Dynasty: A Biblical Theology of the Hebrew Bible*, New Studies in Biblical Theology (Downers Grove, IL: InterVarsity, 2003), 191.

fesses the identity she has found in Naomi's people and Naomi's God: "Your people shall be my people, and your God my God" (Ruth 1:16).

Eventually Ruth marries a relative of Naomi's husband Elimelech, named Boaz, who acts as a kinsman redeemer. At the wedding, the people of Israel pronounce a wish of blessing upon Boaz and Ruth that turns out to be prophetic: "May the LORD make the woman, who is coming into your house, like Rachel and Leah, who together built up the house of Israel. . . . and may your house be like the house of Perez, whom Tamar bore to Judah, because of the offspring that the LORD will give you by this young woman" (Ruth 4:11–12).

The echoes to Rachel and Leah show that Boaz and Ruth will build the house of Israel, while the echo of Perez, the son of Judah and Tamar, highlights the messianic anticipation of Genesis 49 and a royal king coming from Judah. After the wedding, Ruth gives birth to a son, named Obed. As if to make the point unmistakable, the narrator immediately adds, "He was the father of Jesse, the father of David" (Ruth 4:17).

Many students of the Bible have noted that this pronouncement effectively places the little story of Ruth into the larger canonical story. The point is not merely to show the continuance of the line of David, but also to show its continuance in the midst of dire circumstances. As such it provides a fitting analogy to the exile that Israel has experienced. Dempster explains, "Even David's royal line experienced exile, in some ways necessary to further the divine purposes. There seemed no hope for any progeny in the Davidic line, since most of the male heirs died in exile. But from such bleak situations hope was born."[2]

PSALMS

The promise of David's descendant in the book of Ruth helps to prepare us for the book of Psalms. Dempster says it is like moving from "the little book of David" to "the large book of David." The book's fivefold division cannot help but call to mind the fivefold structure of the Pentateuch, and the seventy-three psalms listed as Davidic psalms keep the focus on David.

---

[2] Ibid., 193.

PSALMS 1–2

The first two psalms are like a gateway into the rest of the Psalter. The first psalm focuses on the blessing of walking not in the ways of the wicked, but in the way of the Lord as a steward of the law of the Lord. The relationship between stewarding and effect is clear once again (fig. 9):

Figure 9. Stewarding the law and its effect in Psalm 1:2–3

Stewarding (Ps. 1:2)	Effect (Ps. 1:3)
"His delight is in the law of the LORD, / and on his law he meditates day and night."	"He is like a tree / planted by streams of water / that yields its fruit in its season, / and . . . [i]n all that he does, he prospers."

Psalm 2 takes the reader back to hope in the coming Davidic King, who is the Messiah or "Anointed" of the Lord (2:2), the "King" on Zion (2:6), and the one called the "Son" (2:7, 12):

I will tell of the decree:
The LORD said to me, "You are my Son;
   today I have begotten you." (2:7)

Kiss the Son,
   lest he be angry, and you perish in the way,
   for his wrath is quickly kindled.
Blessed are all who take refuge in him. (2:12)

These two psalms arrest the attention of the reader with a dual blessing. The first verse of the first psalm highlights the "blessed" (Ps. 1:1) task of stewarding the word of God, while the second psalm ends with a call to keep faith alive in the coming messianic King and to experience the "blessed" state of taking refuge in him (Ps. 2:12). The second word for "Son" (*bar*) is a striking one because it is a rare Aramaic word that serves to draw attention to the description of the Messiah in Daniel 7:13: the one coming on the clouds of heaven looking like a "Son" of Man.

The Psalms address many aspects of the word. For example, Psalm 29 stresses that

the voice of the Lord is powerful;
    the voice of the Lord is full of majesty. (29:4)

The rest of the psalm shows how God's powerful voice is the means by which he reigns and he "sits enthroned as king forever" (29:10). Though this kind of study could be multiplied, I will limit myself to tracing the two themes of Psalms 1–2 in more detail: (1) the blessed delight of stewarding the word, and (2) the blessed hope of the coming Davidic King.

THE DELIGHT OF STEWARDSHIP

Psalms 1, 19, and 119 stand out in the Psalter for their exalted celebrations of God's law. In other words, the sweetness of stewarding God's word comes to the forefront. We have briefly dealt with Psalm 1, and so we turn attention to Psalms 19 and 119.

Psalm 19 naturally divides into two sections concerning God's revelation: God's world (19:1–6) and God's word (19:7–11). That second section contains one of the most striking descriptions of the relationship between what the word is and what the word does (fig. 10).

Figure 10. What the word is and does in Psalm 19:7–11

The Word Is	The Word Does
Law of the Lord is perfect,	reviving the soul.
The testimony of the Lord is sure,	making wise the simple.
The precepts of the Lord are right,	rejoicing the heart.
The commandment of the Lord is pure,	enlightening the eyes.
The fear of the Lord is clean,	enduring forever.

Psalm 119 is one of the acrostic psalms. Each section stands for a letter from the Hebrew alphabet, and thus each line within the section begins with that letter. This psalm is not merely a love psalm for the law; it also points to the psalmist's struggle with suffering and sorrow. For example, the psalmist cries out in anguish that his "soul melts away for sorrow" (119:28). His struggle, however, is not simply sorrow. The psalmist confesses that his soul "clings to the dust" (119:25). "Dust" here is not a generic metaphorical way of saying that he is struggling. It is a pointed theological reminder of the brokenness that comes from humanity's fallen state. The psalmist, like us, finds himself struggling with the effects that flow from his own fallen, broken state.

Psalm 119 alludes here to Genesis 2:7 in mentioning dust and the life-giving breath of God: "Then the Lord God formed the man of *dust* from the ground and breathed into his nostrils the *breath of life*, and the man became a *living* creature." The original creation of man happened when God directly breathed his breath of life into Adam, who became a living soul.

The judgment of the fall brings a stinging word to our souls:

> . . . till you return to the ground,
>> for out of it you were taken;
> for you are *dust*,
>> and to *dust* you shall return. (Gen. 3:19)

But the fall is not the final word. We can find hope to delight in God again, even in a fallen world. The stanza of Psalm 119 in view opens with the psalmist "cling[ing] to the dust," but it ends with the psalmist running in the way of God's commandments because God has enlarged his heart (119:32). How can we move from clinging to running?

The answer lies in the *life-giving power of God's word*. The opening verse of the stanza (Ps. 119:25) consists of both a confession and a prayer: "My soul clings to the dust" (confession); "give me life according to your word!" (prayer). The same structure is seen in verse 28: "My soul melts away for sorrow" (confession); "strengthen me according to your word!" (prayer). Paul also testifies that Scripture is God's breath of life (2 Tim. 3:16).

The psalmist prays through this spiritual blindness and believes that wonderful things are there if he has eyes to see:

> Open my eyes, that I may behold
>> wondrous things out of your law. (Ps. 119:18)

God sovereignly causes the psalmist to hope in his word:

> Remember your word to your servant,
>> in which you have made me hope.
> This is my comfort in my affliction,
>> that your promise gives me life. (119:49–50)

The psalmist's prayers for opened eyes that he might see wonderful things in the law are answered many times. The result is delight in the sweetness of what he sees:

> Oh how I love your law!
>> It is my meditation all the day. (119:97)

> How sweet are your words to my taste,
>> sweeter than honey to my mouth! (119:103)

The psalmist sees that if these prayers for opened eyes and a satisfied soul were not answered, his suffering would be too great:

> If your law had not been my delight,
>> I would have perished in my affliction. (119:92)

The psalmist perseveres in hope for God's salvation and waits for comfort:

> My soul longs for your salvation;
>> I hope in your word.
> My eyes long for your promise;
>> I ask, "When will you comfort me?" (119:81–82)

APPLICATION: UNDERSTANDING FOR OBEDIENCE

One of the most challenging aspects of Psalm 119 for me is the rationale for understanding God's word. The psalmist prays for understanding for the sake of obedience:

> Teach me, O Lord, the way of your statutes;
>> and I will keep it to the end.

Give me understanding, that I may keep your law
and observe it with my whole heart. (119:33–34)

I once tried to address the problem of one of my children not listening very well to me.[3] In response, I asked him if he knew how to get to his room. He said yes. I said, "Could you draw me a map?" He did. I tore it up and then asked again if he could draw me a map. He looked at me with a confused look, and then drew another map. I tore it up and asked if he would draw me another map. He started crying and said, "Why would I do that? You don't really want to know!" I explained that his response was the way that I feel when I take the time to explain things and then he does not listen. After we reconciled and I restored him, I went into my room and knelt by my bed and, with tears, asked God to forgive me for all the times that I had prayed to understand something and had not been serious about obeying it.

THE HOPE OF THE KING

Why is there delight in stewarding the word? The answer to this question involves the content of what is stewarded. The delight of stewardship comes from stewarding the *promise of a coming Davidic King*. The strategic place of Psalm 2 means that the Psalter begins with "an eschatological expectation of the Messiah's rule over the entire earth."[4] This focus on the Davidic King also receives further reinforcement in two ways: (1) a whole host of Davidic psalms (Psalms 3–9; 11–32; 34–41; 138–145) and (2) strategic hope for a Davidic King at the seams of the Psalter.

The first division of the Psalter consists mainly of psalms of lament (Psalms 3–41), but the first and last of the division (Psalms 3 and 41) emphasize that God gives victory to the king despite the treacherous rejection of others. The second division of the Psalter (Psalms 42–72) also features many lament psalms, but the last psalm (Psalms 72) shows that the Davidic King will come. His coming will fulfill the Law and

---

[3] My approach was based on an idea from Christopher Ash, *Bible Delight: Heartbeat of the Word of God* (Ross-shire, Scotland: Christian Focus, 2008). I modified it in an attempt to help my child understand the importance of listening.

[4] Dempster, *Dominion and Dynasty*, 195.

the Prophets. The blessing of Abraham (Gen. 12:1) will come because "all nations" will "be blessed in him," and they will "call him blessed!" (Ps. 72:17). Isaiah's prophecy will come true (Isa. 60:1–22) when his enemies will lick the dust and kings will worship him (Ps. 72:10–11). Zechariah's prophecy (Zech. 9:10) will be fulfilled by his coming because his kingdom reign will stretch

> from sea to sea,
> and from the River to the ends of the earth! (Ps. 72:8)

The refrain of the prophets (Isa. 6:3; 11:9; Hab. 2:14) will receive its answer when the whole earth will be filled with his glory (Ps. 72:20).

The next division (Psalms 73–89) once again reflects on the suffering of exile (Psalm 73), but again the promise of a Davidic King stands secure (Psalm 89). Psalm 73 testifies to the dissonance one feels between the view from below and the view from above. The view from below may cause God's people to stumble as they see the prosperity of the wicked, but gazing into God's sanctuary gives them a glimpse into the unchanging reality of the view from above. The view from above in Psalm 89 reminds the reader that despite appearances to the contrary, God is upholding the everlasting covenant promise of 2 Samuel 7 (Ps. 89:4). The psalmist alludes to the prophesy of Amos (Amos 9:11) and cries out because of the breached fences of the Davidic covenant (Ps. 89:41). He also alludes to Isaiah's prophecy (Isa. 55:3) when he looks for the mercies sworn to David (Ps. 89:50). The fourth division (Psalms 90–106) also emphasizes the reign of God through a just Davidic King.

The last division (Psalms 107–150) celebrates a return from exile based on the steadfast love of the Lord. The steadfast love of the Lord "endures forever" (Ps. 107:1), and thus the redeemed will be

> gathered in from the lands,
>> from the east and from the west,
>> from the north and from the south. (107:3)

The psalms of ascent (120–134) highlight that the return from exile will take the redeemed up to Mount Zion and the city of God.

PROVERBS, ECCLESIASTES, AND SONG OF SONGS

Many scholars treat Proverbs, Ecclesiastes, and Song of Songs together because of their links with Solomon. All three books call for wise stewardship as God speaks through his creation. Proverbs focuses on normal functioning in a fallen world. It especially highlights the stewardship theme of receiving instruction and walking in wisdom. The two paths of wisdom and folly are constantly set before our eyes in the book of Proverbs.[5]

Ecclesiastes focuses on the futility that comes from the fall, which is like trying to shepherd the wind. The enigma of the world forces the reader to see the need for one wise shepherd to lead them and overcome the enigma (Eccles. 12:11).[6] The need for this shepherd fits the shepherd theme in the rest of the Writings (e.g., Psalm 23) and the "one shepherd" theme of the New Testament (John 10:16). This one shepherd will be the eternal shepherd of the redeemed (Rev. 7:17).

Song of Songs celebrates one aspect of what is still good in a fallen world. The man and the woman are back in the garden (note how garden imagery abounds); they are naked and not ashamed.

JOB, LAMENTATIONS, AND ESTHER

The books of Job, Lamentations, and Esther speak into the realities of suffering with deep and profound wrestling concerning the sting of suffering and exile. Job is an example of patience in suffering because of his trust in the coming deliverer. Apostolic commentary reinforces this assessment: "Behold, we consider those blessed who remained steadfast. You have heard of the steadfastness of Job, and you have seen the purpose of the Lord, how the Lord is compassionate and merciful" (James 5:11).

Paul describes his own faith while in prison by borrowing Job's example of faith. "Yes, and I will rejoice," Paul says, "for I know that through your prayers and the help of the Spirit of Jesus Christ this will turn out for my deliverance" (Phil. 1:18–19). Paul is not rejoic-

---

[5] See especially Daniel J. Estes, *Hear, My Son: Teaching and Learning in Proverbs 1–9*, New Studies in Biblical Theology (Grand Rapids: Eerdmans, 1997).

[6] See Jason S. DeRouchie, "Shepherding Wind and One Wise Shepherd: Grasping for Breath in Ecclesiastes," *The Southern Baptist Journal of Theology* 15, no. 3 (2011): 4–25. DeRouchie also highlights that the word "one" for the one shepherd is probably an allusion back to *Yahweh* as the one God in Deut. 6:4 (13).

ing because he thinks he has a good chance of getting out of jail. He is completely confident in his salvation and God's work to help him make much of Christ by life or by death. He borrows the language of Job 13:13–18:

> Be silent so that I may speak and relieve my anger. . . . Though the Mighty One should lay hand on me, . . . I will speak, and plead before him. And this will turn out for my salvation [*touto moi apobēsetai eis sōtērian*], since deceit will not come before him. . . . Behold I am near judgment: I know that I will appear just. (LXX)

Job is a righteous sufferer caught up in a spiritual battle. He is the Old Testament example of what Paul says in Ephesians 6:11 about standing "against the schemes of the devil." Job is not aware of all that is going on behind the spiritual veil, but Paul's words are an apt description of his experience: "We do not wrestle against flesh and blood, but against the rulers, against the authorities, against the cosmic powers over this present darkness, against the spiritual forces of evil in the heavenly places" (Eph. 6:12).

Job knows that he will win this battle. Notice the connection between his faith in the resurrection and his faith in God's power:

> For I know that my Redeemer lives,
>   and at the last he will stand upon the earth.
> And after my skin has been thus destroyed,
>   yet in my flesh I shall see God,
> whom I shall see for myself,
>   and my eyes shall behold, and not another. (Job 19:25–27)

Job can hold to this hope because he can confess,

> I know that you can do all things,
>   and that no purpose of yours can be thwarted. (Job 42:2)

DANIEL

The spiritual nature of the battle between God's kingdom and Satan's kingdom continues in Daniel. An angel comes to Daniel and informs him of this battle:

Fear not, Daniel, for from the first day that you set your heart to understand and humbled yourself before your God, your words have been heard, and I have come because of your words. The prince of the kingdom of Persia withstood me twenty-one days, but Michael, one of the chief princes, came to help me, for I was left there with the kings of Persia, and came to make you understand what is to happen to your people in the latter days. (Dan. 10:12–14)

The book of Revelation draws upon the book of Daniel at too many points to address here in detail concerning the future kingdom conflict. The reader notes the frequency with which the kingdoms and kings of the nations operate within the wider sovereignty of God's absolute rule. There are times when kings are brought to this realization so that the heralds of the earthly king and the heralds of the heavenly King come into conflict.

A herald for King Nebuchadnezzar appears in Daniel 3. Notice how the words of the herald and the decree of the king are synonymous in the subsequent verses:

And *the herald proclaimed aloud*, "You are commanded, O peoples, nations, and languages, that when you hear the sound of the horn, pipe, lyre, trigon, harp, bagpipe, and every kind of music, you are to fall down and worship the golden image that King Nebuchadnezzar has set up. And whoever does not fall down and worship shall immediately be cast into a burning fiery furnace." (Dan 3:4–6)

You, O king, have made a decree, that every man who hears the sound of the horn, pipe, lyre, trigon, harp, bagpipe, and every kind of music, shall fall down and worship the golden image. And whoever does not fall down and worship shall be cast into a burning fiery furnace. (Dan. 3:10–11)

Notice that God also has his stewards and heralds, and they speak to the king concerning the places where his kingdom is at odds with God's kingdom. Shadrach, Meshach, Abednego, and Daniel all stand up to pagan kings when forced to display their ultimate allegiance. Through the work of these stewards and heralds, the rulers of Babylon are often forced to acknowledge God's sovereign rule over their own. Nebuchadnezzar confesses,

His dominion is an everlasting dominion,
    and his kingdom endures from generation to generation;
all the inhabitants of the earth are accounted as nothing,
    and he does according to his will among the host of heaven
    and among the inhabitants of the earth;
and none can stay his hand
    or say to him, "What have you done?" (Dan. 4:34–35)

King Darius reaches the same conclusion two chapters later:

He is the living God,
    enduring forever;
his kingdom shall never be destroyed,
    and his dominion shall be to the end.
He delivers and rescues;
    he works signs and wonders
    in heaven and on earth,
he who has saved Daniel
    from the power of the lions. (Dan. 6:26–27)

ESTHER

The book of Esther follows Daniel in the Hebrew Bible. Esther documents the plight of the Jewish nation in exile under the rule of the Persians. The Persian Empire was the ram that Daniel saw (Dan. 8:20). Therefore, Esther is set in a context of Daniel's reminder that though the ram of Persia looks powerful, God's kingdom plan is still advancing.

The battle rages between Mordecai and Haman. Mordecai (a Jew) will not bow down before Haman, a Persian official and a descendant of Agag. Agag was an Amalekite king that Saul infamously spared (1 Sam. 15:9). In other words, the battle between Persia and Israel comes down to a battle between a true steward and a counterfeit.

Mordecai helps Esther see that she has come into the kingdom to save the Jewish people (Est. 4:13–15). Haman's own wife tells him that he cannot win because Mordecai is a Jew (Est. 6:13). Her words come true in Esther 7 as Esther goes to the king and foils Haman's plan. In a great reversal, Haman is hanged on the gallows he prepared for Mordecai (7:10). In a larger reversal, on the day on which the enemies of the Jews hoped to gain mastery over them, "the reverse occurred: the Jews gained mastery over those who hated them" (Est. 9:1).

EZRA AND NEHEMIAH

God's kingdom comes to the forefront in Ezra and Nehemiah as the Lord works in the hearts of pagan rulers to carry out his will for the people's return to the land of Israel. Ezra and Nehemiah are godly stewards and heralds who respond positively to God's work of restoration and return to the land of Israel to rebuild the temple. They lead the people to overcome opposition in accomplishing God's purposes. Ezra in particular leads a renewal movement in which people hear the word of God in the law of Moses and respond to God's voice.

Ezra was a remarkable *steward* of the word. The "good hand of his God was on him" because he "had set his heart to study the Law of the LORD, and to do it and to teach his statutes and rules in Israel" (Ezra 7:9–10). As a scribe, Ezra was trained in the study of the law of Moses, but he had also engaged with the message at the personal level of obedience.

This stewarding led to heralding. Ezra the priest and scribe "stood on a wooden platform" and read from the Book of the Law (Neh. 8:2, 4). The Levites "helped the people to understand the Law, while the people remained in their places" (8:7). How did they help? "They read from the book, from the Law of God, clearly, and they gave the sense, so that the people understood the reading" (8:8).

Ezra was also a *reverent* steward and herald. Ezra could lead corporately in confession (Ezra 9:3–15), and he could lead in corporate worship (Neh. 8:6). The effects were remarkable. Ezra's personal confession led the people to corporate confession and action (Ezra 10:1–17). The ministry of reading the law and giving the sense led people to respond. All the people answered, "Amen, Amen," lifting up their hands. "And they bowed their heads and worshiped the LORD with their faces to the ground" (Neh. 8:6).

APPLICATION: PARALLEL TO PULPIT PREACHING

The account in Nehemiah 8 is perhaps the closest Old Testament parallel to pulpit preaching today. Ezra stood on a wooden platform above the people (8:4–5). He read from the book and did a continuous exposition, not a topical message. The Levites "gave the sense" with the result that the people could understand the reading (8:8).

The stewardship paradigm of Ezra the scribe, with his calling to study, do, and teach (Ezra 7:10), is instructive for ministers of the gospel today. The word entrusted to Ezra was the law of God written by Moses. There is a gap between the original writing and the time of Ezra, and thus he must work hard at *study*. He is a precursor of the calling Paul gives to Timothy of *studying* to show himself approved in order to rightly handle the word of truth (2 Tim. 2:15).

CHRONICLES

It is a grand understatement to say that Chronicles focuses on David. The future hope of Israel remains firm only as Israel continues to focus on the promise of a Davidic King.

The order of Ezra and Nehemiah before Chronicles is instructive for the underlying canonical message. Ezra and Nehemiah narrate events that happened after Chronicles, and this is for a reason. Ezra and Nehemiah cannot be reduced to lessons on good leadership principles. The undercurrent of these books shows that Israel's return to her land pales in comparison to the grand return pictured in the Latter Prophets. The work in Ezra and Nehemiah is a genuine work of God, but it is not *the* work of God to which the prophets point. Chronicles narrates the time of the kingship in which all eyes are on David. All prior kings prove that they are not the promised King. A new King must come in the future who will bring the return and restoration promised in the Prophets. That is why the Hebrew canon ends with the call of Cyrus for the people to return.

PICTURES OF THE MESSIAH

We have already referenced the messianic seams within the Psalter. The first two psalms set the stage for the rest of the Psalter. The Messiah is a servant of God's word who delights in and meditates upon the law of the Lord. The "Son" of Psalm 2 is the messianic King that the Lord has installed in Zion. The rest of the psalms bear the stamp of this same type of reading. Psalm 45 celebrates a King addressed as

"God." "Your throne, O God, is forever" (45:6). Hebrews shows that this King ultimately is a picture of the Son of God (Heb. 1:8).

Many psalms feature a focus on the righteous suffering of the Psalmist, especially what we could call a Davidic sufferer. Psalm 22 is a great example of this suffering, as many of its details appear again in the crucifixion accounts of the Gospels.

The enigma of suffering, curse, and devastation in Job, Lamentations, and Ecclesiastes also focuses hope on a coming deliverer. Job puts his faith in a living Redeemer who will defeat death. Ecclesiastes points to the need for a singular shepherd to lead God's people to find hope amid a cursed world. Lamentations calls God's people to call his mercy to mind so that they can have resolute hope.

> The steadfast love of the LORD never ceases;
>   his mercies never come to an end;
> they are new every morning. (Lam. 3:22–23)

Ezra and Nehemiah anticipate a perfect leader who will shepherd God's people and lead them in a return from exile. The call of Cyrus for the people to return awaits an answer at the end of Chronicles. The answer comes in the Gospels.

13

THE STEWARDSHIP OF THE SON, PART 1

Paradigm 8

> Long ago, at many times and in many ways, God spoke to our
> fathers by the prophets, but in these last days he has spoken
> to us by his Son.
>
> *Hebrews 1:1–2*

THE UNIQUENESS OF JESUS

We come now to the hinge of this study. The coming of Christ represents the climax of mediated revelation. He is the ultimate steward and
herald of God's word. He is, in fact, the very incarnation of the Word
of God. All that the Law, the Prophets, and the Writings anticipated
from a distance has drawn near in perfect fulfillment in him. All the
various strands of our survey now come together in Christ.

Jesus is unique in myriad ways. He images the Father perfectly.
When Philip says, "show us the Father," Jesus responds in a way that
should take our breath away: "Have I been with you so long, and you
still do not know me, Philip? Whoever has seen me has seen the Father. How can you say, 'Show us the Father'?" (John 14:9).

Preachers attempt to make God known through stewarding and
heralding his entrusted word, but Jesus is in a different class altogether. Only Jesus can say, "Whoever has seen me has seen the Father."
Everything Jesus says and does is revelation because he is the incarnate
revelation of God.

One day we will have no more need for the light of the sun because the Lamb will be our lamp. The end of the Bible says, "And the city has no need of sun or moon to shine on it, for the glory of God gives it light, and its lamp is the Lamb" (Rev. 21:23). The lamp is the Lamb!

Let it stagger your mind for a moment that *Jesus is the perfect intersection of all excellencies.* They seamlessly and sinlessly come together in an unparalleled way in one person. This statement has three astonishing affirmations within it that are like glory upon glory upon glory!

First, each excellency is unparalleled in perfection—no one else comes close. Second, he combines in one person *all* of the excellencies that we could imagine and more. All the excellencies. Third, there is even more. He is the perfect combination of all the perfect excellencies. They never clash or contradict each other. They fit together like a puzzle, seamlessly and beautifully. For example, he always knows the right time for either tender mercy or fierce justice to be displayed. He is not tender toward unrepentant sinners when it is time for judgment to fall. He does not drive repentant sinners into the ground beneath the crushing weight of justice. No, he will not cast out a broken sinner who comes running to him in repentance.

There are some obvious answers as to why Jesus is unique as a steward and herald of the word. His deity and sinlessness set him apart from past stewards and heralds. It is striking to think that in our entire survey he is the only example of what sinless stewardship and sinless heralding look like.

One of the neglected points concerning Jesus's ministry of the word is the twofold way he stewards the word: Jesus not only *preaches* the good news promised in the Old Testament, but he also *purchases* it. He is not merely a sinless steward; he is a sinless sacrifice. As steward and herald, he is the *bearer of good news*, but as the perfect Savior he also *bore our sins* on the cross to purchase this good news for us. This chapter will focus mainly on Jesus's stewardship of *preaching* the gospel, while the next chapter will look at the stewardship of *purchasing* the gospel.

JOHN 3:31–36 AS A PARADIGM

John attempts to widen the gap between Jesus the heavenly steward and herald and all earthly ministers. Jesus has a preeminent status as a steward of God's word because he is "from above" and thus is "above all" (John 3:31). Those of the earth speak in "an earthly way" (3:31). In other words, earthly ministers are limited because their words do not transcend the boundaries of earth. By way of contrast, only one speaks in a transcendent way because only one "comes from heaven" (3:31) and "bears witness to what he has seen and heard" (3:32).

Notice the stress on the link between calling, stewarding, and heralding in verse 34: "For he whom God has sent utters the words of God." God called and sent Jesus from heaven, unlike the messengers God sent who came from the earth. Therefore, Jesus utters the words of God in a unique way in the sense that he speaks of the heavenly realities "he has seen and heard" (3:32). He is unique in another way as well. Other messengers from God have had a measure of the Spirit, but Jesus has the Spirit "without measure" (3:34). This assessment fits with the next phrase: "The Father loves the Son and has given all things into his hand" (3:35), including the Spirit.

This unique status results in a unique duty to respond to Jesus (John 3:36). Receiving the words of Jesus is a testimony to the truth of God's word. Failing to receive Jesus and his words is a flat-out rejection of God that makes God out to be a liar. God's wrath remains on all those who reject Jesus.

When we put the pieces together, a paradigmatic picture of Jesus emerges (fig. 11).

Figure 11. Jesus's calling and heralding and their effects

Calling/Sending	Heralding	Effects
Jesus "comes from above" (3:31).	He "bears witness to what he has seen and heard" (3:32).	"Yet no one receives his testimony" (3:32).
Jesus "comes from heaven" (3:31).		
		"Whoever receives his testimony" testifies that "God is true"(3:33).

Calling/Sending	Heralding	Effects
Jesus is "he whom God . . . sent" (3:34).	He "utters the words of God" (3:34).	"Whoever believes in the Son has eternal life; whoever does not obey the Son shall not see life, but the wrath of God remains on him" (3:36).

In what follows, we will examine the paradigm of calling, stewarding and heralding, and effects in more detail.

JESUS'S CALLING

Five different events in Matthew's introductory narrative have a fulfillment formula that showcases how the details of Jesus's birth and infancy "fulfill" Scripture: (1) Jesus's virgin birth (Matt. 1:22–23; cf. Isa. 7:10), (2) Jesus's birth in Bethlehem (Matt. 2:5–6; cf. Mic. 5:2); (3) the journey to Egypt (Matt. 2:14–15; cf. Hos. 11:1); (4) the massacre of children and resulting mourning (Matt. 2:17–18; cf. Jer. 31:15), and (5) the move to Nazareth (Matt. 2:23, with its reference to the "prophets").

These "fulfillment" passages require some in-depth exegetical explanation, which would take too much space to unpack here. Fortunately, there are some good resources that treat the nuances of these passages.[1] Perhaps the best thing to recognize at this point is that these five fulfillment passages are part of a wider narrative dynamic in Matthew 1:18–2:23. This passage consists of six scenes. The discerning reader will catch a repeated rhythm of God's revelation, a human response, and a statement of scriptural fulfillment. Rather than exposit this section in detail, it may be helpful to picture it at a glance in figure 12.

Figure 12. Revelation, response, and fulfillment in Matthew's introductory narrative

Scene	Revelation	Response	Fulfillment
Scene 1	1:20–21	1:24–25	1:22–23 (Isa. 7:10)
Scene 2	2:2	2:2 (magi)	2:5–6 (Mic. 5:2)
		2:3 (Herod/Jerusalem)	

---

[1] See Craig L. Blomberg, "Matthew," in *Commentary on the New Testament Use of the Old Testament*, ed. G. K. Beale and D. A. Carson (Grand Rapids: Baker Academic, 2007).

Scene	Revelation	Response	Fulfillment
Scene 3	2:5–6	2:7–8 (Herod)	
	2:9	2:10 (magi)	
Scene 4	2:11	2:11	Isaiah 60:1–6?
	2:12	2:12	
Scene 5	2:13	2:14–15 (Joseph)	2:15 (Hos. 11:1)
		2:16 (Herod)	2:17–18 (Jer. 31:15)
Scene 6	2:19–20	2:21	
	2:22	2:22–23	2:23 ("prophets")

Luke's introductory narrative takes a different approach than the Gospel of Matthew does. Luke chooses to highlight the relationship between John the Baptist and Jesus. He accomplishes this comparison through a structural feature that presents parallel events for John and Jesus, which Luke follows with a bridge event that brings them together. In each case, Luke stresses the uniqueness and superiority of Jesus's calling in relation to John's calling (Luke 1–2:40). Figure 13 provides a visual of Luke's comparison of John and Jesus.

Figure 13. Parallel events and bridge events regarding John and Jesus

Type of Event	John	Jesus
Parallel	Birth of John foretold (Luke 1:5–25)	Birth of Jesus foretold (1:26–38)
Bridge	John and Jesus "meet" while in the wombs of their mothers (1:39–56).	
Parallel	Birth of John (1:57–80)	Birth of Jesus (2:1–52)
Bridge	John preaches Jesus (3:1–20) and then baptizes Jesus (3:21–22).	

Even in making this comparison, however, we would be off base if we thought that Luke's purpose was for John and Jesus to share the limelight. Because John is the forerunner, the details of his birth pave the way for us to understand the greatness of Jesus's birth. John is born to a barren woman (Luke 1:7), but Jesus is born to a virgin (1:27). An angel visits John's parents and says he will be great as one who prepares people for the Lord (1:15–17), but the same angel visits Jesus's parents and says that he will be great as the Son of the Most High, whose kingdom will never end (1:32–33). Furthermore, in the first bridge section, when Elizabeth meets Mary, John leaps for joy in the womb of Elizabeth, and Elizabeth finds great joy in being with Mary because she is the mother of Elizabeth's "Lord" (1:41–44).

The birth section continues this focus on the greatness of Jesus. John's birth (Luke 1:57–80) receives less sustained attention than the birth of Jesus (Luke 2:1–52). The narrative shows that John is a prophet of the Most High (Luke 1:76), but Jesus is the "Savior, . . . Christ the Lord" (Luke 2:11). Simeon is looking for "the Lord's Christ" (2:26), and he recognizes by the Spirit that Jesus is the Lord's Christ so that he can say, "My eyes have seen your salvation" (2:30).

One should not miss Luke's stress on the work of other faithful stewards here in the birth narrative.[2] Luke highlights the faithful stewardship of Mary,[3] while Matthew emphasizes Joseph's faithful stewardship.[4] Luke also shows that many respond positively to this stewardship of the word.[5]

While the Gospels are remarkably silent about the years between Jesus's birth and his baptism, Luke makes it clear that Jesus comes to

---

[2] One also should not miss how Luke provides a sketch of individual stewards in Luke 1–2, such as Zechariah, Elizabeth, Simeon, and Anna. Luke highlights their faithful character (1:6; 2:25, 37), their advanced age (1:7; 2:26, 29, 36–37), and the fact that they are waiting for the fulfillment of God's promises (2:25–26). Luke also stresses the presence of the Holy Spirit (1:41, 67; 2:25, 26, 27). The Spirit led these saints to prophesy or speak (1:41–45, 67–79; 2:29–35, 38), or recognize the identity of the Messiah (1:43; 2:27). These characters are carryovers from the old era (notice again their advanced age), and they are watching and waiting for the fulfillment of God's promises (the new era of fulfillment). People near the temple respond with reverence to the Lord's loosing of Zechariah's tongue while they ponder in their hearts what the Lord is doing (1:65–66). Likewise, those listening to Anna speak are "waiting for the redemption of Israel" (2:38).

[3] Luke puts the most stress on Mary's stewardship. He records her humble response to the revelation of the angel (1:38), and Elizabeth declares Mary blessed because she "believed that there would be a fulfillment of what was spoken to her from the Lord"—1:45). Luke includes Mary's song of response to God's revelation (1:46–55). Simeon addresses her and says that a sword will pierce her soul (2:34–35). Twice Luke tells us that she responded to God's revelation of Jesus by treasuring these things in her heart (2:19, 51) and pondering their meaning (2:19). Luke also highlights the righteous character and the responses of Joseph and Mary. They marvel at the things they hear (2:33). They also obediently carry out the requirements of the law (2:21–24, 27, 39).

[4] I marvel at the immediate and meticulous obedience of Joseph. He responds to God's revelation without hesitation or questioning each time. Joseph is a model for stewards of God's word today.

[5] Others respond positively as stewards of what God has revealed as well. The shepherds make haste to go and see what the angels revealed to them (2:15–16) and they share what the angels revealed with those gathered (2:17). All who have heard their report wonder at their words (2:18). After seeing Jesus, they respond by glorifying and praising God (2:20).

understand the calling upon his life even in his childhood. The one event that Luke records from Jesus's childhood, when he is twelve, is a strategic one. Twelve years old was a coming of age of sorts, and Jesus takes this one opportunity to declare his true identity and reveal to his parents where his true allegiance rests. Jesus appears to disobey his parents by not returning home with them so that they have to search for him frantically. They find him in the temple and ask, "Son, why have you treated us so? Behold, your father and I have been searching for you in great distress" (Luke 2:48).

The underlying charge is that he should not treat them in that way and should have returned home with them. Jesus corrects this charge by saying that he was at home with his Father in his Father's house: "And he said to them, 'Why were you looking for me? Did you not know that I must be in my Father's house?'" (Luke 2:49). His earthly parents do not understand, but Luke tells us that after this point Jesus is submissive to them again (2:51). In other words, Jesus is submissive to his earthly parents in an unbroken way with the exception of this one moment in time. This one event in his childhood is a personal declaration, a kind of coming of age in which he declares his ultimate submission to his heavenly Father.

JESUS'S STEWARDING AND HERALDING

All of the Synoptic Gospels record what transpires at Jesus's baptism and temptation.[6] They highlight that the Spirit comes upon Jesus at his baptism (Matt. 3:16; Mark 1:10; Luke 3:22), and the voice of God the Father affirms that Jesus is his beloved Son in whom he is well pleased (Matt. 3:17; Mark 1:11; Luke 3:22).

The Spirit then thrusts him into the wilderness in order to face the Devil and his temptations (Matt. 4:1; Mark 1:11; Luke 4:1). The wilderness theme sounds off strongly here because Jesus is the new Israel. He is in the wilderness for forty days just as Israel was in the wilderness for forty years. His facing Satan as the tempter echoes the

---

[6] Even though all of the Synoptic Gospels record these events, they do so in a way that maintains their own unique points of emphasis. Matthew depicts Jesus's baptism in a way that brings out his overall narrative emphasis on fulfillment and righteousness. John can baptize Jesus (even though John should be baptized by Jesus) because it is fitting as a way of fulfilling all righteousness (John 3:15). After the temptation, Jesus moves to the territory of Zebulun and Naphtali, which Matthew informs us is the fulfillment of Isa. 9:2 (4:13–16).

fact that Jesus is also the new Adam who must succeed where the first Adam failed.

The stewardship theme sounds extra loud as Jesus overcomes all of Satan's temptations by citing Scripture as the authority in obeying God's word. Thus, there is no fall narrative! Jesus corrects Satan's Scripture twisting (Matt. 4:5–7; Luke 4:9–12). Jesus quotes the very lesson that Moses said Israel should have learned in the wilderness (Deut. 8:4) but failed to take to heart: "Man shall not live by bread alone" (Matt. 4:4a; Luke 4:4), "but by every word that comes from the mouth of God" (Matt. 4:4b). In fact, Moses said that what Israel experienced was God's testing of them to see if they would obey his commandments (Deut. 8:3). Jesus has overcome Satan's temptation and passed the test that God gave to Israel in the wilderness.

As we turn to look at Jesus's preaching, our goal is not to examine his sermons in detail, but to see the things he stressed and the categories he used in his preaching. The Synoptic Gospels stress that Jesus's sermons are expositions of what the Old Testament anticipated. He shows that what the Old Testament envisioned has arrived with him. He presents himself as Isaiah's end-time herald (Isa. 52:7) because his phrase "the gospel of the kingdom" (Matt. 4:23; 9:35) preaches the "good news" of "Your God reigns" from Isaiah 52:7.

Jesus's coming also fulfills Isaiah's anticipated Spirit-anointed Messiah (Isa. 61:1). Luke presents Jesus teaching in the synagogues with the result that people marvel at his ministry and glorify him (Luke 4:15). Luke then chooses one sermon as an example of this teaching. Jesus reads the first part of Isaiah 61 and declares that it has now been fulfilled in the people's hearing.

> And the scroll of the prophet Isaiah was given to him. He unrolled the scroll and found the place where it was written,
>
> > "The Spirit of the Lord is upon me,
> >   because he has anointed me
> >   to proclaim good news to the poor.
> > He has sent me to proclaim liberty to the captives
> >   and recovering of sight to the blind,
> >   to set at liberty those who are oppressed,
> > to proclaim the year of the Lord's favor."

And he rolled up the scroll and gave it back to the attendant and sat down. And the eyes of all in the synagogue were fixed on him. And he began to say to them, "Today this Scripture has been fulfilled in your hearing." (Luke 4:17–21)

Jesus also fulfills the Old Testament not just in his person, but in his teaching. This comes to the forefront in one of the most well-known examples of Jesus's preaching: the Sermon on the Mount (Matthew 5–7). The sermon consists of an introduction (5:1–16), a body (5:17–7:12), and a conclusion (7:13–27). The body of the sermon begins and ends with a reference to the Law and the Prophets (5:17; 7:12). Jesus claims that his teaching is the culmination of all that the Law and the Prophets anticipated.

If the Synoptics present Jesus in terms of Isaiah's end-time herald and Messiah, John's Gospel stresses the stewardship of Jesus as Son. As Son, he does not speak on his own authority; he speaks what he sees and hears from the Father (John 8:26, 28; 12:49–50; 14:10). He speaks on the basis of the Father's authority because he seeks the glory of the Father (John 7:18). As a sinless steward and herald, Jesus perfectly preaches the gospel of God because he alone fully says what the Father commands him to say in a sinless way. Consider for example, John 12:49–50: "I have not spoken on my own authority, but the Father who sent me has himself given me a commandment—what to say and what to speak. And I know that his commandment is eternal life. What I say, therefore, I say as the Father has told me." Jesus speaks about himself even when he appears to talk about others.

Jesus appears to be teaching the crowds about John the Baptist in Matthew 11:7–11. In verses 7–10, Jesus clarifies that John's mission as defined by Isaiah 40:3 is to prepare the way for the Lord. Jesus could simply close the discussion by saying, "And here I am. I am the 'Lord' for whom John prepared you." But he chooses not to say it that way. Rather, he says, "Truly, I say to you, among those born of women there has arisen no one greater than John the Baptist" (Matt. 11:11). In other words, at first glance, verse 11 looks like a statement of John's greatness. Jesus's next statement puts this assessment into perspective: "Yet the one who is least in the kingdom of heaven is greater than he"

(11:11). Now it looks like Jesus is saying something about the greatness of those who come after John in the kingdom of heaven.

The key here is to ascertain what makes John greater than anyone prior to him and what makes anyone coming after John greater than he. Why is John greater than Moses, Abraham, David, or Isaiah? Why are those in the kingdom after John greater than Moses, Abraham, David, Isaiah, and even John himself? This answer, like every answer in our survey, hinges upon Jesus. John is greater than anyone who came before because others saw the Messiah and pointed to his coming from a distance, while John sees the Messiah face-to-face and points to him in the present by saying, "Here he is." Figure 14 illustrates this logic.

Figure 14. The narrowing gap between prophets and fulfillment of prophecies in Jesus

John the Baptist	Jesus
Isaiah	Jesus
Elijah	Jesus
David	Jesus
Moses	Jesus
Abraham	Jesus

This way of reckoning shows that greatness hinges on the proximity of the prophet to Jesus. The nearer the prophet, the greater the privilege of closeness to Jesus as each prophet points to him. But those who succeed John in the kingdom of heaven see more of Jesus than John ever did (fig. 15).

Figure 15. The greater proximity of the "least in the kingdom"

	Jesus—"least in the kingdom"
John the Baptist	Jesus
Isaiah	Jesus
Elijah	Jesus
David	Jesus
Moses	Jesus
Abraham	Jesus

Even those who are least in the kingdom will see more of Jesus than John does. They will see more of his miracles, hear more of his teaching, and even witness his death and resurrection. In the final analysis, Jesus teaches the crowds about John's limited greatness so that he can teach the crowd about his own unlimited greatness.

D. A. Carson offers an illustration of what Jesus's logic might sound like today. Imagine someone (we will call him Bill) is introducing you to a crowd to whom you are about to preach. After the introduction, you come up to the platform and say, "Among those born of women, no one is greater than Bill, because he got to introduce *ME*."

We laugh at this snobbish, self-aggrandizing way of talking. It would be ridiculous for you to speak this way because it would just be a not-so-clever means of talking about yourself. It is ridiculous and sinful for you or I to talk this way simply because it is totally and patently false. But it is not sinful for Jesus to talk this way precisely because it is totally true. Unbelieving humanity may reject it as ridiculous, but those with eyes to see and ears to hear recognize that Jesus is telling the truth. He is the hinge of all redemptive history, and thus he is the center of his own sermons. He says that all of God's prior revelation points to him.

EFFECTS IN THE GOSPELS

Jesus's word has supreme power in the Gospels. He is able to command the sea to be still (Matt. 8:26). He calls for unclean spirits to flee (8:32), dead legs to walk (Matt. 9:6), blind eyes to see (9:29), and dead men to live (John 11:43). The story of the centurion's faith further illustrates Jesus's authority. He can simply say the word and the centurion's servant will be healed (Matt. 8:13).

What is most surprising in the Gospels is not the power of Jesus's word in healing and nature, but the people's hard-hearted rejection of his word. His words certainly have positive effects. They are "light" for those who walk in darkness (John 8:12) and they cleanse (John 15:3) and produce belief (John 8:30), joy (John 15:11; 17:13), and peace (John 16:33). But far more often we see that Jesus's words bring judgment on people. They serve as the basis of judgment for those who hear them (John 12:48), and they produce guilt (John 15:22).

The Gospels stress that the natural person cannot understand or receive what Jesus says unless the person's spiritual blindness and deadness are removed. For example, his preaching of the parables reveals more than the word of God; it also reveals the state of the people's hearts:

> To you has been given the secret of the kingdom of God, but for those outside everything is in parables, so that
>
> > "they may indeed see but not perceive,
> > and may indeed hear but not understand,
> > lest they should turn and be forgiven." (Mark 4:11–12)

Notice that Mark 4:12 quotes from Isaiah 6:9, which talks about Israel's hardness. Jesus's preaching further consigns some to their hardened state. Jesus makes the effectual link between speaking and judgment explicit in John 15:22: "If I had not come and spoken to them, they would not have been guilty of sin, but now they have no excuse for their sin." John 8:45 is even more striking in stressing a causal connection between the truth spoken and the unbelief that results: "But *because* I tell the truth, you do not believe me."

Jesus has large crowds following his teaching, and many claim to be believers, but Jesus looks beyond the numbers and sees the hearts. For example, John tells us that "many believed in his name when they saw the signs that he was doing" (John 2:23). John adds that "Jesus on his part did not entrust himself to them, because he knew all people and needed no one to bear witness about man, for he himself knew what was in man" (2:24–25).

The next story illustrates this dynamic. The transition is clear if one eliminates the chapter divisions: Jesus "knew what was in *man*." "Now there was a *man* . . . named Nicodemus" (John 3:1). He is an example like those in John 2:23 who believe on account of the *signs*. He says, "Rabbi, we know that you are a teacher come from God, for no one can do these *signs* that you do unless God is with him" (John 3:2).

Jesus tells him that he, Nicodemus, does not know how to interpret the signs; he does not see them rightly: "Truly, truly, I say to you, unless one is born again he cannot see the kingdom of God" (John 3:3). Nicodemus claims to see, but Jesus tells him that he does not even see the kingdom of God because he is not born again. Jesus makes plain the truth of Ezekiel's vision of complete heart change (3:5), but Nicodemus (even though he is Israel's teacher) does not understand. One must be born of the Spirit to understand Jesus (3:8).

This new birth means that we must regard saving faith as an absolute miracle. Martin Luther notes that Jesus marveled at the centurion's faith. Even though two miracles happened (healing of the centurion's servant and the faith of the centurion), Jesus marvels only at the miracle of faith. Luther says:

> People deem it a great miracle that He made the blind see, the deaf hear, and the lepers clean. And certainly, they are great miracles. But Christ thinks much higher of that which comes to pass within the soul than of that which happens to the body. Therefore, by so much as the soul is more precious than the body, so great and so much greater is the miracle to be regarded which he praises here, than other miracles that happen to the body. . . . It is a miracle, a great miracle, that a man should have such fine strong faith; therefore Christ exalts this centurion's faith as if it were a miracle above all miracles.[7]

The parable of the sower highlights how Jesus understands the hearts of those in the crowds that follow him (Mark 4:3–9). The parable explains the effect of the seed (the word) upon the soil (the heart). The seed does not penetrate the first soil at all. These hearts represent those who, like the scribes and Pharisees, immediately reject Jesus's teaching. The next two soils have the seed penetrate more, but it does not bear any fruit because the soil is either shallow (and the seed gets scorched by the sun) or crowded (and the seed gets choked by the weeds). Only one soil is declared good: the soil that the seed penetrates, producing a harvest.

Jesus also tells a parable in Luke 16 to stress the power of the word, which undergirds the priority of preaching. Jesus describes a rich man who is dressed in fine clothes and has the best things in life. On the other hand, there is a poor man named Lazarus, who doesn't have anything. He longs to eat from the scraps that fall from the rich man's table, but the only company he has are dogs to lick his sores. Dogs in the ancient world were not the cute cuddly things we have as pets;

---

[7] Martin Luther, *Day by Day We Magnify Thee: Daily Readings* (Philadelphia, Fortress: 1982), 68.

they were mangy, flea-ridden, wild animals. They were not man's best friend in this story.

Both the rich man and Lazarus die, and what they have in life is reversed in eternity. And so the rich man is now suffering as a poor man in the agony of the flames of hell. Lazarus is now richly comforted by Abraham in heaven. And though there is a gulf fixed between the two, the rich man wants Lazarus to come down and just cool his tongue, which is burning, with a drop of water. Hell has not changed the rich man; he still thinks he can call the shots and run the show—even from there! Father Abraham reminds him of the fixed gulf and God's justice.

So in Luke 16:27–28 the rich man weighs the situation and asks Abraham to send Lazarus to his father's house because he has five brothers. The man wants to warn them in order that they might not come into this place of torment. Abraham answers that they have Moses and the Prophets; let them hear them. But the rich man responds in verse 30, "No, father Abraham, but if someone goes to them from the dead, they will repent." Abraham replies in verse 31, "If they do not hear Moses and the Prophets, neither will they be convinced if someone should rise from the dead."

Do you see what Jesus believes about the power of God's word? It is more powerful than a sensational testimony from a person returning from the grave.

EFFECTS IN REVELATION

Jesus's ministry of the word and as the Word is not impressive in the Gospels in terms of mass conversions! His preaching pronounces judgment upon Israel's hard-heartedness. Jesus's word ministry in the book of Revelation is startling in its powerful effects. Whereas he pronounces judgment in the Gospels, he enacts judgment in Revelation. Jesus "is clothed in a robe dipped in blood, and *the name by which he is called is The Word of God*" (Rev. 19:13). He crushes the enemies of God with a royal scepter like a rod of iron. He has the sharp sword of the word that comes "from his mouth." He treads "the winepress of the fury of the wrath of God the Almighty" (19:15). He vanquishes the Beast and the false prophet and throws them into the lake of fire (19:20) along with Satan (Rev. 20:7–10).

FALSE SHEPHERDS AND STEWARDS IN THE GOSPELS

It is also instructive to see the transition from the false shepherds and true messianic shepherd of Ezekiel 34 to the Pharisees (false shepherds) and Jesus (true shepherd) of Matthew 6 and 22, Mark 6, and John 10. Many passages in the Gospels feature a stinging denunciation of the Pharisees and the rulers of Israel. The life of the preacher matters in preaching, but the Pharisees preach without practicing what they preach (Matt. 23:3).

Jesus's condemnation of the Pharisees is strong and striking, but Jesus shows that Satan is really behind all of their lies and unbelieving false stewardship. Listen to John 8:43–45:

> Why do you not understand what I say? It is because you cannot bear to hear my word. You are of your father the devil, and your will is to do your father's desires. He was a murderer from the beginning, and does not stand in the truth, because there is no truth in him. When he lies, he speaks out of his own character, for he is a liar and the father of lies. But because I tell the truth, you do not believe me.

In this regard, it is important to see how often Jesus makes reference to Satan's work against the word (Matt. 4:1–11; 13:39; Mark 4:15; Luke 8:12; 22:3; John 6:7).

Jesus also condemns the false stewardship of the Sadducees. Matthew 22:29–32 makes a strong case against their stewardship. They deny the resurrection, Jesus says, "because you know neither the Scriptures nor the power of God" (22:29). Notice how the Scriptures and the power of God are linked together. The Sadducees are unbelievers and thus they cannot properly steward the Scriptures. They fundamentally err when they read the Scriptures because they do not believe in God's almighty power.

Recall, by way of contrast, the link between Job's faith in the resurrection and his faith in God's power:

> For I know that my Redeemer lives,
>   and at the last he will stand upon the earth.
> And after my skin has been thus destroyed,
>   yet in my flesh I shall see God,

whom I shall see for myself,
    and my eyes shall behold, and not another. (Job 19:25–27)

Job held to this hope because he could confess,

I know that you can do all things,
    and that no purpose of yours can be thwarted. (Job 42:2)

Jesus denounces the Pharisees and Sadducees together. They are both spiritually blind ("you cannot interpret the signs of the times"—Matt. 16:3) and spiritually wicked and unbelieving ("an evil and adulterous generation seeks for a sign"—16:4). John the Baptist says that they are children of snakes ("brood of vipers"—probably a reference to the seed of the serpent) and spiritually presumptive ("Do not presume to say to yourselves . . ."—Matt. 3:7–9).

APPLICATION 1: THE SUFFICIENCY OF SCRIPTURE OVER SENSATIONALISM

Jesus's words in Luke 16 should demolish our bent to trust in sensationalism. Charles Dickens writes famously of Ebenezer Scrooge's being visited by the ghost of his friend Jacob Marley. Scrooge repents and "keeps Christmas in his heart all year long" because of the impact of the three spirits that visit him. Too many people have similar views of what it would take to change a person's mind about heaven and hell. Do you think that if someone came back from the dead and preached about hell that it would suddenly arrest the attention of more people and automatically produce conviction? Do you think that kind of powerful, sensational experience would lead more people to faith and into heaven?

Jesus speaks a clear and forceful *no* to this line of thinking. In fact, the parable presents that way of thinking as the summary of how unbelievers view the word of God. Unbelievers think that the word is not enough; people need more than Moses and the Prophets. By holding up "Moses and the Prophets" as a benchmark, Jesus presents the way a believer thinks about the power of the word. It is more powerful than a sensational testimony from someone returning from the grave. Do we know the Scriptures and God's power (Matt. 22:29)? Or are we unbelieving like the Sadducees?

APPLICATION 2: NO SUCH THING AS "SET IT AND FORGET IT" CHRISTIANITY

The parable of the sower reminds us that Jesus does not share our modern-day obsession with numbers and crowds. Jesus sees behind the façade and speaks the plain truth about perseverance and discipleship. I am reminded of the popular advertisements for the Ronco Showtime Rotisserie grill that used to frequent television infomercials. The catch phrase in those days was, "Set it and forget it." I received one for Christmas but was shocked to read in the instruction booklet's fine print that I was not to take "set it and forget it" *literally*.

Not taking it literally meant heeding the warning to stay with my meat at all times while it was cooking. My first thought was that this was false advertising. Later I came to see that this kind of false advertising runs rampant in the church as well. Well-meaning preachers proclaim a kind of "set it and forget it" Christianity that says it is sufficient to sign a card, walk an aisle, or raise a hand. Many preachers maintain an approach aimed at seeing the resulting "converts" grow in the faith, but if no progress or growth in godliness comes, these preachers are very slow to insist upon transformation or discipleship as evidence of salvation. Some even tell their "converts" not to worry about transformation and sanctification.

These approaches are out of touch with Jesus's teaching. Jesus called for followers or disciples (Matt. 28:20; Mark 8:34), not just decisions. "Set it and forget it" Christianity is false advertising.

Therefore, Jesus's teaching reminds us of the folly of judging the success of a sermon by the immediate responses. His words also warn preachers against hastily gauging success in ministry by the swelling or falling numbers of the crowds. Jesus's perspective must inform how we evaluate responses to sermons.

Jesus also teaches us how to think about the role of the preacher in producing the effects of the word upon the hearer. He reminds people that the seed does not grow in direct response to the work of the farmer. The seed is at work even when the farmer is not at work (Mark 4:27). As Paul declares, "God gave the growth" (1 Cor. 3:6). The preacher who plants or waters the seed should not be our main focus because God gives the growth (3:7). Inflated views of the preacher have no place in biblical preaching; biblical preaching emphasizes an exalted view of God and the integral part that he plays in preaching.

What a wonder to have Jesus's ministry of the word as the Word recorded for us in the Gospels. He is the perfect sinless steward and herald of the word of God in a unique, unparalleled way because he is the very Word of God. The Gospels should make us long to have the mind of Christ. The first two stanzas of the song "May the Mind of Christ My Savior" (by Kate B. Wilkinson) make a prayerful plea for this very reality:

> May the mind of Christ, my Savior,
> Live in me from day to day,
> By His love and power controlling
> All I do and say.
>
> May the Word of God dwell richly
> In my heart from hour to hour,
> So that all may see I triumph
> Only through His power.

14

THE STEWARDSHIP OF THE SON, PART 2

Paradigm 8 (continued)

> And then all three children were staring with open mouths. What they were seeing may be hard to believe when you read it in print, but it was almost as hard to believe when you saw it happening. The things in the picture were moving. It didn't look at all like a cinema either; the colors were too real and clean and out-of-doors for that.
>
> *C. S. Lewis*

The last chapter covered Jesus's preaching of the word. He pronounced judgment through preaching at his first coming and will enact judgment by the word at his second coming. In between those two things, something colossal happened that opened the floodgates of salvation: the cross. In this chapter we look at Jesus's purchase of the good news of the word. Rather than juggle multiple Gospel accounts, I will focus on Mark's presentation of Jesus's death.

I fear that the cross has become so commonplace in Christian thinking that we can lose the wonder of the story. The phrase "Christ crucified" is like a still photo of Jesus's death in the same way that the painting on the wall of Eustace's home captures the Dawn Treader in a moment in time, as C. S. Lewis describes in *The Voyage of the Dawn Treader*. Lucy and Edmund cannot help but stare at its beauty, and before they know it the picture comes to life and they find themselves entering the story. They experience the drama of the narrative in its highs and lows and share in the adventure with the characters of the story.

My prayer is that this chapter will make the drama of the cross and the wonder of Christ's love come alive. The reader will enter the story as it moves back and forth from irony to rejection to fulfillment of the Scriptures.

THE PURPOSE OF IRONY IN MARK'S PASSION NARRATIVE

Irony is often easier to spot than to define. One simple definition is that irony highlights a difference between appearance and reality. Irony normally conveys a clash between the surface meaning and the deeper meaning of a text. This clash can take place at two different levels: irony that is found "in the narrative" and irony that is "carried by the narrative."[1] Sometimes the characters in the story are able to discern the irony of an event or statement, but at other times the deeper meaning is available to the reader but hidden from the characters.

Both of these dynamics are certainly at work in the mockery of the soldiers leading up to the crucifixion (Mark 15:18). On the one hand, it is obvious to them and to Jesus that "what they *mean* is in balanced dissonance to what they *say*."[2] The "homage" they pay to Jesus as "King of the Jews" is intended as an affront to Jesus and the Jewish nation. However, they are not aware of the deeper meaning of the irony carried by the narrative. Mark's readers know that "Jesus [is the Christ], the Son of God" (Mark 1:1). Therefore, Mark's readers see the unsettling irony of the soldiers' mockery in that what they say is truer than what they know. Jesus is the divine Son of God, and thus they should treat him as royalty, pay him homage, and bow before their King.

Why would an author use irony? Some authors stress the sociological function of irony in that it forces readers to take sides in a narrative. Will they side with or against the characters in the story? Irony "creates a sense of community" that vindicates certain values or practices and divides readers into "insiders" and "outsiders."[3]

---

[1] Jerry Camery-Hoggart, *Irony in Mark's Gospel: Text and Subtext*, Society for New Testament Studies Monograph Series 72 (Cambridge: Cambridge University Press, 1992), 2. Camery-Hoggart says that sometimes irony is so thoroughly embedded in the narrative that the readers of the story have access to it in a way that completely excludes the characters of the story.
[2] Ibid.
[3] Ibid.

I would agree that irony forces the reader to reach a verdict concerning the events of a narrative. The sociological function of irony fits the Gospel of Mark, but it does not go far enough. I want to argue for a divine dimension to irony that highlights God's sovereign control of the events of the cross. God's sovereignty is on display, but only some have eyes to see it. The passion narrative continues to emphasize the theme of spiritual blindness (cf. Mark 4:10–12; 8:11–21, 22–33).

Therefore, irony forces readers to decide if they are going to reject Jesus (as virtually everyone else in the narrative does) or affirm God's hand behind all of the events. Will they interpret the events as coincidence (seemingly random correspondence) or the will of God (intended and planned choices from the author of history)? The ironic interplay of divine sovereignty and human rejection is grounded in Isaiah 53. There is human rejection because Isaiah 53:3 says,

> He was despised and rejected by men;
>   a man of sorrows, and acquainted with grief.

There is irony because God is sovereign over the despising, the rejection, and the grief. Isaiah 53:10 says that

> it was the will of the Lord to crush him;
>   he has put him to grief.

These two points (human rejection and providential irony) are put in back-to-back succession in Acts 4:27–28: "For truly in this city there were gathered together against your holy servant Jesus, whom you anointed, both Herod and Pontius Pilate, along with the Gentiles and the peoples of Israel, to do whatever your hand and your plan had predestined to take place."

In what follows, I highlight the interplay or symmetry between irony and an escalating sense of rejection and suffering in Mark's passion narrative.

IRONY 1: WHY WAS JESUS CAPTURED NOW AND NOT BEFORE?

Jesus takes it upon himself to reveal the first element of irony in the passion narrative. The Jewish authorities come with their swords and clubs. He chides them for forgetting that he has conducted his ministry of teaching (not robbing) in plain sight of everyone (not in secrecy): "Day after day I was with you in the temple teaching, and you did not seize me" (Mark 14:49a). In other words, Jesus forces the authorities (and the readers) to come to grips with the reason for the present state of affairs. Has he been an outlaw on the run from them, and now they have finally caught up with him? Has he been a notorious threat to society as a lawbreaker or robber so that it will take a squad of heavily armed authorities to capture him? No, Jesus is not outmaneuvered and overpowered. He offers a different explanation: "But let the Scriptures be fulfilled" (14:49b). The authorities may think that they have Jesus and the situation in hand, but Jesus points to an unseen hand steering the course of the unfolding drama.[4]

REJECTION 1: REJECTION BY THE DISCIPLES

Mark also documents the first moment of rejection in the next two verses. All the disciples leave Jesus and flee, including a young man who runs away naked (Mark 14:50–52). This rejection does not take Jesus by surprise, as can be seen in his prophecy in Mark 14:27. The sheep scatter when the shepherd is struck.

IRONY 2: JESUS'S "TRIAL"—WHO IS GUILTY OF BLASPHEMY, JESUS OR THE SANHEDRIN?

Jesus the shepherd now becomes Jesus the Lamb of God at his trial as he remains silent, just as a lamb before his shearers is silent (Isa. 53:7). The authorities finally bring this silent Lamb to speak a word of self-

---

[4] Justice was certainly not served at the Jewish judicial proceedings. The trial was more like a travesty of justice. Jewish leaders sought out any testimony that would condemn Jesus, but all of the testimonies were contradictory or false. Much has been written concerning the so-called illegal aspects of this trial. Some scholars look at the Sanhedrin rules governing capital trials and note that (1) trials are to be conducted during the day and have the sentence rendered during the day, (2) they should begin with reasons for acquittal and not with reasons for conviction (*m. Sanh.* 4:1), (3) they should not be held on the eve of the Sabbath or a festival day (*m. Sanh.* 4:1), (4) they could reach an acquittal on the same day, but verdicts of conviction must be confirmed on the following day after a night's sleep (*m. Sanh.* 4:1), (5) they required the evidence of two witnesses for verdicts of condemnation (evidence became null and void if the witnesses disagreed; furthermore, false witnesses were required to suffer the same death penalty to which the accused had been made liable), and (6) they were supposed to be held in the temple, not the high priest's home. See David Garland, "Mark," in the *Zondervan Bible Background Commentary*, vol. 1 (Grand Rapids: Zondervan, 2005), 291. Garland rightly adds that these rules reflect the idealized thoughts of a later era. There is no way to know whether these rules really represent the historical procedures for the Sanhedrin in the era of Jesus or any other era. The fact remains, however, that the religious leaders held a hasty, prejudicial trial aimed at conviction.

identity. He confesses that he is the Messiah, the Son of the Blessed One (Mark 14:61–62). The high priest claims that Jesus is guilty of the charge of blasphemy (14:63–64). The Sanhedrin confirms the charge and begins to carry out "justice" by spitting on him and hitting him with many blows to the face.

However, the reader knows that Jesus is who he says he is (Mark 1:1). Therefore, Jesus is also correct in stating that his and the high priest's roles will be reversed in the final judgment because Jesus is the son of man in Daniel's vision, and thus the rebellious Jewish authorities will see him sitting at the right hand of power, coming on the clouds of heaven as the Judge. They stand in judgment of him at this meeting, but Jesus will stand in judgment over them at their next meeting. It is difficult to know whether the Sanhedrin has caught the pointed element of irony. The Jewish court has convicted Jesus of blasphemy, but the heavenly court has convicted them of blasphemy, and their roles will be reversed at the coming of the son of man.

REJECTION 2: REJECTION BY THE JEWISH LEADERS

Mark takes pains to inform us that Jesus faces trial alone. Peter follows at a distance in the courtyard. "Many" bear false witness (Mark 14:56), and "all" condemn him as deserving death (14:64). Mark does not record the voice of anyone who defends Jesus. He stands trial all alone and everyone renders a verdict against him.

IRONY 3: PETER'S "TRIAL"—THE FAILURE OF PETER'S WORDS AND THE VINDICATION OF JESUS'S WORDS

In contrast to Jesus's "official" trial before the Jewish high priest, Peter has an unofficial trial before the servant girl "of the high priest"[5] and some of the bystanders. Three times Peter denies knowing Jesus (Mark 14:68, 70, 71), even putting himself under "oath" and calling down a curse on himself (14:71). The irony here is that Peter's claim not to be a disciple of Jesus or to know Jesus is partially true. Would a real disciple deny Jesus? Would someone who really knows Jesus's true divine identity fail to confess him before a lowly servant girl?

---

[5] Mark alone adds the clarification that it is the servant girl of the high priest.

The second irony at work in this story relates to the last word spoken by the Sanhedrin in the previous story: "Prophesy!" (Mark 14:65). While the Sanhedrin mockingly asks Jesus to prophesy, the reader witnesses the vindication of Jesus's prophecy uttered back in Mark 14:30. The validity of Jesus's words stands in stark contrast to the failure of Peter's earlier prediction: "Even though they all fall away, I will not" (14:29); "If I must die with you, I will not deny you" (14:31).

REJECTION 3: REJECTION BY PETER

It is not hard to see the rejection at this juncture, as it is remarkably personal and pointed. Peter, the disciple who swore with the most bravado that he would not fall away (Mark 14:31), denies Jesus in the most detailed, repeated way (14:68, 70, 71). The *how* (the oath and the curse), the *how many* (three times), and the *before whom* (a lowly servant girl) of his denial make the rejection all the more stunning.

IRONY 4: JESUS'S TRIAL BEFORE PILATE—WHO IS ON TRIAL AND WHO IS GUILTY, JESUS OR THE JEWS?

Next the Jewish leaders hand Jesus over to the Gentile leaders. The reader has access to Pilate's private verdict: Pilate knows that Jesus is innocent because he sees that the priests have handed him over because of their "envy" (Mark 15:10). Mark emphasizes that even a pagan Gentile can see Jesus's innocence and the falsehood of the chief priests.

Mark not only drives home the innocence of Jesus; he also stresses the guilt of the chief priests and the crowd.[6] The charge shifts from the religious sphere (blasphemy—Mark 14:64) to the political sphere (King of the Jews—Mark 15:2). Pilate thinks that he has found an ingenious, politically expedient way to exonerate Jesus before the Jewish crowd. He takes advantage of the tradition on the Passover feast of releasing one prisoner. He presents to them a notoriously guilty murderer and forces a verdict by making them choose between the "innocent" Jesus and the "guilty" Barabbas (15:6–10). The chief priests stir up the crowds

---

[6] Matthew makes this point even more explicit. Pilate announces that he is innocent of Jesus's blood, but the crowd exclaims, "His blood be on us and on our children!" (Matt. 27:25).

to choose Barabbas. When Pilate asks them what they want to do with Jesus, they cry out for his crucifixion (15:13).

Surprisingly, the private verdict of Pilate now becomes public. The "pagan Gentile" judge now functions as the public defense attorney for God's true "Son" before the crowd composed of those who are supposed to be "God's children."[7] Pilate comes to Jesus's defense with an interrogating question for the crowd concerning the supposed "evil" that Jesus has done that could possibly justify the charge of crucifixion (Mark 15:14). The fact that he is asking the crowd to defend their "verdict" shows that he does not see Jesus as an evildoer. The crowd refuses to produce any evidence; they simply shout more for Jesus's death (15:14). This lack of evidence turns out to be the clearest evidence against the crowd, which proves their guilt.

REJECTION 4: REJECTION BY THE CHIEF PRIESTS, THE CROWD, AND PILATE

Once again, in the narrative Mark does not record a single Jewish voice in Jesus's defense. He emphasizes that the chief priests and the crowd as a whole are unified in their rejection of Jesus. If any of the onlookers do not support the death penalty, they remain silent in Mark's narrative.

As mentioned above, the pagan Gentile Pilate is the only one to come to Jesus's defense. One would think that the verdict would be favorable for Jesus since the judge of the trial has become his advocate. However, in a spineless perversion of justice, Pilate orders Jesus to be scourged and then releases him to the crowd to satisfy its bloodthirsty cries for crucifixion (Mark 15:15). Jesus's one-time advocate rejects him because Pilate cares more for the reign of Caesar and its demands on him than for the reign of "the King of the Jews."

The intensity of Jesus's rejection and suffering now escalates to a new level with the report of his scourging. Mark allots one sentence to a scene that seems to last an eternity in the movie *The Passion of the Christ*. Some have argued that Mel Gibson exaggerated the intensity

---

[7] Jesus himself points out the irony of this response in John's Gospel. To those who claim to be the children of Abraham (8:33, 39) and God (8:41), he declares that they want to kill him and therefore they are *not* acting like their professed fathers, Abraham (8:39–40) and God (8:42), but are acting like their real father, the Devil (8:44).

and duration of the scourging, but one could counter that the historical reality was actually worse. The Romans, unlike the Jews, were not limited by how many blows they could inflict (thirty-nine lashes—cf. 2 Cor. 11:24). It was up to the whim of the torturer.

IRONY 5: THE TRUTH BEHIND THE SOLDIERS' MOCKING SCORN

Now it is the soldiers' turn to mock the apparent messianic pretender.

> They clothed him in a purple cloak, and twisting together a crown of thorns, they put it on him. And they began to salute him, "Hail, King of the Jews!" And they were striking his head with a reed and spitting on him and kneeling down in homage to him. And when they had mocked him, they stripped him of the purple cloak and put his own clothes on him. And they led him out to crucify him. (Mark 15:17–20)

The irony is unmistakable. The purple robe, the crown of thorns, the chanting and acclaiming as "King of the Jews," the reed, the anointing (spitting), the kneeling and bowing all bear royal connotations. The soldiers are clearly mocking Jesus, but just as clearly the reader recognizes the truth hidden behind the scorn. He *is* royalty and thus he *should* be dressed in royal robes with a crown and a reed. They *should* anoint him, hail him as King, and bow before him. The truth of his deity is suppressed, but at the same time they almost can't help expressing it, if in a twisted and perverted way.

REJECTION 5: REJECTION BY THE SOLDIERS

The Roman soldiers do not carry out their orders in a workmanlike way. They energetically join in the rejection of Jesus. It seems that they take sadistic delight in ensuring that Jesus is mocked to the maximum degree. Imagine a crown of thorns pressed into one's scull like a series of nails hammered into place. The manifold disgrace that the soldiers heap upon Jesus probably exceeds the punishment for capital crimes of common criminals. Adding insult, the soldiers cast lots for his clothes, as Psalm 22:18 said they would (Mark 15:24).

IRONY 6: THE IRONIC TRUTH BEHIND
THE MOCKING AT THE CROSS

"Those who passed by derided him, wagging their heads and saying, 'Aha! You who would destroy the temple and rebuild it in three days, save yourself, and come down from the cross!'" (Mark 15:29–30). These passersby speak more truth than they know when they mock Jesus as the one who will destroy the temple and rebuild it in three days. If Jesus is speaking of the temple of his body, then they are indeed witnessing the destruction of the temple. But the passing gawkers will not stay long enough to witness the rebuilding of the temple when Jesus is raised on the third day.

The chief priests join the fray once again and mock Jesus on the cross. They are more intimately connected with the events of the crucifixion than are the transient spectators, and geographically closer to the cross. They say more than they know when they declare, "He saved others; he cannot save himself. Let the Christ, the King of Israel, come down now from the cross that we may see and believe" (Mark 15:31–32).

They are right. Jesus cannot save others *and* save himself. He can only save others by staying on the cross. If he comes down, there will be no salvation to believe in. They cannot grasp the fact that the nails are not what keep him there on the cross.

REJECTION 6: THE CRESCENDO OF
REJECTION AT THE CROSS

This scene at the cross also features a final crescendo of rejection and agony. The crescendo builds as the narration moves closer and closer to the cross. The progression of rejection and pain for Jesus starts on the outside with those who pass by and moves inward as those nearest to Jesus join in the rejection. First, the mockers passing by on the road are the furthest from the cross, and they do not come close to watch the drama of Jesus's death. And yet, even though they have no intention to stick around, they cannot resist the urge to hurl insults at Jesus like drive-by hecklers. They are moved to join the rejection and they give voice to it, even if from a distance. They wag their heads and taunt him the way Psalm 22:7–8 said they would.

This rejection intensifies as Jesus's original accusers pile abuse on him once again. The chief priests seem to hang around to watch the brutal results of their involvement in the plot to destroy Jesus. They have already expressed their rejection of Jesus, but they can't resist the opportunity to repeat their rejection of him whenever the moment presents itself.

The last act of human insult is likely the most painful. This final wave of human rejection comes crashing down upon Jesus as his fellow criminals mock him. The pointed nature of their rejection is stunning. Victims on the cross die by suffocating. One has to push up with his legs and suffer the pain of the nail through the feet in order to catch a breath and stay alive. It is all the more amazing, then, that the other convicts can't resist the urge to use their dying breath to mock Jesus.

At this point, I marvel that Jesus does not come down from the cross and call legions of angels from heaven to destroy this mass of wicked sinners scorning their sinless Creator.

Let me try to put this pain in perspective. I am ashamed to tell you of the time I played basketball with my eighth-grade neighbor. I was trying to witness to him because he came over one day and was boasting that he watched *The Passion of the Christ* without crying at all—as if his not being moved by the cross would impress me! So, in the interest of building a relationship, I determined that I would let him win as we were playing. But by the end of our pick-up game my pride simply would not let an eighth grader beat me.

How pathetic am I? Because of that experience, I marvel even more at the fact that Jesus let his creation crucify him. The people around him—instead of mocking him for staying on the cross so that he could save them—should have marveled that he didn't come down from the cross so that he could destroy them.

However, we have not yet arrived at the ultimate pain. The crescendo reaches its peak with the alienation of Jesus from the One closest to him, his own heavenly Father: "And at the ninth hour Jesus cried out with a loud voice, 'Eloi, Eloi, lema sabachthani?' which means, 'My God, my God, why have you forsaken me?'" (Mark 15:33–34).

This cry from the cross has been called the "scream of the damned."

It represents the deepest possible pain. Jesus and his Father have had perfect, unbroken harmony and fellowship in the Trinity for all eternity—until now. In the climactic moment, the Father places the sin of the world upon Jesus, the Lamb of God. The Father, who has eyes too pure to behold sin, turns his face away from his Son for the first and only time. Jesus is now enduring not only the pain of mocking, scourging, and crucifixion—he is also experiencing something akin to the pain of hell: separation from God. He cries out asking why God has forsaken him, just as Psalm 22:1 said he would.

THE RESURRECTION

When the accounts in the Synoptic Gospels stress that God raised Jesus from the dead, they use the passive voice ("he was raised"). This is important because the resurrection is Jesus's vindication (1 Tim. 3:16). The resurrection is the proof or evidence that all of Jesus's claims are true. God the Father puts his stamp of approval on everything that Jesus said and did. The resurrection becomes a touchstone of later apostolic preaching, as we will see in the next chapter. Before we turn there, let us reflect on these truths together.

APPLICATION 1: PREACH THE CROSS TO YOURSELF FIRST, THEN TO OTHERS

Jesus is the perfect steward and herald, and thus he is a shining example for all present and future stewards and heralds. However, every sinful preacher knows that he needs more than just a model for his preaching; he needs a Savior. Jesus is not simply the model of faith; he is also the object of faith. He is the perfect sacrifice for imperfect stewards and heralds like us. Hallelujah, what a Savior!

Preach to yourself often that Jesus has swallowed the wrath of God in your behalf. The significance of Jesus's tasting hell and swallowing up the wrath of God can be seen powerfully in a story from the recent California wildfires. One family waited too long to abandon their home as the flames quickly came upon them. The blazing fires surrounded them and blocked every escape route. The desperate dad had an idea. He had recently burned part of the field next to their home. They went to the burned area. The children lay down first, then the mother covered the children, and the father put his body on top over all of them. The fires raged around them and they felt the intense heat, but the fire stopped at the spot that had been burned the previous week because there was nothing left to burn. The family was saved from the fire.

In the same way, we are saved from the fires of hell and the wrath of God when we run to the cross and rest there, because it is the place where God's wrath already fell. The cross is the only safe place for sinners to stay. Therefore, remember that you preach while standing on singed ground. Do not let the cross ever become "ho hum" in your preaching. Let the singed ground you are standing on fill your preaching with great gravity and gladness. Jesus had to die for us to preach what we preach.

APPLICATION 2: REJOICING IN OUR SALVATION

Think of the times in the Gospels when Jesus rejoices. What causes him to rejoice? What does he call his disciples to celebrate? Luke 10 may provide the clearest answer.

In that chapter the disciples return with joy from their mission. They seem especially to rejoice that the demons were subject to them in Jesus's name (Luke 10:17). Jesus affirms the truth of his authority over all the power of the enemy, but he also redirects their rejoicing: "Nevertheless, do not rejoice in this, that the spirits are subject to you, but rejoice that your names are written in heaven" (10:20). Salvation is a greater miracle than a power encounter over a demon.

Jesus further illustrates this principle with his own rejoicing:

> In that same hour he rejoiced in the Holy Spirit and said, "I thank you, Father, Lord of heaven and earth, that you have hidden these things from the wise and understanding and revealed them to little children; yes, Father, for such was your gracious will. All things have been handed over to me by my Father, and no one knows who the Son is except the Father, or who the Father is except the Son and anyone to whom the Son chooses to reveal him." (Luke 10:21–22)

Jesus rejoices in God's sovereignty in salvation. God hides things from the wise and understanding and reveals them to little children—

such as the disciples (Luke 10:23). The Son also takes part in this sovereign process because no one knows who the Father is "except the Son and anyone to whom the Son chooses to reveal him." The miracle of faith and salvation is the miracle that both Jesus and his disciples celebrate.

An example from the life of Martyn Lloyd-Jones made rejoicing in our salvation hit home for me. At the end of his life, Lloyd-Jones was so sick that it took him a very long time to shuffle from his couch to his bed. A friend saw him one day and said, "How do you keep going every day? You used to be a powerful presence in the pulpit, and now it takes all you have to shuffle to your bed." Lloyd-Jones simply quoted a Bible verse: "Nevertheless, do not rejoice in this, that the spirits are subject to you, but rejoice that your names are written in heaven" (Luke 10:20). In other words, Lloyd-Jones said, "Why should I be depressed? I am no less saved today than I was when I was preaching the gospel. In fact, salvation is nearer to me than when I first believed."

The cross keeps us from being too inflated by ministry success (i.e., the demons submitting to your name, or people liking your sermons) or being too deflated by a lack of ministry success (i.e., attendance is down). Our name cannot be tied to ministry successes or failures. The cross helps us to rejoice completely in our salvation by seeing everything in the light of Jesus's wounds. As Stuart Townend and Keith Getty so well remind us in the song "The Power of the Cross," our names are "written in the wounds."

15

THE STEWARDSHIP
OF THE APOSTLES

Paradigm 9

The glorious company of the Apostles praise thee.

"Te Deum" or "Ambrosian Hymn"

Two texts in Luke-Acts make massive claims about what the Old Testament anticipated (Luke 24:44–49; Acts 26:23). Namely, the Old Testament predicted both the advent of the Messiah and the coming of those after him who would herald him. Both Luke 24 and Acts 26 say that (1) the Christ will suffer and rise, and then (2) what he has done will be proclaimed—first by the Christ himself and then by others. These texts stress that *both* of these things were written in Scripture. The Old Testament contains a focus on both the Messiah *and* the future preaching of the Messiah.

Romans 10:14–17 highlights the same reality. Paul quotes Isaiah 52:7 in his discussion of the apostolic imperative to preach. God's heralds must preach because they have been sent: "How beautiful are the feet of those who preach the good news!" (Rom. 10:15). Paul's quotation differs from Isaiah 52:7 in one specific detail. Paul speaks of heralds in the plural, whereas Isaiah spoke of a singular herald. I would argue that the Messiah is the one in view as the end-time herald. Paul can make it plural because Jesus himself commanded the continuation of his ministry on this side of the age of fulfillment. This heraldic ministry is a ministry that focuses on how Jesus has come as the culminating fulfillment of all the promises of God.

Paul does something similar with texts in Isaiah concerning the servant. The apostle views Isaiah 49:6 as a command for himself from the Lord saying, "I have made you a light for the Gentiles, that you may bring salvation to the ends of the earth" (Acts 13:47). Even though Jesus fulfills the servant songs in an ultimate sense, he sets in motion a movement of his ambassadors who will be servants of the word.

This servant theme continues in Acts 26:15. The risen Lord Jesus gives Paul a commandment and commission:

> But rise and stand upon your feet, for I have appeared to you for this purpose, to appoint you as a servant and witness to the things in which you have seen me and to those in which I will appear to you, delivering you from your people and from the Gentiles—to whom I am sending you to open their eyes, so that they may turn from darkness to light and from the power of Satan to God, that they may receive forgiveness of sins and a place among those who are sanctified by faith in me. (26:16–18)

Luke 24 also helps answer a crucial question. Think back to what Jesus did with the two disciples on the road to Emmaus and later with the eleven. He taught them what all the Scriptures said about him (24:27, 44–45). The disciples had an Old Testament survey class taught by Jesus! I would sign up for that class in a heartbeat. I used to wish that we had a recording of those talks. What Scriptures did Jesus address? How did he explain them?

I once heard James Montgomery Boice say that we already know the texts. For all practical purposes, we have much of the recording because we have the preaching of the apostles in the book of Acts. For example, think about Peter's first two sermons. Have you ever wondered how he learned to preach Christ from Psalm 16:8–11 (Acts 2:25–31), Psalm 110:1 (Acts 2:24–35), Deuteronomy 18:15, 18, and 19 (Acts 3:22–23), and Genesis 22:18 (Acts 4:25)? The answer is simple. He learned how to preach those texts from Jesus in Luke 24. Furthermore, Jesus was with the disciples for forty days after his resurrection, and he spoke with them about the kingdom of God (Acts 1:3). They were not talking about the weather in first-century Palestine. They talked about Jesus's fulfillment of the Scriptures.

In other words, we should interpret the work of the apostles as what Jesus continues to do and teach through them (Acts 1:1). The apostolic ministry of the word centers on two main tasks: evangelistic preaching and authoritative guidance for the churches. Let us look at the apostles' ministry of the word in more detail through the paradigm of calling, stewarding and heralding, and effects.

APOSTOLIC CALLING

The Gospels record how Jesus called the disciples to become fishers of men (Matt. 4:18–22; 9:9; Luke 5:1–11). Jesus spent all night in prayer before choosing the Twelve (Luke 6:12–16). Jesus called the disciples to "be with him" (Mark 3:14) so that they could learn from him. He commissioned them to preach and teach about the kingdom (e.g., Mark 3:14; 6:12). Peter laid down the ground rules for joining the apostles in Acts 1: Judas's replacement had to be "one of the men who have accompanied us during all the time that the Lord Jesus went in and out among us, beginning from the baptism of John until the day when he was taken up from us" (Acts 1:21–22).

Paul highlights that the Lord appeared to Peter, the Twelve, James, the rest of the apostles, and last of all to Paul himself. Paul often narrates his experience of this divine calling and commissioning (Acts 9:1–19; 22:1–21; 26:3–23; Gal. 1:11–24). Paul's calling was so strong that he even says: "Necessity is laid upon me. Woe to me if I do not preach the gospel. For if I do this of my own will, I have a reward, but if not of my own will, I am still entrusted with a stewardship" (1 Cor. 9:16–17).

APOSTOLIC STEWARDING AND HERALDING

STEWARDING

It is striking how many times the summary term for what the apostles stewarded or preached is the "word" (Acts 4:4, 29, 31; 6:2, 4, 7; 8:4, 15, 25; 10:36, 44; 11:1, 16, 19; 12:24; 13:5, 7, 15, 44, 46, 48, 49; 14:3, 25; 15:7, 15, 35, 36; 16:6, 32; 17:11, 13; 18:5, 11; 19:10, 20; 20:32, 35; Rom. 3:4; 4:23; 9:6; 10:8, 17–18; 13:9; 1 Cor. 1:18; 2:4, 13; 14:36; 15:2; 2 Cor. 2:17; 4:2; Gal. 5:14; 6:6; Eph. 5:26; 6:17; Col. 1:25; 3:16; 4:3; 1 Thess. 1:5, 6, 8; 2:13; 4:15;

2 Thess. 3:1; 1 Tim. 4:5–6; 6:3; 2 Tim. 2:9; Titus 1:3; Heb. 4:12; 5:13; 6:5). At other times the gospel is identified explicitly as the "word" (Eph. 1:13; Col. 1:5). We have space to take a few examples.

Acts 6:4 and 6 make it clear that the apostles devoted themselves mainly to stewarding the word and the ministry of prayer. Paul also summarizes his ministry in a short, pithy way in 1 Corinthians 4:2: "This is how one should regard us, as servants of Christ and stewards of the mysteries of God. Moreover, *it is required of stewards that they be found faithful*" (1 Cor. 4:1–2).

Paul says that a steward is one who has been entrusted with something (i.e., the *what*) and so he must be found faithful (i.e., the *how*) with respect to what has been entrusted. Paul's "stewardship from God" is "to make the word of God fully known" (Col. 1:25; cf. Eph. 3:2). Paul also claims that the Lord Jesus appointed Paul to be a preacher and "entrusted" him "with the gospel of the glory of the blessed God" (1 Tim. 1:11; cf. 2:7). He was entrusted with the gospel (Gal. 2:7; 1 Thess. 2:4) and the "message of reconciliation" (2 Cor. 5:19).

The apostle John speaks in similar terms. The apostles were entrusted with the word of life, whom they heard, saw, and touched (1 John 1:1–3). John stewarded the word of God and the testimony of Jesus (Rev. 1:1–2).

As mentioned above, the apostolic ministry of the word focuses on evangelistic preaching and authoritative guidance for the churches. I will begin with authoritative guidance and then examine the evangelistic preaching of the apostles.

The apostles had a commission of stewardship and oversight over churches. Paul experienced much physical suffering in his ministry (2 Cor. 11:23–27), but his oversight of the churches produced a different kind of pain: anxiety. "And, apart from other things, there is the daily pressure on me of my *anxiety* for all the churches. Who is weak, and I am not weak? Who is made to fall, and I am not indignant?" (11:28–29). This anxiety does not contradict the command of Jesus or Paul not to be anxious (Matt. 6:25–34; Phil. 4:6); Paul is indeed seeking first the kingdom (Matt. 6:33) and making his requests known to God by prayer and supplication with thanksgiving (Phil. 4:6; cf. the "thanksgiving" sections of his letters).

Paul's passionate care and concern for the churches shows up constantly. First Thessalonians 2–3 is an excellent paradigm in this regard. He describes his nurturing gentleness to be like a mother's (2:7) and his admonishing love like a father's (2:11). His ministry consists not only of sharing the gospel with the Thessalonians, but also of sharing himself with them because of how "very dear" they are to him and how "affectionately desirous" he is of them (2:8). They are torn away "in person not in heart" (2:17). They are his "hope," "joy," and "crown of boasting" before Jesus at his coming (2:19).

Paul often experienced distress while waiting for reports from members of his ministry team, such as Timothy. Paul suffered much anxiety over their faith, "for fear that somehow the tempter had tempted [them] and our labor would be in vain" (1 Thess. 3:5). Paul sent Timothy to the Thessalonians when he "could bear it no longer" (3:5), and Timothy brought back a good report. As a result, Paul's "distress and affliction" were comforted (3:6–7). He exults by saying, "For now we live, if you are standing fast in the Lord" (3:8). He offers thanksgiving to God for "all the joy we feel for your sake before our God" (3:9). This thanksgiving and joy come in the midst of praying "earnestly night and day that we may see you face to face and supply what is lacking in your faith" (3:10).

Interactions like these between congregations and apostles could be multiplied. Sometimes Paul has to respond to reports about a church (1 Cor. 1:10) or answer a congregation's questions (1 Cor. 7:1). Sometimes interactions are more than offering guidance or direction; they are disciplinary in nature. In some cases Paul has to make many a "painful visit" (2 Cor. 2:1) or write a painful letter that causes grief (2 Cor. 7:8–9). He does not "spare" those who have sinned (2 Cor. 13:2). He sometimes has to practice church discipline and hand people over to Satan in the hope that they will be restored (1 Cor. 5:3–4; 1 Tim. 1:20).

In all of these interactions, Paul prays for and rejoices over restoration (2 Cor. 7:8–13; 13:9). Paul does not enjoy making the hard visit or writing the hard letter, but he rejoices when doing so brings repentance and fear and earnestness for God (2 Cor. 7:8–13). He does not want to be severe in his use of the authority the Lord has given him for building up and not for tearing down (2 Cor. 13:10). In all of his interactions, he comes alongside his congregations and shares their joy of faith in Jesus (2 Cor. 1:24–2:4; Phil. 1:25).

HERALDING

The apostolic practice of evangelistic preaching is simple, but far from simplistic. The apostles are to (1) open their mouths and make Christ and the gospel known and (2) trust the divine power of the Spirit and the word to create faith, so that people would call on the name of the Lord and be saved. I will address the first point in this section and deal with the second in the "effects" section.

The fundamental part the apostles play in evangelistic preaching is to preach Christ and the gospel faithfully and fearlessly.[1] This summary holds true in both Acts (2:22–36; 3:13–26; 4:5–12; 5:27–32, 42; 8:12; 9:20, 22, 27–28; 10:34–43; 11:20; 13:27–41; 14:21; 16:10, 31; 17:3, 18, 31–32; 18:5; 20:20) and the Epistles (1 Cor. 1:17; 2 Cor. 1:19; 5:20; Gal. 1:6; 3:1; Col. 1:28; 1 Thess. 2:2). Perhaps the most picturesque term for Paul's preaching comes in Galatians 3:1: "It was before your eyes that Jesus Christ was publicly portrayed as crucified." The apostolic preaching placards Jesus Christ as crucified so vividly that the hearers see it ("before your eyes").

This proclamation is fearless. The Acts narrative makes this plain after a healing happens in the name of Jesus, and Peter preaches in the name of Jesus. The Jewish leaders cannot deny the reality of the healing, and so they aim their attack squarely upon the preaching of the name of Jesus. This event foreshadows a storm of persecution over the name of Jesus: "'But in order that it may spread no further among the people, let us warn them to speak no more to anyone in this name.' So [the ruling council] called [Peter and John] and charged them not to speak or teach at all in the name of Jesus" (Act 4:17–18).

The disciples realize that this command clashes with the stewardship that they have received from God himself. They resolutely respond

---

[1] I am not including here the people who preach what Jesus has done for them (Mark 1:45; 5:20; 7:36). This proclamation is more of a personal testimony, not an exposition of the word or the gospel. The Gospel writers highlight this difference by using a different set of terms. For example, Mark uses *apangellō* as a term for a "report" (Mark 5:14, 19; 6:30). Jesus tells the Gerasene demoniac to "report" (Mark 5:19—*apangellō*) what Jesus has done for him. This reporting sometimes happens despite Jesus's repeated injunctions against it (Mark 1:45; 7:36). In fact, the author tells the reader in Mark 7:36 that "the more he charged them, the more zealously they proclaimed it."

by saying that they "must obey God rather than men" (Acts 5:29). God has given them a stewardship of serving as witnesses, and thus they cannot deny what they have seen and heard (Acts 4:20). They continue to preach in Jesus's name no matter what the cost because "there is salvation in no one else, for there is no other name under heaven given among men by which we must be saved" (4:12). The disciples have come to see that the salvation is bound up in the name of Jesus alone.

Paul stresses this point when he lays out the necessary process of preaching in Romans 10:14–17. He declares that "everyone who calls on the name of the Lord will be saved" (10:13). But Paul recognizes that this introduces a problem. People would have to call upon *the name of the Lord* to be saved. How will they come to know that name? Paul stresses that people cannot call upon someone of whom they have never heard. What they need is preaching in order to hear. But there would be no preachers without God's sending.

God has done everything necessary for people to call upon the name of the Lord for salvation. He has done the sending (Isa. 52:7), and his heralds have gone out to preach so that people can hear. But how will they come to faith? Paul answers that the source of faith is none other than the powerful word of Christ: "So faith comes from hearing, and hearing through the word of Christ" (Rom. 10:17).

Paul preaches the gospel and suffers for it (2 Tim. 2:8–9). He is treated like a criminal and imprisoned with chains, but the word cannot be bound (2:9). Now, even at the end of his life, he still has a passion for stewardship as he begs Timothy to bring "the books, and above all the parchments" (2 Tim. 4:13).

First Corinthians 2 is a central passage for understanding preaching. In the context Paul is correcting the worldly ways in which the Corinthians look at the cross (1:18–31), the preaching of the cross (2:1–5), and ministers of the cross (chs. 3–4). Duane Litfin summarizes the Greco-Roman backdrop that contributed to a worldly view of preaching:

> It is our thesis that perceived deficiencies in Paul's preaching, when measured against Greco-Roman eloquence, precipitated many of Paul's difficulties in Corinth. These were the deficiencies which prompted a section of the Corinthian congregation to complain about Paul's

preaching and declare their independence from him. As we shall see, the existence of such complaints is what energizes Paul's argument in 1 Cor. 1–4 and gives it coherence.[2]

Why does Paul renounce playing the game of preaching by the rules of the rhetoricians? Depending on the dynamics of rhetoric would have allowed Paul to manufacture a response that "would have been rooted in his own facility as an orator."[3] As James Denney has said, "No man can give the impression that he himself is clever and that Christ is mighty to save."[4] Paul desperately wants to circumvent any possibility that the faith of his listeners is a human creation rather than a divine creation. Paul does not need to depend upon a power-packed rhetorical flourish because the gospel has a power all of its own: it is the power of God for salvation (Rom. 1:16; 1 Cor. 1:18).

Putting stress on the Spirit's ability to produce saving faith is key in understanding Paul's opposition to eloquence. Eloquence is not evil in and of itself. The contrast is not between speaking that is good and speaking that is bad—or else he would be saying that bad speaking is good and good speaking is bad. The crucial distinction is between being clever and being clear.

Paul's resolve to know nothing except Christ and him crucified (1 Cor. 2:3) represents an ambition to make Christ *clear*. Paul does not want to cancel this aim by being *clever*. What is the difference? Someone wants clear speech so that *what* he preaches will be clearly recognized; someone uses clever speech so that *how* he preaches will be clearly recognized. Paul wants his preaching to point to Christ, not himself. The ambition of his preaching is to preach Christ clearly so that Christ is clearly seen.

What is wrong with clever speech? Clever speech implies that one makes the truth real by how one says it. The speaker trusts in his ability to shape words that will move audiences. Clear speech implies trust in the Spirit to make the truth real. Paul contrasts his communication calculus with the one that orators utilize:

---

[2] Duane Litfin, *St. Paul's Theology of Proclamation: 1 Corinthians 1–4 and Greco-Roman Rhetoric* (Cambridge: Cambridge University Press, 1994), 187.
[3] Ibid., 192.
[4] Quoted in John Piper, *The Supremacy of God in Preaching*, rev. ed. (Grand Rapids: Baker, 2004), 59.

Orator: concept + clever communication = conviction
Paul: word of God + clear communication + Spirit's work = conviction

Litfin provides a table to summarize the fundamental difference between Paul and the orators of his day in 1 Corinthians 2:1–5.[5] The rhetoricians of Paul's day look at the message as the independent variable. They start with the response they want to create, and then they craft the message to reach that result.

Paul's approach is exactly the opposite. The message is precisely the thing that cannot change. It is a precious stewardship that must be heralded faithfully. Paul chooses to preach the message faithfully and puts his trust in God's Spirit to produce the results (fig. 16).

Figure 16. Litfin's table on Paul versus the orators of Paul's day

Speaker	Audience	Orator's Efforts	Results
Greco-Roman Rhetorician	A given dependent	Independent variable	Given dependent
Paul	A given	A constant	Dependent variable

Litfin's assessment is worth quoting in full:

Paul's determination to hold his preaching constant threw the variability in the equation to the end. Hence for Paul the results became the equation's *dependent variable*, a factor which could scarcely even be addressed until after the fact. Each time Paul preached the Gospel he perceived himself to be introducing the *Constant*, the message of Christ crucified, but it was the Spirit who would use this message to distinguish between οἱ ἀπολλύμενοι [those being destroyed] and οἱ κλητοί [the called]. The former would find the simply proclaimed Gospel foolish, or even offensive, but the latter would come to view it, through the supernatural force of the Spirit's conviction, as the truth of their own salvation. In this way Paul's unchanging message of the cross carried the stench of death to the one, but became a fragrance of life to the other, depending strictly upon the work of the Spirit. Paul could not know beforehand which listeners were which, of course; it was only afterwards as he observed and assessed the

[5] Litfin, *St. Paul's Theology of Proclamation*, 205.

consequences of the preaching that he could reach any conclusions
(1 Thess. 1.4–5, 2.13).[6]

APOSTOLIC EFFECTS

As noted above, the apostles' preaching strategy is straightforward:
they lift high the name of Jesus, and people call on the name of the
Lord to be saved by the *faith-creating power of the Spirit and the word*. We
will look at apostolic commentary on this (Rom. 10:17; 1 Thess. 1:4; 2:13;
2 Tim. 2:9; James 1:18; 1 Peter 1:23, 25), but first we will see a picture of
the power of the word and the Spirit in the narrative of Acts.

THE POWER OF THE SPIRIT OF GOD IN ACTS

Some very important changes happen in the transition from the Gospels to the book of Acts. Think about all that the disciples have already
experienced before Acts chapter 2. They have been with Jesus in person. They have seen his miracles and heard his teaching. They have
already had practice in ministry as Jesus has sent them out to heal
and to preach. They have even witnessed his death and resurrection!
Furthermore, he has opened their minds to understand the Scriptures
after his resurrection so that they can see him in all the Law, Prophets,
and Writings. Thus it is all the more striking that they are told to wait
for something else.

They still need something else because the Great Commission
could never succeed in their strength. That "something else" is the
sending of the Spirit at Pentecost by the ascended Christ. The power
of the Spirit produces a tremendous change in the disciples. They go
from fearful followers of Jesus to bold preachers of the gospel of Jesus.

Acts also highlights the power of the word of God conquering the
nations as the gospel spreads. The kingdom of God advances as the
Spirit empowers witnesses to preach Jesus in Jerusalem, Judea and
Samaria, and even to the ends of the earth (Acts 1:8). Pentecost marks
the birthday of the church as the Spirit baptizes many Jewish believers
into the one body at the opening of Acts. By the end of the book, the
Spirit has baptized many Gentile believers as well into the one body.

Acts does not simply attribute the spread of the gospel to the

---

[6] Ibid., 249–50.

power of the Spirit. It is vitally important to note that Acts follows the rest of the Scriptures in linking both the Spirit of God and *the word of God*.

THE POWER OF THE WORD OF GOD IN ACTS

The word's conquest of the nations means that the book of Acts compares closely with the Old Testament book of Joshua. Joshua is a conquest narrative in which the twelve tribes of Israel conquer the Gentile nations with a physical sword. The book of Acts has the twelve disciples as a reconstituted Israel conquering with the sword of the Spirit: the word of God. Luke has many different ways of documenting the word's conquest. In what follows, I will highlight several of them.

First, Luke situates summary phrases throughout the narrative that cause the ministry of the word to stand out to the reader:

> And the word of God continued to increase, and the number of the disciples multiplied greatly in Jerusalem, and a great many of the priests became obedient to the faith. (Acts 6:7)

> So the church throughout all Judea and Galilee and Samaria had peace and was being built up. And walking in the fear of the Lord and in the comfort of the Holy Spirit, it multiplied. (Acts 9:31)

> But the word of God increased and multiplied. (Acts 12:24)

> And the word of the Lord was spreading throughout the whole region. (Acts 13:49)

> So the churches were strengthened in the faith, and they increased in numbers daily. (Acts 16:5)

> So the word of the Lord continued to increase and prevail mightily. (Acts 19:20)

Some have even made this theme an explicit structural feature of Acts, which they have labeled "panels of progress."[7]

---

[7] "Panel 1: Earliest Days of the Church—2:42–6:7; Panel 2: Events in the Lives of 3 Pivotal Figures—6:8–9:31; Panel 3: Advances of the Gospel in Palestine-Syria—9:32–12:24; Panel 4: Missionary Campaign 1 & Jerusalem Council—12:25–16:5; Panel 5: Missionary Campaign 2 & 3—16:6–19:20; Panel 6:

Second, the book begins with a picture of the word's conquest through Peter's sermon. Acts 2:5–13 highlights the presence of devout Jews from "every nation under heaven" (2:5). The multitude hear the sound of the disciples speaking the mighty works of God in their own languages and they respond with both amazement/perplexity (2:12) and mocking (2:13). These Jews from the nations have not been conquered by the word yet because it has not been preached. But what a difference after Peter preaches the word in the power of the Spirit! Three thousand Jews from every nation under heaven are "cut to the heart" (2:37), and they respond by receiving the word and being baptized (2:41). Verse 38 makes it clear that theirs is a baptism into "the name of Jesus Christ."

Third, Acts ends on the same note of the progress of the proclaimed word. Paul lived in Rome for two years on house arrest, but the word of God was not chained or hindered. Paul "welcomed all who came to him, proclaiming the kingdom of God and teaching about the Lord Jesus Christ with all boldness and *without hindrance*" (Acts 28:30–31). Fourth, Luke included many summaries of sermons to show that it was the apostolic preaching of the word that led to the conquest of the nations (e.g., Acts 3:12–26; 10:34–43; 13:16–41; 17:22–31).

POWER OF THE WORD OF GOD IN THE EPISTLES

Paul's epistles also show the triumph of the word even when it looks like the citizens of this world have won. Paul may be in a prison and appear to have lost, but he tells the Philippians that the gospel has advanced (Phil. 1:12–26). He expresses the gospel's advance even among the Romans at the beginning and the end of his letter to the Philippian church. Paul opens by telling how his imprisonment has actually caused the name of Christ to became well known throughout the Praetorian guard (1:13). He closes his letter by highlighting the greeting of saints in Caesar's household (Phil. 4:22). The gospel has even penetrated the most powerful family in the world while Paul has been in prison! Paul may be bound with chains like a criminal, but "the word of God is not bound" (2 Tim. 2:9).

To Jerusalem and Thence to Rome—19:21–28:31." Richard N. Longenecker, "The Acts of the Apostles," in Merrill C. Tenney and Richard N. Longenecker, *John–Acts*, vol. 9 in *The Expositor's Bible Commentary* (Grand Rapids: Zondervan, 1981), 234.

Romans 10:17 states that the word of Christ is the source of faith. The word is the divine power that causes new spiritual life. Christians are born again "through the living and abiding word of God" (1 Pet. 1:23), which Peter defines as the gospel that was preached to them (1:25). James 1:18 also testifies that God brought believers forth from "the word of truth." Paul thanks God that the Thessalonians received the word of God not as the word of men "but as what it really is, the word of God, which is at work in you believers" (1 Thess. 2:13).

Paul will not allow a bifurcation between the power of the word and the power of the Spirit. The evidence of election is that the gospel comes not merely as words of promise but also as words of "power and in the Holy Spirit with full conviction" (1 Thess. 1:4–5). Paul can even call the word of God "the sword of the Spirit" (Eph. 6:17).

FALSE STEWARDS: FALSE APOSTLES

The working of miracles does not prove that one's ministry is successful. In fact, miracles do not even prove that one is a Christian, according to Jesus!

> Not everyone who says to me, "Lord, Lord," will enter the kingdom of heaven, but the one who does the will of my Father who is in heaven. On that day many will say to me, "Lord, Lord, did we not prophesy in your name, and cast out demons in your name, and do many mighty works in your name?" And then will I declare to them, "I never knew you; depart from me, you workers of lawlessness." (Matt. 7:21–23)

Jesus faults them not for the work of their lips (i.e., "Lord, Lord"—7:21), or the working of miracles (7:22), but for the working of lawlessness (7:23). He knows that they are false prophets because of their works, and in the same way we will know false prophets by their fruits (7:15–20). The internal spiritual display of a changed life is a bigger witness to someone's spiritual state than a miracle as an external spiritual display.

Satan once again stands behind false apostles and false stewards. Judas was a false apostle, whom Jesus called a devil (John 6:70). Satan entered Judas in order to carry out his murderous schemes (Luke 22:3; John 13:27). Paul responded to the opposition of Elymas the magician by saying, "You son of the devil, you enemy of all righteousness, full of all deceit and villainy, will you not stop making crooked the straight paths of the Lord?" (Acts 13:10).

Paul put false apostles in the same category:

> For such men are false apostles, deceitful workmen, disguising them-selves as apostles of Christ. And no wonder, for even Satan disguises himself as an angel of light. So it is no surprise if his servants, also, disguise themselves as servants of righteousness. Their end will cor-respond to their deeds. (2 Cor. 11:13–15)

Paul likens the work of false apostles to the serpent's act of deceiving Eve by cunning (11:3). The false apostles are leading the Corinthians away from a "sincere and pure devotion to Christ" by proclaiming another Jesus and another gospel (11:3–4).

APPLICATION 1: EMPOWERMENT OF THE HOLY SPIRIT

Once again, when we pause to take inventory of all that the disciples had before Pentecost, it staggers the imagination. They had been with Jesus in person. They had seen his miracles and heard his teaching. They already had practice in ministry as Jesus had sent them out to heal and to preach. They had even witnessed his death and resur-rection! Furthermore, he had opened their minds to understand the Scriptures after his resurrection so that they could see him in all the Law, Prophets, and Writings. And thus it is all the more striking that they are told to wait for something else: the power of the Spirit.

Martyn Lloyd-Jones stresses the "how much more" of our need:

> You would have thought these men therefore were now in a perfect position to go out to preach; but according to our Lord's teaching they were not. They seem to have all the necessary knowledge, but that knowledge is not sufficient, something further is needed, is indeed essential. The knowledge indeed is vital for you cannot be witnesses without it, but to be effective witnesses you need the power and the unction and the demonstration of the Spirit in addition. Now if this was necessary for these men, how much more is it necessary for all others who try to preach these things?[8]

---

[8] D. Martyn Lloyd-Jones, *Preaching and Preachers* (Grand Rapids: Zondervan, 1971), 307–8.

APPLICATION 2: LET THE NAME OF THE PREACHER PERISH, IF ONLY CHRIST BE GLORIFIED

If people preached the true gospel of Christ, Paul did not care about what happened to his own name; rather, he rejoiced that Christ was proclaimed (Phil. 1:18). Paul's desire was to make much of Christ, not to make much of himself (1:20). The passionate longing to make much of Christ will cause us to rejoice when others proclaim Christ's name powerfully. This rejoicing can save us from the sin that is almost a vocational sin in Christian ministry: envying the ministry success of others.

I was recently asked in an interview whether I had aspirations for a significant global ministry (e.g., speaking and writing, like my predecessor) or whether my ministry would focus more on the local church? I tried to answer in a way that affirmed my desire to be a local church pastor. I also pointed out that the desire to have a global ministry is a good thing as long as a clear distinction is made between having a global ministry and wanting global recognition. All world Christians want the earth to be filled with the knowledge of Christ's glory. Christ is a global Savior, not a tribal deity. We want him to be named globally. A craving for global recognition makes us vulnerable to the snare of the Devil and the stronghold of pride.

It is far better to aspire to faithfulness and obedience as an unworthy servant who simply does what he is commanded (Luke 17:10). God can give global recognition to whomever he wills; I do not think it is something we can plan or will. I am a firm believer that "a person cannot receive even one thing unless it is given him from heaven" (John 3:27). For John the Baptist, this meant taking a decreasing role with a fullness of joy that gladly confesses, "He must increase, but I must decrease" (3:30).

My main motivation is epitomized by something Whitefield said when he gave the reigns of leadership of the Methodist movement to Wesley. Whitefield's followers warned him that his name might be forgotten. He replied, "My name? Let the name of Whitefield perish if only the name of Christ be glorified."[9] The singular passion of a faithful Christian minister is to make much of *the name of Christ*.

---

[9] Arnold Dallimore, "Whitefield, George," in *New Dictionary of Theology*, ed. Sinclair B. Ferguson, David F. Wright, and J. I. Packer (Downers Grove, IL: InterVarsity, 1988), 721.

16

THE STEWARDSHIP
OF THE PASTOR

Paradigm 10

I charge you in the presence of God and of Christ Jesus, who is to judge the living and the dead, and by his appearing and his kingdom: preach the word; be ready in season and out of season; reprove, rebuke, and exhort, with complete patience and teaching.

2 Timothy 4:1–2

A shift takes place in Acts and the Epistles away from the direct preaching and teaching of the apostles themselves (such as Paul) to pastoral shepherds and elders who continue to preach the apostles' teaching. In other words, we begin to witness a strong shift to today's paradigm of stewardship: pastoral preaching. Please note that the shift is not away from the content of the apostles' teaching—that remains constant. Apostolic emissaries such as Timothy and Titus are called and equipped to preach the word, combat false teaching, and appoint pastoral shepherds who continue the work. They labor in study to rightly divide the word so that they can fulfill the call to preach the word. The word calls for study and exposition because it is the word passed down from the apostles.

Pastoral preaching does not have a different content than apostolic preaching! We could say that the two have precisely the same content. The difference is that pastors now preach the entrusted message of the apostles to specific congregations of believers. The locus of what is proclaimed is "the word." These pastors are called to study the word and rightly handle it in their preaching. The apostles' teaching serves as the great norm for assessing teaching as either true (healthy) or false, which is a constant theme in the Epistles. I will try to make some of these points clear through the categories of calling, stewarding and heralding, and effects.

PASTORAL CALLING

It is important to note that elders are also called to ministry. Paul appoints elders in every city. In a speech to the Ephesian elders, he highlights the responsibilities of their ministry. He stresses that the Holy Spirit has made them overseers (Acts 20:28). The call to serve comes in many texts as an appointment, but some texts complement this point by emphasizing the inward desire for this calling. Elders should desire the eldership (1 Tim. 3:1).

Part of the call of an elder finds expression in character qualifications. The Pastorals document a detailed list of qualifications for the pastoral shepherd. Most of the qualifications are character-based. Our biblical survey of stewards has shown how these characteristics have marked all true stewards of the word (e.g., not a lover of money). These character qualities are on display for congregational viewing. Hebrews 13:7 commands the congregation in view (and us) to "consider the outcome" of its leaders' "way of life" and to "imitate their faith."

Among the qualifications for elders in 1 Timothy and Titus, two stand out most: ability to teach (1 Tim. 3:2) and ability to manage one's household and keep his children submissive (3:4). The logic of household management is made explicit: "If someone does not know how to manage his own household, how will he care for God's church" (3:5).

PASTORAL STEWARDING AND HERALDING

STEWARDING MEANS STUDYING THE WORD

The stewardship of the pastor is unique in some important respects. The locus of the message heralded is crucial. The message entrusted to pastoral heralds is the whole counsel of God as contained in written form throughout Scripture. This written message calls for careful study and careful exposition. A pastor must command and teach and devote himself to the public reading of Scripture and exhortation and teaching (1 Tim. 4:11–12). He is not to neglect the gift that was given to him by prophecy when the council of elders laid their hands on him (4:14). Instead, he must take it and fan it into flame (2 Tim. 1:6). He must practice and immerse himself in the word so that all may see his progress (1 Tim. 4:15). He must keep a close watch on himself and on his teaching. This charge carries great gravity with it. He must persist in this twofold watch because, Paul says, "by so doing you will save both yourself and your hearers" (4:16).

Paul commands Timothy, "Follow the pattern of the sound words that you have heard from me" (2 Tim. 1:13). Timothy must "keep the commandment unstained and free from reproach" (1 Tim. 6:14) and "guard the deposit entrusted" to him (6:20). Timothy is to teach and also entrust the teaching to "faithful men who will be able to teach others also" (2 Tim. 2:2). He must rightly handle the word and understand the nature of Scripture.

> Do your best to present yourself to God as one approved, a worker who has no need to be ashamed, rightly handling the word of truth. (2:15)

> All Scripture is breathed out by God and profitable for teaching, for reproof, for correction, and for training in righteousness, that the man of God may be complete, equipped for every good work. (3:16–17)

In Titus, Paul presents himself as a steward entrusted with the task of preaching as a command from God. God promised the hope of eternal life in ages past, which is now "at the proper time manifested in his word through the preaching with which I have been entrusted [*pisteuō*] by the command of God our Savior" (Titus 1:3). Paul goes on to show how Titus needs to appoint elders in every city because the pastoral shepherd is also God's steward: "For an overseer, as God's steward [*oikonomos*], must be above reproach" (1:7). Part of his stewardship is the stewarding and heralding of the trustworthy word: "He must hold firm to the trustworthy word as taught, so that he may be able to give instruction in sound doctrine and also to rebuke those who contradict it" (1:9).

STEWARDING MEANS STUDYING THE CONGREGATION

However, the pastor must avoid studying only the ancient text. He must exposit both ancient text and his contemporary audience in order to discover the most powerful points of contact. These points of contact may be poignant moments of confrontation and rebuke or they may be moments of tender encouragement. The pastor seeks to bring together the two things that he has studied: a specific passage of the word of God and the specific flock God has entrusted to his care and oversight.

Pastoral shepherds are distinct from apostles in that elders are called to a particular flock. Therefore, the preaching that one sees reflected in the Pastoral Epistles is distinct from the preaching in Acts. Preaching in Acts is primarily evangelistic and itinerants. The apostles were servants of the word, but they were not primarily pastors preaching to a congregation of believers. Preaching in the Pastorals is preaching by pastors to a flock entrusted to their charge.

Acts 20 says to elders, "Pay careful attention to yourselves and to all the flock, in which the Holy Spirit has made you overseers, to care for the church of God, which he obtained with his own blood" (20:28). Attentiveness is warranted because "fierce wolves will come in among you, not sparing the flock; and from among your own selves will arise men speaking twisted things, to draw away the disciples after them" (20:29–30). Hebrews 13:17 calls the congregation to obey its leaders and submit to them, "for they are keeping watch over your souls, as those who will have to give an account." They are to do this "with joy and not with groaning, for that would be of no advantage to you" (13:17).

First Peter likewise says, "Shepherd the flock of God that is among you, exercising oversight, not under compulsion, but willingly, as God would have you; not for shameful gain, but eagerly; not domineering over those in your charge, but being examples to the flock" (1 Pet. 5:2–3).

PASTORAL HERALDING

Heralding continues to be a central calling for the ministry of the word. Timothy must "preach the word; be ready in season and out of season; reprove, rebuke, and exhort, with complete patience and teaching" (2 Tim. 4:2).

This is not a calling for the faint of heart, as is seen by the variety of expressions used for what ministers must do with authority: forms of the words "teach" (1 Tim. 4:11, 13; 6:2; 2 Tim. 3:16; 4:2), "exhort" (1 Tim. 4:13; 2 Tim. 4:2), "urge" (1 Tim. 6:2), "charge" (1 Tim. 1:3; 6:17; 2 Tim. 2:14), "reprove" (2 Tim. 3:16; 4:2), "rebuke" (1 Tim. 5:20; 2 Tim. 4:2), "command" (1 Tim. 4:11), "remind" (2 Tim. 2:14), give "correction" (2 Tim. 3:16). They must charge people not "to teach any different doctrine" (1 Tim. 1:3); they must promote "the stewardship from God that is by faith" (1 Tim. 1:4). Timothy is called to teach people how "to behave in the household of God" (1 Tim. 3:15).

Hebrews 13:7 urges the congregation to remember its leaders, namely, "those who spoke to you the word of God." Paul in 1 Timothy 5:17 speaks of those elders who labor hard in preaching and teaching.

EFFECTS

While opposition to the word in Acts tends to come from outside the church, from crowds that are often hostile to the gospel, the opposition in the Epistles comes largely from inside of the church (see e.g., 2 Tim. 2:24–26). Paul's epistles also highlight that the health of the churches is measured by their adherence to the apostolic teaching in contrast to false teaching. Therefore, pastoral shepherds play a vital role in that they will lead a congregation either toward or away from the apostolic teaching. People can overcome a supernatural opponent like Satan only through the supernatural weapon of the word of God (1 John 2:14).

Paul can speak sweepingly of those who rejected his teaching: "You are aware that all who are in Asia turned away from me" (2 Tim. 1:15). False teaching "will spread like gangrene" (2 Tim. 2:17), "upsetting the faith of some" (2:18). Some "have swerved from the faith" (1 Tim. 6:21). However, Timothy can be confident that God's firm foundation will stand because the "Lord knows who are his" (2 Tim. 2:19).

The General Epistles continue the theme of true versus false teaching and true versus false teachers. The contrast in 2 Peter 2:1 is instructive. Peter draws the link between the false prophets in former times and false teachers in his time. Both arise from among the people and both fail miserably as stewards of God's word. There is a decided spiritual drift at work in the churches as people have an appetite for false teaching and a distaste for the apostles' teaching. The truth of the apostle's teaching did not originate with the apostles; it is a word coming from the beginning (1 John 1:1, 7) and stretching throughout the progression of redemptive history. Stewardship stands or falls in terms of fidelity to that word. All of this opposition means that the pastoral shepherd must prepare for suffering (e.g., 2 Tim. 1:8; 2:3).

REPEATING THE CYCLE OF STEWARDSHIP

One of the most important effects of the ministry of the word is the principle of repetition. The ministry of the word done well on the part of the pastoral shepherd leads to an effective ministry of the word on the part of the congregation. Hebrews 3:12 issues a warning and calls for congregational action: "*take care, brothers*, lest there be in any of you an evil, unbelieving heart, leading you to fall away from the living God." This action is defined in terms of a congregational ministry of the word practiced daily: "But *exhort one another every day*, as long as it is called 'today,' that none of you may be hardened by the deceitfulness of sin" (Heb. 3:13).

The author of Hebrews also points to the relationship between what the word is and what the word does as an encouragement in this ministry of the word (fig. 17).

Figure 17. What the word is and does according to Hebrews 4:12

What the Word Is	What the Word Does
"For the word of God is living and active, sharper than any two-edged sword,"	"piercing to the division of soul and of spirit, of joints and of marrow, and discerning the thoughts and intentions of the heart."

The nature of the word keeps the ministry of the word grounded in the hope of what God can do, and thus it keeps people from focusing on the limitations of what their words can do. Someone may read Hebrews 3:12 and justifiably wonder, "How can I possibly speak a word that would penetrate past all of the defenses of a sick, unbelieving heart?" Hebrews 4:12 gives the answer. Our words cannot perform heart surgery, but God's word can. The solution is to speak God's word with faith in its ability to cut past all of the defensive layers and discern "the thoughts and intentions of the heart." As we noted earlier, the Bible is a book like no other. We read it, but it also reads us.

FALSE STEWARDS

Satan shows up once more as the one behind the scenes in all false stewardship. Paul warns that elders must not be recent converts and risk being puffed up so that they fall under the condemnation of the Devil and get caught in his snare (1 Tim. 3:6–7). Timothy's opponents are caught "in the snare of the devil" and have been "captured by him to do his will" (2 Tim. 2:26).

Paul highlights the demonic source of false teaching: "Now the Spirit expressly says that in later times some will depart from the faith by devoting themselves to deceitful spirits and teachings of demons" (1 Tim. 4:1). In the same breath, he also mentions the human element in these false demonic doctrines. They come from insincere "liars whose consciences are seared" (4:2) and who teach, for instance, that marriage and certain foods are not good (4:3).

Paul names explicit individuals in some of his letters. Hymenaeus and Alexander "made shipwreck of their faith," and Paul "handed [them] over to Satan that they may learn not to blaspheme" (1 Tim. 1:19–20). Some teach different doctrines that do "not agree with the sound words of our Lord Jesus Christ and the teaching that accords with godliness" (1 Tim. 6:3). Rather they are "puffed up with conceit" and have "an unhealthy craving for controversy and for quarrels about words" (6:4).

The central importance of 2 Timothy 3 necessitates a more extended exposition of this passage. Here the role of the word in the conflict between true and false stewards stands out clearly. Paul's instructions in this chapter of 2 Timothy are very instructive for pastoral shepherds today, as they were for Timothy in his time.

A CLOSER LOOK AT 2 TIMOTHY 3

Paul calls believers to two things: (1) *know* the times and the opposition (2 Tim. 3:1–9), and (2) *persevere* in the course of Scripture (3:10–14). Paul then gives three reasons for staying the course of Scripture: (1) the message of Scripture (3:15), (2) the inspiration of Scripture (3:16a), and

(3) the sufficiency of Scripture (3:16b–17). I will unpack these points under three headings below.

KNOW WHAT WE ARE UP AGAINST (2 TIM. 3:1–9)

If we are to win the battle for the Bible, we need to know the enemy and know the times so that we do not get caught off guard. Paul alerts Timothy to the perilous nature of this battle in the last days. Students of the Bible know that the "last days" in Scripture has one of two meanings: (1) the time immediately preceding the second coming, and (2) the time between the first coming and the second coming. It appears that Paul speaks of the second option, the time between the first and second comings, because even though he speaks of the future in verses 1–5, he concludes by commanding Timothy to avoid certain people in his current experience (3:5).

It does not take long to figure out why these last days are so difficult. Look at the eighteen vices Paul identifies in three verses (3:2–4)! The two foundational descriptions are "lovers of self" and "lovers of money" (3:2). Today we face the same kind of narcissism and materialism in our society. Narcissism is named after the mythological Narcissus, who fell in love with his own reflection and starved to death (there are varying accounts of this legend). Thus, narcissism is another name for self-centeredness. This kind of behavior is coupled with a selfish pursuit of material things. Is there any worse combination than self-centeredness and selfishness? This kind of activity is even encouraged today. Look out for number one, go for the gusto, get it while the getting is good, get the rewards you deserve, indulge yourself.

The next two vices also go together: boastfulness and arrogance. One vice focuses on words and the other on thoughts. Men who brag obviously have overly exalted estimates of themselves. They also speak abusive, blasphemous words, a fifth vice. We are so wrapped up in our culture that the sixth vice may surprise us: disobedience to parents. Has there even been a time in history where children were more rebellious against parental authority than they are today? Rebellious kids are celebrated on TV all the time.

The next eight vices all begin with what we call an alpha privative (usually translated as "un"), except one. People are ungrateful, unholy, unloving, unforgiving, slanderous (*diaboloi*), uncontrolled, cruel, and not lovers of good.

In addition, they are treacherous, reckless, and conceited. Notice that the list ends the same way it began, with the use of "love" (*philos*). They are lovers of pleasure, rather than lovers of God. There are really only two options: you can be self-centered or God-centered. A self-centered approach to life includes the selfish pursuit of wealth and pleasure, but a God-centered approach to life involves going hard after God for our joy and for his glory. We live for his fame and his name, not ours. Which approach and pursuit do you follow?

One problem needs to be addressed if we are to understand this text: Why are these last times so perilous? Haven't people always acted like this? People have always been self-centered, selfish, and unloving, ever since Cain murdered Abel. Verse 5 gives us the answer. This is a description not of people in the world, but of people in the church. They have a form of godliness, but they deny its power. They have a Christian shell, but no Christian substance, power, life, or vitality. They are imposters and fakes—their lives contradict their words and give them away.

You might think at this point that we are finished with this first point by now: we know the times and the enemy. Worldly people have infiltrated the church. However, let me return to the word "slanderous" (*diaboloi*). This same word appears in the immediately preceding section. Paul tells Timothy to avoid foolish speculations, which lead to quarreling (*machas*, 2:23), and then he reminds Timothy that the Lord's servant must not be quarrelsome (*machesthai*) in verse 24. He must not go around trying to pick a fight; he must be kind to everyone and gently correct those in opposition. Only God can ultimately intervene and overcome their opposition by granting them repentance and new life (2:25) so that they will come to their senses and escape from the Devil's (*diabolou*) snare and captivity (2:26).

Therefore, the beginning of chapter 3 shows that the opponents act as they do (3:1–4) because they are living in bondage to the Devil. In other words, the opponents are not the enemy; they are victims of the enemy. First Timothy 4:1 offers complementary commentary on this verse: "Now the Spirit expressly says that in later times some will depart from the faith by devoting themselves to deceitful spirits and teachings of demons." This point clarifies the nature of our warfare.

Since 9/11 some people have had the misconceived notion that Muslims are our enemies; they are victims of the enemy. Some think that liberal judges or those who would take "one Nation under God" out of the pledge of allegiance are the enemy; they are merely victims of the enemy, Satan. We are to bless them and not curse them; we are to pray for them and do good to them and pray for their salvation and release from the captivity and blindness caused by Satan.

Now that we know the opposition, we can move on to the second point: staying the course of Scripture (2 Tim. 3:10–14).

PERSEVERE IN THE COURSE OF SCRIPTURE (2 TIM. 3:10–14)

Paul first reminds Timothy of his own example. He promises that Timothy, like everyone else who attempts to live the Christian life, will experience opposition and persecution (3:12). Timothy should not be surprised by the intensity of the warfare: it will go from bad to worse. People will go from being deceived to deceiving others (3:13).

One is tempted to look for a secret weapon at this point. There must be a new strategy to counteract the increased opposition of these days. As a kid, I grew up loving Transformers. I can still remember watching *The Transformers: The Movie* in the theater. The animated autobots had something called the Matrix, which was supposed to come to their rescue in their darkest moments like a secret weapon.

Many today in the church are looking for this elusive Matrix. Some try to find it in managing techniques or the latest church-growth strategy. The proposed "answers" are staggering: more modern music, better sound systems, Starbucks served in the service, better child care, less preaching and more dialogue, small groups—the list goes on. Paul's message to Timothy cuts through this fog of confusion in verse 14: remain steadfast in the things you have learned.

WHAT THE WORD SAYS, IS, AND DOES: ITS MESSAGE, INSPIRATION, AND SUFFICIENCY (2 TIM. 3:15–17)

Paul reminds Timothy to stay the course of Scripture for three main reasons: (1) Scripture alone reveals God's plan of salvation (3:15),

(2) Scripture alone is inspired (3:16), and (3) Scripture alone is sufficient (3:16–17).

First, the word teaches salvation through faith in Jesus Christ (3:15). This plan of salvation that we need is not written in the stars, and God does not whisper it into anyone's ears. Scripture alone contains the message of salvation, and so Scripture alone grants the wisdom necessary to understand and receive salvation.

John Wesley echoes the importance of the word of God with respect to salvation:

> I have thought, I am a creature of a day, passing through life, as an arrow through the air. I am a spirit come from God, and returning to God: just hovering over the great gulf; till a few moments hence, I am no more seen! I drop into an unchangeable eternity! I want to know one thing, the way to heaven: how to land safe on that happy shore. God himself has condescended to teach the way; for this very end he came from heaven. He hath written it down in a book! Oh give me that book! At any price, give me the book of God.[1]

The weapon specifically crafted for the present conflict is not new. God got it right the first time: the answer to our deepest need is still the eternal and abiding word of God.

A second reason to stay with Scripture is that it is the word inspired by God (i.e., breathed out by God). Verse 16 sometimes does not pack the punch that it should. We think of the Scriptures as "inspired," but we are often not sure what that really means. *Inspired* means "breathed in." *Expired* means "breathed out." Which one is Scripture? We do not want to say "expired" because that reminds us of an expiration date, which implies that it is past its shelf life. The word used here means what the ESV translates: "breathed out by God." Scripture is the very breath of God.

To understand this dynamic, let's take a couple of steps back in the canon. First, Genesis 2:7 says: "Then the LORD God formed the man of *dust* from the ground and breathed into his nostrils the *breath of life*, and the man became a *living* creature." The original creation of man happened when God directly breathed his breath of life into Adam,

---

[1] John Wesley, preface to *Sermons on Several Occasions*, 2 vols. (New York: Waugh and Mason, 1836), 1:6.

who became a living soul. Genesis 2 helps us understand the wonder of the word of God. The Bible is now the place where we find God's breath of life. He breathes his breath of life into a book. When we read it, memorize it, meditate on it, we breathe God's breath of life into ourselves. We share it with others because we want them to breathe in God's breath of life.

John Calvin understood this dynamic. He movingly reminds us about what we find when we turn to Scripture:

> Nor do we do this as those miserable men who habitually bind over their minds to the thralldom of superstition; but we feel that the undoubted power of his divine majesty lives and breathes there. By this power we are drawn and inflamed, knowingly and willingly, to obey him, yet also more vitally and more effectively than by mere human willing or knowing![2]

It is at this point that our inconsistency in reading Scripture feels foolish. Let me illustrate. Even a liberal, unbelieving Bible teacher like Bart Ehrman can see our evangelical inconsistency. He asks his survey of the New Testament class at the University of North Carolina three questions. First, how many of you believe that the Bible is inspired? Just about everyone raises their hands. Second, how many of you have read Dan Brown's *Da Vinci Code*? Almost everyone raises their hands. Third, how many of you have read the whole Bible? No one raises a hand. And so he says, in effect, "I understand why you have read *The Da Vinci Code*. Dan Brown is a good author. But there is something I do not understand. You are telling me that you think that God wrote a book and you have not read it?"

A penetrating question helps us take the next step in the study of our text: What good does it do to have an inspired Bible if we are not going to read, memorize, and study it? In many places within evangelicalism, the battle for the inspiration of the Bible has been won. It is our settled conviction that the Bible is breathed out by God—his truth without any mixture of error. The main battlefront for many evangelical churches is not the inspiration of Scripture, but the sufficiency of

---

[2] John Calvin, *The Institutes of the Christian Religion*, ed. John T. McNeill, trans. Ford Lewis Battles, 2 vols. (Philadelphia: Westminster, 1960), 1.7.5.

Scripture. This question leads us to Paul's next point: the connection between what the word is and what the word does.

Third, then, look at what the word does (2 Tim. 3:16–17). It is useful for four things, and it therefore equips one for "every good work" (3:17). The four things that Paul focuses on are structured in pairs of two: the first and last words ("teaching" and "training") focus on instilling truth, while the middle words ("reproof" and "correction") refer to refuting error.

Verse 17 is doubly emphatic. Paul uses two words together (a noun and a verb from the same root) that mean the same thing: "that the man of God may be *complete, equipped* for every good work."

Support for this belief in the sufficiency of Scripture comes from many places in Scripture. Recall the relationship between what the word is and what the word does from our discussion of Psalm 19:7–11 (fig. 18).

Figure 18. What the word is and does in Psalm 19:7–11

The Word Is	The Word Does
Law of the LORD is perfect,	reviving the soul.
The testimony of the LORD is sure,	making wise the simple.
The precepts of the LORD are right,	rejoicing the heart.
The commandment of the LORD is pure,	enlightening the eyes.
The fear of the LORD is clean,	enduring forever.

The ten paradigms in these eleven chapters serve to undergird a proper understanding of preaching with pervasive biblical support. We have now reached the moment of truth: it is time to take what we have learned and apply it today.

PART THREE

EXPOSITORY PREACHING TODAY

17

THE *WHAT* OF EXPOSITORY PREACHING TODAY

Holy Scripture . . . may truly be
described as God preaching.

J. I. Packer

In this chapter, I aim to bring the survey of preaching *in Scripture* to bear on the issue of preaching *from Scripture* today. Making this transition is difficult because there is little agreement among adherents of expository preaching concerning definition or practice. This state of affairs raises an important question: Who gets to decide how to define expository preaching so that, in turn, one can determine who fits the description of an expository preacher? The real problem here is that the Bible never directly defines expository preaching because it never explicitly uses that phrase. Thus, it is no wonder definitions vary and differences of practice are sometimes even more striking.[1]

TWO HAZARDS TO AVOID

To help us negotiate this transition, I will try to walk a narrow path that avoids two hazardous ditches for expository preaching: (1) a rigid blueprint for preaching that spells out every step in detail and thus becomes a new law for preaching, or (2) an "anything goes, everyone

[1] "While most preachers tip their hats to expository preaching, their practice gives them away." Haddon W. Robinson, *Biblical Preaching: The Development and Delivery of Expository Messages* (Grand Rapids: Baker, 1980), 19.

does what is right in his own eyes" type of expository preaching. One could picture this path as shown in figure 19.

Figure 19. A narrow road between two hazardous paths

Hazard on the Left	Narrow Road	Hazard on the Right
Mechanical devotion to rules.	Biblical convictions with corresponding principles.	Everyone crafts his own approach, and anything goes.

In other words, my goal is to focus on biblical convictions and their corresponding principles of method. People must first agree on the *philosophy* of expository preaching if they are ever to agree on the *practice* of expository preaching.

TWO DISTINCTIONS TO MAKE

My definition of preaching in part one of this book attempted to capture the dynamics of biblical preaching in a single sentence. Recall that I defined preaching in Scripture as *stewarding and heralding God's word in such a way that people encounter God through his word.* This definition recognizes that there are three phases of preaching: (1) the stewarding phase, (2) the heralding phase, and (3) the response phase. The good news at this juncture is that the essential elements of this definition fit both the context of Scripture and our contemporary context. The bad news is that the definition must be nuanced because some crucial distinctions must be made as we move from Scripture to today.

Our contemporary situation introduces two determinative factors: a completed canon and noninspired interpretations. First, God is no longer speaking as he did in the past, in the sense that he is not adding authoritative revelation to Scripture. The canon is now complete. God's inspired, inerrant word is found in the completed canon alone. Second, though the Scripture is inspired and inerrant, our interpretations of Scripture are not. Scripture cannot err, but sermons certainly can and do err.

Another way to state the difference involves a famous comment about Scripture from J. I. Packer: "Holy Scripture . . . may truly be described as God preaching."[2] God has revealed himself *in* his word, and thus he reveals himself to us *through* his word. John Frame has stressed that God's word is not only *propositional* revelation, but also *personal* revelation. He says, "My thesis is that God's word, in all of its qualities and aspects, is a personal communication from him to us."[3]

Therefore, Scripture is God's authoritative word that comes to us as personal communication or "God preaching." It is "God preaching" in a complete and unqualified way because Scripture is free of error. Our preaching is not. A preacher cannot claim that people have heard from God simply because they have heard the preacher's sermon! We cannot equate God's preaching and our preaching. The question then arises, can people discern when they are hearing God's voice and when they are not in a sermon?

We need also to distinguish between *what God can sovereignly do* through preaching, even flawed preaching such as saying the right things from the wrong texts, and *what we are responsible to do*: preach what is true according to the content and purpose of Scripture. While God can and does sovereignly work through flawed means, we remain responsible for handling his word with utmost care and according to its intended meaning and use.

With these two distinctions in mind, how do we move from the study of preaching *in* Scripture to the study of preaching *from* Scripture that takes account of these distinctions?

A DEFINITION FOR TODAY: THREE *R*'S

The phrase *expository preaching* is a way of expressing the vital connection between the terms *stewarding* and *heralding*. One could say that the word *heralding* focuses on the preaching aspect or the type of delivery, while the word *stewarding* places stress on the act of exegeting and explaining the entrusted word. Preaching focuses on the tone or type of delivery, while teaching stresses the exegetical nature of the content being heralded. Once we understand the link between stewarding and heralding in the concept of expository preaching, we are ready to craft

---

[2]J. I. Packer, *Truth and Power: The Place of Scripture in the Christian Life* (Downers Grove, IL: InterVarsity, 1999), 123.

[3]John M. Frame, *The Doctrine of the Word of God* (Phillipsburg, NJ: P&R, 2010), 3.

240 Expository Preaching Today

a definition for expository preaching. Preaching today has three *r*'s: re-present, represent, and respond. Preaching must: *(1) re-present the word of God in such a way that the preacher (2) represents the God of the word (3) so that people respond to God.*

First, the preacher *re-presents* the word because Scripture is God preaching. The preacher also invites correction on the basis of God's word. Second, this calling requires the preacher to handle the word reverently and accurately because the preacher is an ambassador who must *represent* the God of the word. Third, the *response* phase is vital because both the preacher and the hearer are interpreters. They are both charged with coming to grips with what God says and with who God is. The hearers must test the sermon by the word of God, and the preacher must invite correction on the basis of the word of God.

What I am saying in terms of re-presenting and representing is very close to what D. A. Carson calls the dynamic of "re-revelation." He explains, "When that Word is re-announced, there is a sense in which God, who revealed himself by that Word in the past, is re-revealing himself by that same Word once again."[4] This "re-revelation" of God's word creates "a revelatory event, a moment when God discloses himself afresh, a time when the people of God know that they have met with the living God."[5]

Though the words "reveal" and "re-reveal" are both helpful, I chose "represent" because of the play on words within the term itself. On the one hand, a lawyer or mediator is called to represent another party. On the other hand, one may be hired to re-present or convey the will and words of another. In fact, a person may be called to *re-present* the words of someone he or she is called to *represent*. If a preacher is to represent God well, he must re-present the will and words of God faithfully.

Reverent and accurate re-presenting of Scripture will allow people to hear God speak and will seek to represent God himself. Scripture is personal and authoritative communication from God to us (again, God preaching). First Samuel is paradigmatic here once again: "And the LORD appeared again at Shiloh, for the LORD revealed himself to

---

[4] D. A. Carson, "Challenges for the Twenty-first Century Pulpit," in *Preach the Word: Essays on Expository Preaching in Honor of R. Kent Hughes*, ed. Leland Ryken and Todd Wilson (Wheaton, IL: Crossway, 2007), 176.
[5] Ibid.

Samuel at Shiloh by the word of the L ORD" (1 Sam. 3:21). Note that the Lord revealed *himself*, and he did it *by the word of the Lord.*

1. RE-PRESENTING GOD'S WORD

Re-presenting the word of God calls for accuracy, authenticity, and clarity.

Accuracy

The quest for accuracy involves a commitment to textual honesty. The messenger does not have the right to monkey with the message. What I am calling accuracy is what Lloyd-Jones called the "golden rule" of preaching: "At this point there is one golden rule, one absolute demand—honesty. You have got to be honest with your text. I mean by that, that you do not go to a text just to pick out an idea which interests you and then deal with that idea yourself. That is to be dishonest with the text."[6]

The stewardship of God's word calls for accuracy because God does not and cannot lie (Titus 1:2; Heb. 6:18). How can we handle the word of God, who cannot lie, in a dishonest way? Fidelity to the stewarded word demands that the message God intended for the audience is the same message that God first entrusted to the steward. The authority of the herald is derived from the accuracy of his stewardship. Notice the link between authority and accuracy. No one should give heed to his message as authoritative unless it is accurate—a faithful transmission of the original message that came from God.

An open Bible on the pulpit symbolizes a stunning statement of authority: "Your Creator and King has spoken—listen up!" An open Bible on the part of the preacher in the pulpit must correspond to an open Bible in the pew because both are under the authority of God's word.

Accuracy will invoke the principle of verification. In the past, God provided ways to test the validity of prophecy. Recall God's test for a prophet in Jeremiah: if the "word of that prophet comes to pass, then it will be known that the L ORD has truly sent the prophet" (Jer. 28:9; cf. Deuteronomy 18). Even though we do not use identical criteria today

---

[6] D. Martyn Lloyd-Jones, *Preaching and Preachers* (Grand Rapids: Zondervan, 1971), 199.

for preaching, my point is that we still use criteria. The criteria we use today are primarily exegetical and theological.

Preachers ask listeners to check their claims based on what the text actually says. If the preaching is not true to the content and purpose of the passage, then the hearer must be able to discern specific areas of error. The converse is also true. There is a sense in which the hearer has heard from God and needs to respond to God *if* the preaching has been true to the content and purpose of a passage of Scripture.

True preaching always points to God's word and says, "This passage is God's word. God is speaking to you—see for yourself." This is a breathtaking claim, but it need not be an arrogant claim. It should be the humble claim of one under the complete authority of God's word because Scripture commands this way of thinking: ". . . whoever speaks, as one who *speaks oracles of God*" (1 Pet. 4:11). A look at the context shows that 1 Peter 4:10–12 contains the twin themes of stewardship and speaking God's very word:

> As each has received a gift, use it to serve one another, as *good stewards* of God's varied grace: whoever speaks, as one who *speaks oracles of God*; whoever serves, as one who serves by the strength that God supplies— in order that in everything God may be glorified through Jesus Christ. To him belong glory and dominion forever and ever. Amen. (4:10–11)

Peter charges Christians to steward the spiritual gifts of grace that God has given them. He boils the gifts down to two major types: speaking and serving gifts. His focus on the first gift of speaking highlights the way the herald is to speak: "as one who speaks oracles of God" (1 Pet. 4:11).

Three other New Testament uses of the term "oracle" further illuminate the meaning in 1 Peter 4:11. Acts 7:38 highlights that Moses "received living oracles to give to us." Notice the stewardship theme (*received* oracles from God) along with the term "oracles." Paul also focuses on the stewardship theme as he states that the Jews "were *entrusted* with the oracles of God" (Rom. 3:2). The author of Hebrews reminds his readers that they have not been good stewards of the "oracles" of God. They should be teachers by this time, but they still need to be taught again "the basic principles of the oracles of God" (Heb. 5:12).

This brief look at the term "oracles" is somewhat surprising in that the first three New Testament instances have *God speaking them*, but in 1 Peter 4:11 preachers are to believe *they are speaking them*! In other words, the comparison ("as") instructs preachers in how to approach their own preaching. As recipients of God's grace, they should speak *as* speaking the oracles of God. God's gift of grace leads preachers to think of their preaching as "God speaking" his very oracles through them. John Stott states this aim well: "In the ideal sermon it is the Word itself which speaks, or rather God in and through His Word. The less the preacher comes between the Word and its hearers, the better. What really feeds the household is the food which the householder supplies, not the steward who dispenses it."[7]

Accuracy means more than saying the right things; it also includes saying them in the right way. True preaching means that the "message" and "manner" of preaching must match. John Piper gives a rousing plea for making these things match. "Oh, brothers, do not lie about the value of the gospel by the dullness of your demeanor."[8]

Demeanor is one aspect of communication. Tone of voice is another. I will never forget what Charles Spurgeon said about the preacher he called "a bumble bee in a pitcher":

> What a pity that a man who from his heart delivered doctrines of undoubted value, in language the most appropriate, should commit ministerial suicide by harping on one string, when the Lord had given him an instrument of many strings to play upon! Alas! Alas! For that dreary voice, it hummed and hummed, like a mill-wheel, to the same unmusical tune, whether its owner spake of Heaven or hell, eternal life or everlasting wrath. It might be, by accident, a little louder or softer, according to the length of the sentence, but its tone was still the same, a dreary waste of sound, a howling wilderness of speech in which there was no possible relief, no variety, no music, nothing but horrible sameness. When the wind blows through the Aeolian harp, it swells through all the chords, but the Heavenly wind, passing through some men, spends itself upon one string, and that, for the most part, the most out of tune of the whole. Grace alone could enable hearers

---

[7]John Stott, *The Preacher's Portrait: Some New Testament Word Studies* (Grand Rapids: Eerdmans, 1961), 30.
[8]John Piper, "Preaching as Expository Exultation," in Mark Dever et al., *Preaching the Cross* (Wheaton, IL: Crossway, 2007), 115.

244 Expository Preaching Today

to edify under the drum—drum—drum of some divines. I think an impartial jury would bring in a justifiable slumbering in many cases where the sound emanating from the preacher lulls to sleep by its reiterated note.[9]

Spurgeon elsewhere defines preaching in a way that brings message and manner together: "To know truth as it should be known, to love it as it should be loved, and then to proclaim it in the right spirit, and in its proper proportions."[10]

This principle would rule out, for example, saying one thing while gesturing something opposite. John Piper has said, you cannot preach, "Let the little children come to me," with a noninviting gesture, as if to say, "Stop!" with your hands. Tone of voice and nonverbal forms of communication such as facial expressions bear a significant weight in communicating the message. When message and manner are in conflict, the manner often wins, and the congregation loses because God's message can get lost in the process. The preacher must communicate as a whole person, not just with words.

Authenticity

Second, re-presenting God's word calls for authenticity. We came close to authenticity when we talked about the message and the manner matching. Here I want to address the issue of personality in the pulpit. Preachers are not called to be robots. Authentic stewardship is intensely personal, not robotic or mechanical. Philips Brooks gave a definition of preaching in 1877 that has since become one of the most well known. He defined preaching as "truth through personality."[11] The very nature of stewardship means that God's voice will come through the personality and style of the steward and herald.

Clarity

Third, re-presenting God's word also calls for being clear, but not clever. Recall Paul's stress on the Spirit's ability to produce saving faith.

---

[9] Charles Haddon Spurgeon, *Autobiography: The Early Years* (Edinburgh: Banner of Truth, 1962), 48.
[10] Charles Haddon Spurgeon, *An All-Round Ministry* (Edinburgh: Banner of Truth, 1960), 8.
[11] Philips Brooks, *The Joy of Preaching* (Grand Rapids: Kregel, 1989), 26. Brooks first defined it as "the communication of truth by man to men" (25). He further boiled down this definition to its two constituent parts: divine truth and human personality. The result was "truth through personality."

I argued that it was the key in understanding Paul's opposition to eloquence. Paul's resolve to know nothing except Christ and him crucified (1 Cor. 2:3) fuels an ambition to make Christ *clear*. Paul does not want to cancel this aim by being *clever*. What, again, is the difference?

Clever speech implies that one makes the truth real by how one says it. Clear speech implies that the Spirit makes the truth real. The orator thinks that words cleverly communicated will create conviction. Paul believes that God's word clearly communicated and illumined by the Spirit's intervention will create conviction. How tragic when Christian preachers think about preaching in a worldly way! The following diagram illustrates the difference in communication calculus.

> Pulpiteer: word of God + clever communication = conviction
> Preacher: word of God + clear communication + Spirit's work
>   = conviction

In other words, the pulpiteer acts like an orator operating in the realm of human ability from first to last. The preacher puts all trust in the power of the word and the Spirit. The preacher focuses on clarity because he wants the word to be on display, not his "performance."

2. REPRESENTING GOD

The preacher's call to represent the God of the word involves being (1) God-centered, (2) fearless, (3) humble, and (4) worshipful.

God-Centered

For true preaching to represent God, it must always be God-centered in that it always directs people's attention to God and not the preacher. Lloyd-Jones emphasizes this point in one of the most important descriptions of preaching I have ever read:

> [True preaching] addresses us in such a manner as to bring us under judgment; and it deals with us in such a way that we feel our whole life is involved, and we go out saying, "I can never go back and live just as I did before. This has done something to me, it has made a difference to me. I am a different person as the result of listening to this." Epictetus adds that if you do not do this, the utmost praise you get is

when one man says to another, "That was a beautiful passage about Xerses." And the other says, "No, I like that best about the Battle of Thermopylae." In that case, you see, nothing has been done to them at all, but they were just sitting in a detached manner and estimating and judging the speaker. One liked this quotation, the other liked that historical allusion. It had been an entertainment—very interesting, very attractive, very stimulating perhaps for the intellect. But it had done nothing to them, and they went out just praising this or that aspect of the preacher's performance.[12]

The fact that true preaching directs people's focus in a Godward direction changes preaching for both the preacher and the congregation. In terms of the preacher, grasping the God-centered nature of his task will enable him to stay God-centered in his assessment of his preaching. One way to express the difference is that this understanding allows the preacher to die and live in a fuller way than ever before. He can die more fully in the sense of dying to both the smiles and frowns of men (Andrew Fuller). He can live more fully in the sense of living exclusively for the joyful smile of God. Do not forget that God is a happy God—indeed he is the happiest being in all the universe.[13] To experience the smile of God in the study and the pulpit is one of life's sweetest joys.

Concerning sermon listeners, the God-centered focus of preaching will change their assessment of the preacher and the preaching. If people know they have encountered God, they do not praise the preacher. The focus stays on God. They no longer stand over the preacher as a judge of his sermon "performance." Though one moment they are the judge, the next they perceive that they are being judged. This perception should lead to a different diagnostic question in regard to preaching. The question will no longer be, "How was the sermon?" because that question calls for the hearer to judge how the preacher did. Instead it will be, "How did your soul fare under the sermon?" or "How did God address you in the sermon?" That is why the above quote by Lloyd-Jones says preaching is an act that brings "us under judgment."

Paul says that preachers are ambassadors: "Therefore, we are ambassadors for Christ, God making his appeal through us. We implore

---

[12] Lloyd-Jones, *Preaching and Preachers*, 56.
[13] See John Piper, *Desiring God: Meditations of a Christian Hedonist* (Portland, OR: Multnomah, 2003).

you on behalf of Christ, be reconciled to God" (2 Cor. 5:20). It is a stunning thing to think that preachers are God's ambassadors. That is really another way of saying that they are God-centered. God's ambassadors must of necessity be God-centered.

Fearless

Second, representing God means that the preacher will be fearless. The herald ceases to be an ambassador if he shrinks back from speaking as one vested with God's very authority. How can one claim to preach God's very words timidly and hesitantly? Such marks of uncertainty betray a lack of trust in the God-breathed nature of Scripture. The hearer should come away from a sermon with a sense that the herald *really* believed he was saying the very words of God. Are the preacher's words charged with God's grandeur or not? Confidence in God's word creates fearless preaching. This kind of preaching is attractive because many people today want to believe something that is firm and unshakable.

The story is told of the skeptic David Hume going to hear the preaching of the great evangelist George Whitefield. Hume's friends began to chide him because he did not believe the things Whitefield preached. And so they asked him, "Why do you go to hear Whitefield preach if you do not believe the things he preaches?" Hume's response was simple: "Because *he* believes it."

There is something moving when a person preaches something that he believes with all of his being to a person who has given up hope of believing in anything. Fear of man erodes this sense of confidence and hope.

Humble

Third, representing God means that the preacher will be humble. This is really another way of saying that the preaching will be God-centered instead of man-centered. C. S. Lewis gets to the heart of this distinction in saying that the humble man "will not be thinking about humility: he will not be thinking about himself at all."[14] The best way to turn thoughts from yourself is to turn them to God.

---

[14] C. S. Lewis, *Mere Christianity* (San Francisco: Harper & Row, 1980), 114.

The steward and herald must have a humble heart because the one to whom the Lord looks is "humble and contrite in spirit" and "trembles" at the word of the Lord (Isa. 66:2). The ideal dynamic is that the preacher as a humble, trembling steward has heard the voice of God in a way that colors the way he speaks that same word to the people. The preacher as a humble, trembling herald gives the stewarded word of God a voice. Paul reminds us that in his capacity as a preacher, he was with the Corinthians in weakness, fear, and much trembling (1 Cor. 2:3).

Worshipful

Fourth, representing God will make one a worshipful preacher. How can one represent God without worshipping him? The preacher will not typically steward and herald God's word in such a way that people encounter God unless he has *first* encountered God through his word. Lack of worship over the word of God betrays a stunning level of hypocrisy. We claim to have heard from God, but people see that it has not changed us or affected us.

Therefore, above all else, the steward and herald must be a worshipper. As a worshipper, a preacher will seek to lead the people in worshipful celebration over the truth of God's word. The true preacher does not desire people to express their admiration of him; the preacher as worshipper wants the people to express their adoration for the Lord who will not give his glory to another. Church should be a place that shines with God's glory so that people sizzle with fervency to make him known. Preachers should take a vow to raise the affections of their people as high as possible. We cannot raise the affections of our students if our own affections are not soaring with God's glory.

Lloyd-Jones is helpful here once more. He describes preaching as "logic on fire! Eloquent reason! . . . Preaching is theology coming through a man who is on fire."[15] Christopher Ash tells the story of how W. E. Sangster evaluated candidates for the ministry. A nervous young man said that he was shy and thus was not the type that would set the River Thames on fire. "My dear young brother," responded Sangster, "I'm not interested to know if you could set the Thames on fire. What

---

[15] Lloyd-Jones, *Preaching and Preachers*, 97.

I want to know is this: if I picked you up by the scruff of your neck and dropped you into the Thames, would it sizzle?" "Never mind his eloquence," Ash adds; "was he himself on fire?"[16]

The importance of worship in the study will be clearer if we work our way backward when considering a worship service. The preacher as worshipper wants preaching to awaken worship in others as he himself worships over the text. There is little hope of the congregation worshipping over the text if the preacher is not modeling for listeners how to worship over the text. Furthermore, there will be little hope of worshipping over the word of God in the pulpit if the preacher has not worshipped over it in the study. That is why Lloyd-Jones says that the prayer for anointing must come at the beginning of the process and all points in between. The preacher's study must be anointed, not just the pulpit.

God's word is not something to be taken lightly; God's worth causes the preacher to ascribe a corresponding weight of glory to God's word. Piper has stressed this component of preaching more than any other author today. He even defines preaching as "expository exultation." The first half of his definition upholds expositional accuracy because preaching is the "faithful exposition of God's Word."[17] But this exposition fails to be true heralding without "exultation." "Preaching is a public exultation over the truth that it brings. It is not disinterested or cool or neutral. It is not mere explanation. It is manifestly and contagiously passionate about what it says."[18] In other words, true preaching requires a Christian Hedonist in the pulpit.[19]

Many preachers take a "checklist" approach to growing as a preacher. They want easy and practical steps that they can use to improve their sermons. They work on their theory of hermeneutics or sharpen their skill in using historical background or cultural analysis to connect with the audience. These things have their place, but they will not make a preacher. As Lloyd-Jones reminds us, only God can

---

[16] Christopher Ash, *The Priority of Preaching* (Ross-shire, Scotland: Christian Focus, 2009), 67. Ash also adds an illuminating example from John Updike's *Rabbit, Run*: "When on Sunday morning then, when we go out before their faces, we must walk up not worn out with misery but full of Christ, hot . . . with Christ, on *fire: burn* them with the force of our belief" (67).
[17] John Piper, *The Supremacy of God in Preaching*, rev. ed. (Grand Rapids: Baker, 2004), 10.
[18] Ibid., 11.
[19] For the meaning of "Christian Hedonist," see Piper, *Desiring God*.

make a preacher. God creates worshippers. Starting by working your way down a checklist is a poor replacement for being soaked in Scripture and being captivated by the majestic supremacy of God in Christ. A heart that is alive to God and dead to pride will preach far more effectively than an approach to sermon composition that walks through all of the requisite steps of Homiletics 101. If we are to represent God in a reverent way in our preaching, we will need all the help we can get.

3. RESPONDING TO GOD'S WORD

Along with re-presenting God's word and representing God himself, preaching is concerned that people respond to God and his word. The preacher may be seen as an archer aiming at the heart. Much of my thinking on preaching to the heart is indebted to Tim Keller.[20] He rightly insists that true preaching attempts to make the truth not only *clear* but *real*. Many people think that preaching simply shares spiritual principles and that application is for later. In this view, change happens only after the sermon. But true preaching should bring change in the sermon itself, or there will never be any change after the sermon. Keller echoes Jonathan Edwards's emphasis that there must be an experiential knowing that changes one on the spot. One moves from knowing that honey is sweet in a notional sense to knowing honey is sweet in an experiential sense *when it is actually tasted, not just discussed.*[21]

In the same way, true preaching brings God to bear on the heart in such a way that God changes hearers on the spot in the sermon. The preacher recognizes that the problem is not primarily the intellect or the will, but the heart. Preachers often misdiagnose this heart problem. Many think the problem is the intellect. Biblical illiteracy is indeed a problem and the Scriptures must be taught. But this cannot be one's sole approach to preaching. Preaching must be more than teaching biblical principles for application.

This misdiagnosis continues once a pastor senses that these principles are not being applied. The preacher is tempted to conclude that

---

[20] I have benefited from two different sets of lectures by Keller on preaching. He has taught a course with Edmund Clowney at Westminster Theological Seminary (available on iTunes) entitled "Preaching Christ in a Postmodern World." The other set of lectures was given at Gordon-Conwell Theological Seminary and was entitled "Preaching to the Heart."

[21] I first heard Keller make this point in his lecture "Preaching to the Heart."

the real problem is the will. He may start to look at people as though they are just spiritually lazy. Again, spiritual laziness is certainly a problem. However, change does not happen by whaling away at the will. Harping on duty may bring short-term motivation, but it will not produce lasting change. Worse yet, this approach tempts pastors to resort to guilt trips and emotional manipulation from the pulpit.

Keller rightly recognizes that preaching aims for the heart, which he calls the control center of one's life. The heart is the place where the person thinks and tastes. How can someone speak in a way that reaches the heart? One example Keller gives concerns sacrificial giving. Most people in church know that they should give sacrificially. The problem is not with the intellect. Is the problem, then, with the will? Do people just need stronger, more prolonged exhortations reminding them of their responsibility?

No, that will not bring about the needed response. Keller says that the heart needs to taste the sweetness of Christ's sacrificial giving. If this change does not happen in the heart, then sermon listeners will never become sacrificial givers. The work of Christ must capture and control the heart: "For you know the grace of our Lord Jesus Christ, that though he was rich, yet for your sake he became poor, so that you by his poverty might become rich" (2 Cor. 8:9).

When Christ and his sacrifice take control of the command center of one's life, money stops being an idol. Christ is now more real than money, so money just becomes money, not a god. If this kind of change happens during the sermon, then there is every reason to hope that the change will continue after the sermon. If change does not take place during the sermon, there is little hope that people will apply the sermon to their lives in a lasting way afterward. This transformation comes only from the transforming power of the Spirit flowing through the life-giving word of God.

THE PREACHER'S CANONICAL COMPASS: GOD-CENTEREDNESS AND GOSPEL-SATURATION

Preaching must take its proper place in alignment with the supremacy of God and his gospel. The *what* of preaching inevitably drives us to come to grips with the *who* of Scripture. The supremacy of God in

Christ is the point of the canon and all creation. This ultimate reality must serve as a compass and center of gravity that keeps preaching pointed in a God-centered and gospel-saturated direction.

COMPASS COMPONENT 1: GOD-CENTERED PREACHING

All reality is God-centered because God is *ultimate* reality, while everything else is derived and secondary. Romans 11:36 proclaims this truth in an abbreviated way: "From him and through him and to him are all things. To him be the glory forever." The book of Revelation portrays all reality as flowing from a central point: God's throne. Therefore, this core truth must act like a compass to keep our preaching pointed in the right direction: away from ourselves and toward the matchless glory of God in Christ. How can we *re-present* God's message in a way that fails to *represent* God himself? By definition, that type of preaching cannot be true preaching. If preaching gets God wrong, then how can it be true?

What is God like? God is supreme and preeminent to a superlative degree that brings us right up to the limit of what finite language and finite minds can express. God is committed to himself in an unrivaled way because he is no idolater; he has no other god besides himself (Ex. 20:3). He is in the heavens and he does whatever he pleases (Ps. 115:3). He acts for the sake of his own glory. The clearest text in this regard may be Isaiah 48:11:

> For my own sake, for my own sake, I do it,
>   for how should my name be profaned?
>   My glory I will not give to another.

God also exists as one God in three persons. This truth is another point of God's word that pushes us to the limit of what we can comprehend—and goes even beyond. God eternally exists as Father, Son, and Holy Spirit: coequal and coeternal.

A DIAGNOSTIC CHECK FOR GOD-CENTERED PREACHING

The first part of the compass concerning the supremacy of the triune God is also important as a diagnostic test for true preaching. Imagine a scenario in which someone has made the gospel a central part of his sermon. He has called people to repent of their sin and believe in the Lord Jesus Christ to be saved. Isn't that enough? Why do we need the supremacy of God as a test for true preaching?

In short, we need the supremacy of God as a test for true preaching because people can preach the gospel of God in a man-centered way. People can misuse the gospel to boost self-esteem and make much of themselves as the center of the universe. Contemporary Christianity is flooded with feel-good, man-centered messages. Look how much God did for you. He would rather die than to ever live without *you*. God loves *people* more than anything. God took the fall and thought of *you, above all*. We must beware of singing these kinds of messages. The early church understood that what is sung is what will be believed. Messages like these wrongly reinforce the flawed idea that humanity stands at the center of the universe instead of God.

This message is not only unbiblical; it is unloving. Life is not meant to revolve around us. The planets of our lives will spiral out of control unless God is the center of our lives. Then, and only then, will all the planets of our lives fit together in proper orbit. This recognition of God's centrality must not settle as mere raw recognition. The stunning realization that God is supreme over all and central to all should cause the soul to soar to the heights of joyful recognition and thanksgiving.

COMPASS COMPONENT 2: GOSPEL-SATURATED PREACHING

The first component of the compass leads us to the second component: preaching must be gospel-saturated. The Trinitarian nature of God means that the gospel of God is profoundly Trinitarian. God the Father initiates the great plan of redemption revealed in the gospel; the Son of God comes and purchases the good news of the gospel for humanity; and the Holy Spirit takes what the Son has accomplished and exalts the Son by empowering the human heralding of the gospel and by giving life to dead humanity so that people can receive the gospel. True preaching is therefore grounded in the supremacy of the triune God. We cannot rightly respond to that reality without the corresponding reality of the gospel. We dare not try to relate to God another way. The

Father sovereignly planned the gospel, the Son faithfully purchased the gospel, and the Spirit effectually applies the gospel to the lost for their salvation.

This compass keeps our preaching centered on the central things so that we do not lose our bearings and drift in dangerous directions. Woe to the preacher who does not keep checking his compass. Failing to check this compass would be a failure to "watch over" and "persist in" the teaching of Scripture. Gospel watching and persisting are serious in the extreme because salvation is at stake for both preacher and hearer (1 Tim. 4:16). As Piper says, "The fundamental problem of preaching is how a preacher can proclaim hope to sinners in view of God's unimpeachable righteousness."[22] The solution to this problem is not just a fundamental solution; it is a glorious solution of glad tidings for sinners. "The glorious solution to that problem is the cross of Christ."[23]

A DIAGNOSTIC TEST FOR GOSPEL-SATURATED PREACHING

Graeme Goldsworthy has repeatedly stressed that preachers must use the gospel as a diagnostic check for true preaching.[24] He gives a very practical way to account for gospel centrality in our preaching. If a sermon preached by a Christian is acceptable in a synagogue or a mosque, it is not a Christian sermon.[25]

This focus on the centrality of the gospel may cause the discerning reader to wonder what constitutes the content of expository preaching. Do we exposit the passage, or do we preach the gospel every week? Goldsworthy rightly sees this as a false dichotomy. Preaching the gospel of Christ is proclaiming the word of God because the Bible is about Jesus from beginning to end. Goldsworthy claims that the gospel of Christ is the only proper starting point:

> The soundest methodological starting point for doing theology is the gospel since the person of Jesus is set forth as the final and fullest expression of God's revelation of his kingdom. Jesus is the goal and

---

[22] Piper, *The Supremacy of God*, 33–34.
[23] Ibid., 34.
[24] Graeme Goldsworthy, *Preaching the Whole Bible as Christian Scripture* (Grand Rapids: Eerdmans, 2000), 31–45.
[25] Ibid., 32.

fulfillment of the whole Old Testament, and, as the embodiment of the truth of God, he is the interpretive key to the Bible.[26]

We could go a step further in pointing out the many times in Scripture that the "word of God" or the "word of truth" is defined as the gospel. Acts 8:25 gives a parallel picture of preaching as testifying and speaking the "word of the Lord" and preaching the "gospel." The Pauline Epistles show a similar parallelism. Paul can put preaching the "word" and preaching the "gospel" in parallel descriptions (1 Cor. 15:1–4). At other times, he can even identify the "word of truth" as the "gospel" (Eph. 1:13; Col. 1:5). The apostle Peter follows suit when speaking about the living and ever-abiding word of God (1 Pet. 1:23–25; cf. Isa. 40:8). He explicitly says, "This word was the good news that was preached to you" (1 Pet. 1:25).

Jonathan Leeman gives an example of a very specific failure concerning gospel centrality. He points out that a criminal gang in Mexico, *La Familia*, has adopted the message of the book *Wild at Heart*, written by an American evangelical. The leader of the gang, called "The Craziest One," loves the message of the book that "God designed men to be dangerous" and that men have "a battle to fight . . . an adventure to live." Leeman astutely wonders whether the picture of "wild and godly manliness" sketched in the book is "rooted in the foolish gospel of a crucified king." Leaders in a Mexican drug cartel do not seem to catch the offense of the cross in this book.[27] This is what I call a failure to use the centrality of the gospel as a compass in scriptural exposition.

Leeman expands upon this important theme by clarifying how to preach the Samson narrative not merely as a "chest-thumping call to masculinity," but as a gospel-rooted reminder that "Jesus Wins."[28] This "headline" from Scripture functions in a way similar to a sports headline like "Yankees win the World Series." The headline serves as the main point of a news article. The rest of the article fills in the details of the win. To focus on one line of the article in a way that clashes with the headline would be to misunderstand the article as a whole.

---

[26] Ibid., 33.

[27] Jonathan Leeman, *Reverberation: How God's Word Brings Light, Freedom, and Action to His People* (Chicago: Moody, 2011), 126–27.

[28] Ibid., 127–30. Leeman gives three different routes one could take to move from the Samson story to the message of Jesus's victory. See ibid., 130–32.

Leeman calls us to imagine asking someone, "Hey, did you hear about that baseball game last night?" If the person responded, "I did not see it, but I read about that relief pitcher in the 7th inning," you would scratch your head and have serious doubts about that person's grasp of baseball. Focusing exclusively on the relief pitcher would miss the main point of the article, not because he is unimportant, but because his "importance depends entirely on how it affected the outcome of the game."[29]

In the same way, expository preaching that looks for the main point of a passage in isolation from the main point of the rest of Scripture will not do justice to what God has entrusted to the stewards of his canonical word.

The next chapter will delve more deeply into the preacher's stewardship of the word in expository preaching and how that helps hearers grow in stewardship of the word as well.

---

[29] Ibid., 130.

18

THE *HOW* OF EXPOSITORY PREACHING TODAY

It is only as we return to this [expository preaching] that we shall be able to show people the grandeur, glory and majesty of the Scriptures and their message.

Martyn Lloyd-Jones

Expository preaching is a philosophy and not merely a method; it is concerned with one's understanding of the totality of the task of preaching. Though it is not *merely* a method, there is a method nonetheless. I am only saying that one will fail to follow the method of expository preaching in any meaningful sense if one never comes to celebrate the underlying philosophy of expository preaching. One's philosophy (the *what* of expository preaching) will normally determine one's approach or method (the *how* of expository preaching). One can affirm the principles in theory and yet deny them in practice.

The previous chapter answered the *what* question of preaching by focusing on three *r*'s: (1) re-presenting the word of God, (2) representing the God of the word, so that people (3) respond to God. Now the *what* question gives way to the *how* question: How does one preach an expository sermon? We need a method that incorporates what we have learned about re-presenting, representing, and responding.

THE METHOD OF EXPOSITORY PREACHING: THREE *S*'S

One of the best approaches to expository preaching I have heard is from Mark Dever: the way to preach an expository sermon is to make sure "the point of the passage is the point of the sermon, applied to the life of the congregation."[1] This principle is clear and succinct. It addresses both the exposition and the application of the text. I agree with it entirely. In fact, I feel the need to support it further by establishing some guardrails for it. These guardrails will protect us against a simplistic reading of it and a minimalistic practice.

I would like to make the case that a method for expositional preaching should have three *s*'s: (1) share, (2) show, and (3) shepherd. The way to preach an expository sermon is (1) to *share what* the point of the passage is, (2) to *show why* that point is the point from the passage, and (3) to *shepherd* the flock according to *where* the text leads when applied to the present circumstances of the congregation.

Notice that the quotation from Mark Dever makes the first and the last of these elements explicit, but leaves the second element unspoken (i.e., showing the congregation *why* the point of the sermon is the point from the passage). I believe that second element is vital for preaching because it constitutes the principle of verification. The principle demands that we must not only *share what* the main point is *in the text*; we must also *show why* it is the main point *from the text*. I will unpack its importance in what follows.

THE IMPORTANCE OF VERIFICATION: SHOW YOUR HOMEWORK

Another way to state the principle of verification is that *the preacher needs to show enough of his homework so that the people are in a position to agree or disagree.* The people of God need to discern when they have heard from God in order to respond to God. The baton of stewardship passes from preacher to hearer, and the preacher can and must do certain things to help pass the baton. The congregation will need the preacher not only to share the content and purpose *of* the passage, but also to *show* them the content and purpose *from* the passage.

In other words, we must make a case for our reading of the text.

---

[1] Quoted in Jonathan Leeman, *Reverberation: How God's Word Brings Light, Freedom, and Action to His People* (Chicago: Moody, 2011), 114.

We dare not pull rank on people in the pew and say, in effect, "This point is the main point because I say so." We must do everything we can to demonstrate that both preacher and listener are under the authority of God's word. Scripture as "God preaching" is truth with no mixture of error, but our preaching of the word is not. We must put our people in a position where they can *check our claims*.

Let me illustrate. I remember not liking math in school. At times, I just wanted to get done with my homework, and so I would take shortcuts either by asking my friends for the right answers or by looking up the answers in the back of the book. I did not like showing my work, especially when I had cheated by finding the answers while failing to work the problems. I did not even understand what made a right answer right. Sometimes, even if I got the answer right, the teacher would mark the question wrong because I could not show how I got the right answer. I began to see that this was a loving thing for the teacher to do to help get me ready for the exam. If I got the answer right because I knew whom to ask or where to look in the back of the book, I would do poorly on the exam when I was on my own.

Preaching is the same way. Biblical Christians expect their pastor to be under the absolute authority of God's word. This expectation goes beyond mere verbal affirmations from the pastor ("I am under God's word"); it extends to the actions of the pastor (teaching in a way that demonstrates he is under God's word). The way he teaches will also communicate his expectations for the congregation. His actions will say, "I am showing you how I came to this position so that you can see whether it is in Scripture, because we *both* are under the authority of God's word."

Congregations should be skeptical if pastors are not willing to show their work. Shortcuts like looking up the "answers" in a commentary before really wrestling with the passage for themselves will short-circuit the process of stewardship. One should go to commentaries not just for their conclusions, but for their arguments concerning how the commentators arrived at that conclusion. Downloading a sermon from the Internet is an even greater breach of stewardship. Shortcuts that prevent both preacher and hearer from really understanding and seeing the passage for themselves will impoverish a church and rob its members of the joy of hearing and responding to God's life-giving word in a direct and personal way.

Therefore, speaking in way that plays fast and loose with a passage is a sinful power play that says, "Just take my word for it." Almost every evangelical today would say that twisting the Scriptures is wrong. However, I hope I have also convinced you that speaking in a way that does not show our homework is unloving and unbiblical because it says, "Trust my interpretations because I say so." This type of preaching assumes that only the pastor has the responsibility to steward Scripture. But as we have seen, both the pastor and the church have the responsibility to steward God's word.

We want to avoid an approach to preaching that ignores whatever in a passage does not directly contain our main point. We cannot ignore the rest of the passage, because the main point of the passage does not exist in isolation from the rest of the passage. Our charge is not to find the main point or main idea and then buttress it as we see fit. If Scripture is God preaching, then it follows that we should make his main point and purpose our main point and purpose. But if God includes the rest of the passage to support the main point and purpose of the passage, then we should do the same in our sermons.

In an earlier draft of this book, I crafted the verification principle in a way that said the supporting points of the passage should be the supporting points of the message. Stating the principle that way may be misleading because "supporting points" sounds like something from a sermon outline. I am not saying that one's sermon outline needs to conform exactly to one's exegetical outline. I firmly believe that in most cases having the two outlines match is ideal. Having the sermon outline match an exegetical outline of the text helps people see the point and purpose of the passage for themselves, which is important because people learn how to read the Bible from their pastors! However, I do not insist that the two outlines need to match in every case.

SHEPHERDING THE FLOCK ACCORDING TO THE PURPOSE OF THE PASSAGE

It is also important to note that the third element of expository preaching (application) depends upon the first two elements (sharing the point of the passage and showing why it is the point). The reason is simple: the preacher as *steward and herald* must say what the text says, and then the preacher as *shepherd* must lead the people where the text leads.

The faithful steward recognizes that texts are more than points or topics from which a preacher can pick and choose. A text has both content *and* purpose. Stewardship of the word recognizes that God speaks through his word. He says something with the intention of taking his people somewhere. A faithful steward must be true to both the content and purpose of a text by sharing what it says and shepherding listeners in where it leads.

There are right ways and wrong ways to practice expository preaching because some approaches embody stating, showing, and shepherding better than others. In what follows, I will highlight three ways to miss the mark of expository preaching. I will then conclude by giving a test case concerning how to embody the principles better.

THREE WAYS TO MISS THE MARK

One can claim the mantle of expository preaching and yet miss the mark by (1) preaching an expository series with a topical method, (2) preaching an exposition of a passage without the right amount of verification, or (3) preaching an exposition of a passage while ignoring the need for application. Let us take them one at a time before moving on to the right way to practice expository preaching.

MISSING THE MARK 1: EXPOSITORY SERIES WITH TOPICAL METHODOLOGY

Sometimes pastors will preach through a book of the Bible in a topical way. In other words, the passage does not provide the content and purpose of the sermon. The "expository" series in this sense is really just an organizational principle in which each week's passage supplies the preacher with a sermon topic.

For example, the next passage in a series on John may be John 3:1–17. Instead of preaching the specific content and purpose of John 3:1–17, however, the preacher decides that the main topic of the passage is "God's love." He then goes elsewhere in Scripture to talk about

God's love without really getting around to expounding what John 3:1–17 says. At the end of the day, it is a sad reality that some preachers would preach the same sermon on the love of God regardless of what passage was before them. A sermon on the love of God in Romans 8:28–39 or John 3:1–17 should not be the same sermon. If it is, the preacher is not being honest with the text because he has not dealt with its specific content and purpose.

Another version of this problematic approach to expository preaching is something of an irony because even well-known expositors fall into this trap on occasion (in my opinion). At times some of the best-known expositors will go through a book of the Bible so slowly that the passage being preached shrinks down to part of a verse or even part of a phrase. This is not a problem in and of itself, but it can lead to problems if one is not careful. The principle I have observed is this: the smaller the passage, the more the preacher will have to leave the specific context of the passage and go elsewhere in Scripture to explain the phrase or the verse. This makes it difficult for the person in the pew to catch both *the content and the purpose* of the passage. One may learn what "righteousness" or "faith" means in multiple biblical texts, but the listener also needs to see what part the phrase plays in its particular passage and the specific purpose it serves in the argument of the passage.

For example, let us imagine that someone is preaching through the book of Ephesians. On a particular Sunday he is preaching on the phrase "one baptism" (Eph. 4:5c). The preacher may understandably make baptism the focus of the sermon. There is not enough in the context itself to explain the concept of baptism, so the preacher searches all the Scriptures and produces a mini-biblical theology of baptism. There is nothing wrong with this at one level. People in the pew need to know what "baptism" means.

But at another level, the preacher may get the content of baptism right, but lose touch with the purpose of the phrase "one baptism" within its context. Perhaps the sermon explains what baptism is, and the application is "you should be baptized if you are a believer." That is true, but it misses the overall purpose of the passage. Ephesians 4:5c is not interested in merely making a case for the meaning of baptism. It is one piece in Paul's larger case for the oneness of the faith.

Let us look briefly at the passage in its context to support this claim. Paul moves from what God in Christ has done (Ephesians 1–3) and now addresses how believers are to live in light of that great work (Ephesians 4–6). The gospel celebrates the fact that Christ is "seated" at the right hand of God (Eph. 1:20), and as a result of believing in the gospel, the Christian is no longer a child "of wrath" (Eph. 2:3), but a child of God "seated" with Christ (2:6). Therefore, the believer must now "walk" with Christ in a distinctive way (Eph. 4:1, 17; 5:2, 8, 15).

Paul describes one of those distinctive ways of walking with Christ in Ephesians 4:1–6, which is the immediate context for the phrase "one baptism" (4:5c). This text answers three questions in the walk of a believer: *what, how,* and *why.* Paul addresses *what* believers should do (walk worthy of their calling as Christians—4:1), *how* they should do it (with humility, gentleness, love, and unity—4:2–3), and the underlying reasons *why* they should live that way (because of the sevenfold oneness of the faith—4:4–6). The oneness we have as believers (one body, one Spirit, one hope, one Lord, one faith, one baptism, and one Father) supports Paul's call to walk worthy of our calling by living in a gentle, loving, and unified way. Yes, one should be baptized if he or she is a believer. But more to the point in Ephesians 4:5c, believers must be zealous to maintain the unity they have in Christ. The one baptism into Christ is one of the shared realities that functions as a stirring testament to that unity.

I am not saying that it is wrong to preach on a small passage like Ephesians 4:5c. Nor am I saying that it is wrong to use the rest of the Scriptures to explain the meaning of a word, especially when the rest of the context does not provide enough information. I am saying that a sermon falls short of the true sense of the word *expository,* when it misses the point and purpose of a passage, even a "small" passage like Ephesians 4:5c.

MISSING THE MARK 2: EXPOSITORY PREACHING WITH TOO LITTLE OR TOO MUCH VERIFICATION

A second way to miss the mark of expository preaching is to preach the proposed point of the passage in a way that fails to show why it is the point. In other words, this approach to preaching lacks the principle of verification, discussed earlier.

Let us assume that one is convinced he should make the main point of the passage the main point of the message. The preacher goes to a passage of Scripture and says, "This point seems really important—this must be the main point." Having found what he thinks is the big idea of the passage, he finds a creative way to preach it clearly. What would be wrong with that?

My answer is, it depends. The preacher may have found the main point or may have missed it. Faithful stewardship precludes simply picking out a point that *seems* really important and then explaining it in various ways. It is not even enough to go to other places in Scripture to show that this particular point is important elsewhere.

How can the preacher and his people know that a point is indeed *the* point? As we have seen, they need verification because our interpretation of Scripture is fallible. One must, however, walk the path of prudence with regard to verification. Not providing enough verification will miss the aims of expository preaching, but providing too much verification will cause it to misfire as well.

Prudence involves providing just the right amount of verification for our interpretations. In other words, what I have called the verification principle also needs what has been described as the "Goldilocks" principle: not too hot, not too cold, but just right. When it comes to verification, people in the pew need not too little, not too much, but just enough. The path of prudence calls for wisdom on the part of the preacher because the amount of verification needed to be "just enough" will vary from congregation to congregation.

The quickest way to err on the side of too little verification is simply to commit the "because I said so" fallacy. A preacher must examine his expectations: Do I really expect the people to accept what I say without seeing it for themselves? Preachers should want their people to be noble Bereans and search the Scriptures daily to see whether the things preached are true to Scripture (Acts 17:11).

The quickest way to err on the side of too much verification is to commit what I call the "overly zealous seminary student" fallacy. The seminary student sometimes makes the mistake of thinking that he needs to tell people everything he learned in seminary, and in his study, about a passage. Overzealous preachers start talking about the hypostatic union of the human and divine natures of Christ and toss around grammatical labels, such as the "plenary genitive."

Too much emphasis on verification has negative side effects for the sermon. One side effect is a lack of application, which leads us to the third way to miss the mark of expository preaching.

MISSING THE MARK 3: EXPOSITORY PREACHING WITHOUT APPLICATION

Sometimes an overly zealous preacher will put so much time into study and so much verification into the sermon that he leaves no room for application. Too many sermons close with something like, "May the Spirit of God apply what I am saying to your hearts." It is a pious way of a preacher saying, "I did not devote much time to this; I hope you will do better."

It is sad that it took someone with a low view of Scripture like Harry Emerson Fosdick to remind us that evangelicals somehow think people wake up in the morning with a vital interest in knowing who the Jebusites were. Sometimes preachers think that loving to preach means sharing all the historical and exegetical details of a passage. One can love to study these things without genuinely loving people. For some, learning creates a love for the act of preaching in place of a love for the people to whom they preach. Loving people well involves providing just the right amount of both verification and application.

A love for the word of God and the people of God should bring verification and application together in balance. The word of God compels us to serve and love people, while a love for people compels us to go back to the Bible in order to serve and love them well from the Bible. How can one tell if a pastor loves both the text and people?

My answer is simple. If application is an afterthought, then a preacher has not yet learned to love both the text and the congregation. The Book drives us toward people and people drive us back to the Book. The truth of God's word captures the whole preacher, and he in turn wants to deliver its truth directly and lovingly to the whole congregation. Listen to Martyn Lloyd-Jones on this score:

We must ever remember that the Truth of God while meant primarily for the mind is also meant to grip and influence the entire personality. Truth must always be applied, and to handle a portion of Scripture as one might handle a play of Shakespeare in a purely intellectual and analytical manner is to abuse it. People have often complained that commentaries are "as dry as dust." There is surely something seriously wrong if that is the case. Any kind of exposition of "the glorious gospel of the blessed God" should ever produce such an impression. It is my opinion that we have had far too many brief commentaries on and studies in the Scriptures. The greatest need today is a return to expository preaching. That is what happened in the time of the Reformation and the Puritan Revival and the Evangelical Awakening of the 18th Century. It is only as we return to this that we shall be able to show people the grandeur, glory and majesty of the Scriptures and their message.[2]

Providing principles for application would take too much space at this point, and others have done a better job than I would.[3] I will conclude this chapter with a test case concerning how verification and application go together with finding the point of a passage.

A TEST CASE FOR THE PRINCIPLES OF EXPOSITORY PREACHING: MARK 5

The method of expository preaching I sketched above proves to be an effective way to exposit all of Scripture (i.e., narrative, poetry, the Epistles, etc.). For example, if someone preaches Mark 5 so that all of chapter 5 is the "passage," then the first order of business is to find the main point of Mark 5. I think the main point in all three parts of the story (i.e., Gerasene demoniac, the woman with the flow of blood, and Jairus's daughter) is the same: Jesus is unique in that he can do what no one else can do, and therefore he can rescue when no one else can.

---

[2] D. Martyn Lloyd-Jones, *Romans: An Exposition of Chapters 3:20–4:25* (Carlisle, PA: Banner of Truth, 1998), xii, quoted in Mark Dever and Greg Gilbert, *Preach: Theology Meets Practice* (Nashville: B&H, 2012), 116–17.
[3] Daniel M. Doriani, *Putting the Truth to Work: The Theory and Practice of Biblical Application* (Phillipsburg, NJ: P&R, 2001). I have benefited from a lecture by Tim Keller entitled "Applying Christ." It comes from the course he taught with Edmund Clowney at Westminster Seminary (available on iTunes) entitled "Preaching Christ in a Postmodern World." I have also received help from Bryan Chapell, *Christ-Centered Preaching: Redeeming the Expository Sermon*, 2nd ed. (Grand Rapids: Baker, 2005), 209–36; Robert H. Stein, *A Basic Guide to Interpreting the Bible: Playing by the Rules* (Grand Rapids: Baker, 1994), 28; and Mark Dever and Greg Gilbert, *Preach: Theology Meets Practice* (Nashville: B&H, 2012), 112–17. 9Marks Ministries also has a helpful application grid and other resources on their website: www.9marks.org.

The purpose is to show that Jesus is the unique Son of God, who alone can rescue *so that* we will call upon him and receive him by faith; we should respond to him and his words by faith.

In saying this, I have not yet identified the things in the text that support what I claim is the purpose of the passage. Thus, I will try to demonstrate my claim.

Each of the three stories in Mark 5 contains supporting details that make this overarching point and purpose clear (usually in the form of Mark's editorial background information). First, people have tried to "help" the demoniac by taming him or chaining him (5:3–4), but without success. Jesus, however, does not chain him, but frees and heals him. Second, doctors have tried to help the woman with the flow of blood, but she has spent all she had and is worse off than before (5:25–26). Then she is healed with the mere touch of Jesus's garment. Jesus emphasizes that her faith has saved her (5:34). She has reached out to him because she knew he alone could rescue her.

Third, Jairus's daughter is sick to the point that only Jesus can help, so Jairus begs him to come. But before he does, she dies and so some come to them and say, "Why trouble the Teacher any further?" (Mark 5:35). Jesus hears these words of unbelief and brings Jairus (and the reader of the text) to the moment of truth: "do not fear, only believe" (5:36). In their minds, it is too late for anyone to help, even Jesus. They even laugh in unbelief at Jesus's words when he says the child is not dead but sleeping (5:39). But Jesus, by raising her up, demonstrates why he, and he alone, can rescue when no one else can (5:42).

These observations from Mark 5 illustrate how the details of the text reinforce the main point in the expository preaching of a passage. First, notice that the main point and purpose can be found for a smaller passage (e.g., Mark 5:21–34) or for a larger one (e.g., all of Mark 5). In the example above, the main point and purpose are the same in all three parts of the larger passage: Jesus's actions demonstrate his unique authority to do what no one else can do. He has authority over demons, sickness, and even death. Therefore, come to him and receive him by faith.

In fact, the preacher can put these stories together because Mark has provided the necessary clues to show the reader that he wants the stories to be read together. Notice, for example, that Mark sandwiches the story of the woman with the flow of blood within the story of Jairus's daughter. Mark starts 5:22 with the request to help Jairus's daughter, and then the woman with the flow of blood comes into the picture and Jesus heals her, before Mark finally resumes the narrative of the Jairus story.

Second, the point of the passage needs the rest of the text to provide supporting reasons that will help make the main point, or big idea of the passage, clearer (Mark 5:3–4, 25–26, 35–36). It is not wrong to go to other Scriptures to find supporting points, but it is more important to find them in the passage itself so that the congregation can see the main point in the passage for themselves.

Third, the main *point* of the passage should inform the main *application* of the message as well. This method is the only way to steward both the content and the purpose of the passage. In other words, the application of the message should go where the driving force of the message goes. In the case of Mark 5, the main point is that Jesus alone is willing and able to save, and so we should trust in him to save us. The text itself makes much of this call for faith (5:34, 36).

Fourth, the principle of verification should cause the text to cohere throughout all of its various contexts. For example, one can look at the immediate context for verification concerning the main point of Mark 5, as we have illustrated above, but one should also be able to connect that point with the main point or purpose of Mark at the compositional level. Mark begins and ends his Gospel with a confession of faith in Jesus as the divine Son of God (Mark 1:1; 15:39).

This divine identity is revealed in specific ways throughout the narrative of Mark. Jesus's authoritative actions demonstrate his divine nature in Mark 1:1–8:21, while the cross and resurrection serve as the ultimate demonstration of his divine identity in Mark 8:22–16:8. Therefore, one notices that the focus of Mark 5 on Jesus's authoritative actions and divine ability fits the main point of the overall section of Scripture (Mark 1–8) in which it is found.

The next chapter turns to consider the critics of expository preaching. It is not enough to simply cover how to define and practice expository preaching. We must go further and consider the arguments of those who call it into question. I will attempt to show how the preceding survey of preaching in Scripture provides a response to these critics and the crisis of faith that such criticism can cause for expository preaching.

19

THE *WHY* OF EXPOSITORY PREACHING TODAY

Of the many criticisms of contemporary expository preaching, the one that cuts deepest is that it is not biblical—at least not in the sense that it is warranted by apostolic example.

Greg R. Scharf

An important challenge to the cause of expository preaching has remained backstage up to this point, but now must take center stage. This problem needs to be stated fairly so that people feel the force of it. The crisis of faith for expository preaching comes when we are confronted by the question of whether the Bible contains any examples of expositional preaching. In other words, the Bible itself may contain the strongest argument *against* the practice of expository preaching in our day: the biblical preachers did not practice it. Does the Bible we are called to preach actually sound the dreaded death knell for expository preaching?

Greg R. Scharf testifies to the confrontational force of this question. One of his colleagues at Trinity Evangelical Divinity School asked him why he was so "committed to expository preaching when preachers in the Bible don't actually practice it."[1] He rightly says that of the "many criticisms of contemporary expository preaching," this

---

[1]Greg R. Scharf, "Were the Apostles Expository Preachers? Old Testament Exposition in the Book of Acts," *Trinity Journal* 31 (2010): 65.

one is the one that "cuts deepest" because the claim is that it is "not biblical."[2]

This criticism can sow seeds of serious doubt for those who are committed to expositional preaching. If the practice of preaching in Scripture does not promote expository preaching, then proponents of expository preaching today will feel less confident in their own practice of it.

Evangelicals need not foster a defensive posture at this point. True, sometimes the question comes from outside the camp of expositional preaching and may have a mocking or mean-spirited tone. Maybe the charge comes from those who think preaching should be given less prominence in church services and be replaced by something else (more music, more small-group sharing, etc.). This assessment may come as a snide summary from those who think preaching should be eliminated altogether in our media age because a monologue is passé or hopelessly outdated. One does not have to look long or hard for clever contemporary put-downs of preaching.

But the question does not come exclusively from these quarters. It is a genuine question for many evangelicals as well. And I would go so far as to say that it is, in fact, a healthy question that all those who are committed to biblical authority *should* ask. Lovers of God's word should pause to feel the weight of the argument. It will do no good to retreat to tradition or circle the wagons around an evangelical consensus if we cannot confidently and manifestly demonstrate it from Scripture. Protestants, after all, are supposedly the ones who uphold the doctrine that Scripture alone is the final arbiter for faith and practice (*sola Scriptura*). Whatever happened to the Protestant plea of Luther that "my conscience is held captive by God's word"?[3]

THESIS STATEMENT

A preliminary step in addressing the question of biblical precedent is simply to acknowledge that the Bible does not use the phrase "expository" preaching, and so equating biblical preaching with expository preaching is not a simple process. We must first appreciate the

---

[2] Ibid.
[3] Quoted in Roland Bainton, *Here I Stand: A Life of Martin Luther* (Nashville: Abingdon, 1978).

complexity of the question. A second preliminary step would be the frank confession that this challenge continues to thrive in part because most books on preaching have not attempted to address it in a direct or detailed way.

My constructive response to this crisis of faith can be expressed in a thesis statement: *Though the Bible does not contain the phrase "expository preaching," the concept is thoroughly and demonstrably biblical.* I will defend this claim with six interlocking arguments.

SIX ARGUMENTS FOR THE THESIS

Argument 1: Biblical examples and biblical commands point to the concept of expository preaching in seed form. The basic concept and principles of expository preaching appear in prominent places in Scripture via both example and command. I hasten to add that even in these places the concept appears only in seed form; there is not extensive detail or development in these texts. Once this lack of detail is duly noted, however, these instances stand out in a striking way simply because Scripture does not contain many extended sermon examples or models in the first place. In what follows, we will consider the examples of Ezra and Jesus and the command to preach the word in 2 Timothy 4:2.

In terms of examples, one could argue that Ezra and the priests practiced the basic principles of expository preaching in Nehemiah 8:8. They read from the Law and gave the sense so that the people could understand it (Neh. 8:8). In this example, the "passage" or content of exposition is the entire Law of Moses in a kind of continuous exposition. Note here that they did not merely "read" the Law; they also "gave the sense" in order to make God's past word clear to a new generation that did not understand it, owing to its historical distance. The reader also gets an inside look at Ezra's preparation to preach in his commitment as a scribe to study, live, and teach God's word (Ezra 7:10).

Another possible example of expository preaching is Jesus's synagogue sermon in Luke 4. Luke informs the reader that Jesus "taught" (4:15) in many synagogues throughout Galilee, but Luke only gives us a brief glimpse of one of Jesus's sermons in this text: a sermon at Nazareth. The "passage" or content of exposition in the synagogue sermon is the first few phrases of Isaiah 61. Here one could argue that

Jesus preached the main point of the passage as the main point of his sermon: "Today this Scripture has been fulfilled in your hearing" (Luke 4:21). He seems to have preached himself as the main point of the passage because he saw himself (rightly!) as the fulfillment of the passage. Preachers today should preach this same message—with one exception—they will point to Jesus, not themselves, when they say, "Today this prophecy of Isaiah 61 is fulfilled . . . in Jesus."[4]

In terms of commands, Paul's charge to "preach the word" (2 Tim. 4:2) is a compact way of calling for expository preaching because "the word" is the object or the content that is unpacked in preaching. In the immediate context, Paul has reminded Timothy of the God-breathed and sufficient nature of the Old Testament Scriptures (2 Tim. 3:16–17). Now Paul commands Timothy to preach that word.[5] This command stands parallel to Paul's earlier command to "devote yourself to the public reading of Scripture, to exhortation, to teaching" (1 Tim. 4:13) because both passages contain the same Greek word translated "teaching" and forms of the same word translated "exhort" and "exhortation." The first phrase ("the public reading of Scripture") implies that the content of Timothy's exhortation and teaching will include an exposition of the Scripture.

As I argued before, these two commands bear a striking similarity to the example of Ezra's preaching. Both involve reading and teaching God's word. Both Ezra and Timothy have responsibilities in the stewardship phase as well because the reader gets a sneak peek into

---

[4] Luke certainly does not provide the reader with the full transcript of Jesus's sermon from Isaiah 61, and so one must exercise caution in making conclusions. Luke does not give us the rest of Jesus's words in his teaching on this passage. Luke is more interested in providing the people's reaction (Luke 4:22) and Jesus's extended response claiming that a prophet is not well received in his own hometown (4:23–27) and then backing up his claim with examples from Scripture (4:24–27).

[5] Some argue that the "word" (*logos*) here is a very specific reference to the gospel, not the Old Testament Scriptures. See for example, T. D. Lea and H. P. Griffin, *1, 2 Timothy, Titus*, The New American Commentary (Nashville: B&H, 2001), 242. This interpretation is possible because the "word" (*logos*) is sometimes in the Pastorals a reference to the wider body of teaching or doctrine that Paul has passed on to Timothy, which goes by different designations, such as the "gospel" or "sound doctrine" or even "word of truth." The reading that sees the reference as the Old Testament Scriptures remains preferable for a few reasons. The immediate context favors a reference back to Paul's preceding discussion in 2 Tim. 3:15–17 concerning the Old Testament Scriptures. Paul's choice of words demonstrates the repetition of terms, such as the noun and verb forms of "rebuke" (3:16; 4:2), and other words from the same semantic domain, such as "teach/instruct" and "reproof/correction" in both sets of verses. Also the grammar of the passage suggests that the article should be read in an "anaphoric" way (the word "the" signals a reference back to something in the preceding discussion). In other words, "the word" means "that word that I was just talking about a few verses ago"). See Daniel Wallace, *Greek Grammar beyond the Basics* (Grand Rapids: Zondervan, 1996), 220. One must hasten to add that in either reading the Old Testament Scriptures and the gospel message should not be separated, because these very Scriptures "make one wise for salvation through faith in Jesus Christ" (2 Tim. 3:15).

the stewarding phase of preaching the word in Timothy's life. Paul commands Timothy, "Do your best to present yourself to God as one approved, a worker who has no need to be ashamed, *rightly handling the word of truth*" (2 Tim. 2:15).[6]

Some may want to lodge a complaint here and say that none of these three examples *irrefutably* or *explicitly* says that Ezra, Jesus, or Timothy preached the point of a singular passage of Scripture as the point of the message. One may also point to other examples of preaching in Scripture (especially in Acts) that preach from multiple texts in a single sermon and thus do not focus on expositing a single passage of Scripture.

The reader may be surprised to discover that I agree with these observations. None of these three texts is *irrefutable evidence* of today's practice of expository preaching because there is simply not enough explicit detail included in the texts to form a watertight case. I also agree that it does no good to point to certain examples that fit our view of preaching while ignoring or downplaying the "exceptions" that include multiple passages in a single sermon. One should not pit one Scripture against another as if Scripture is at odds with itself. How then should we deal with all of the scriptural evidence so as not to ignore or downplay certain texts?

This question leads to the next piece of my response. I believe that the vital union between the stewarding and the heralding phases of preaching provides the way forward. This approach can do justice to the questions and biblical passages that are on the table for discussion. New vistas come into view when we focus on the link between what is stewarded and what is heralded. The reason for this enlarged view is that even though the Bible does not have many extended *examples* of preaching, it does have a lot to say about the *content* of preaching. In other words, though there are not many extended examples or models of the heralding phase of preaching, there are many examples and models of the stewarding phase of preaching. This vantage point leads

---

[6] One can make a good case here for reading "the word of truth" as the gospel because of the parallels in Eph. 1:13 and Col. 1:5 ("the word of truth, the gospel"). I certainly agree that Paul calls Timothy to handle the gospel rightly in his teaching in contrast to the false teaching of the opponents. One should not, however, sharply distinguish the Old Testament Scriptures from this body of authoritative, apostolic teaching because the teaching of the gospel or sound doctrine flows out of the Old Testament Scriptures.

to my next two arguments supporting the claim that the concept of expository preaching is thoroughly and defensibly biblical.

Argument 2: God spoke specific words and entrusted them to stewards. Here one observes that God's word in Scripture is specific in that God never gives an incomplete message. He does not give the stewards of his word a partial word and then expect them to use their imaginations to supply what is unspecified and undefined. Second Peter makes a case for the completely divine origin of prophecy quite directly: "For *no* prophecy was ever produced by the will of man, but men spoke from God as they were carried along by the Holy Spirit" (2 Pet. 1:21).

Prophecies consist of specific words, and Peter claims that *all* of these words came from God because there was *no* prophecy produced by the will of man. Peter defines prophecy in a way that brings together the human and the divine in a precise way. Some theologians have labeled the joint human and divine activity in prophecy (and Scripture) as "concursus." *Men spoke* (human activity) *from God* (divine activity) because they (the prophets) were carried along by God's Spirit (divine activity).

Peter also points out the parallel nature between the preaching of the prophets and the preaching of the apostles. Just as prophecies were not produced by the *will of man* in times past, Peter also says that the apostolic preaching of Jesus did not come from the *imagination of man*. The apostles did not follow the cleverly invented stories of men when they preached about Christ (2 Pet. 1:16). The apostles preached as eyewitnesses of what they both saw with their own eyes and heard with their own ears (1:17–18). In fact, I am not aware of any place in Scripture where God entrusts someone with an undefined or partial message to share. God's stewards are not left in doubt; God gives them the words to speak, not just an outline or a few suggestions.

In other words, here I am pointing out that God's revelation in the past came with specific words. God does not give people a list of important topics or ten-step models for managing life. The Bible never says, "And then a theme (or ten steps) from the Lord came to the prophet." It says, "And the word of the Lord came to the prophet." God's assignments are always very specific in terms of what God entrusts and thus what his stewards are to herald. This specificity of God's word supports expository preaching.

Argument 3: God's specific words were written in a specific form with God's authorization. The Scriptures attest to the specificity not only of God's spoken words, but also of his written words. God's prior spoken words are *written* with God's authorization as specific words in a specific form. This written word is considered just as much the word of God as God's spoken word. It is also functions just as much as a basis of blessing and judgment as any immediate revelation that God gives for a specific moment. The written word of God takes on an increasingly specified form culminating in a very specific biblical canon.

The fact that God commands his words to be written reinforces the idea of the *corresponding specificity between what has been entrusted and what should be heralded.* God commands preachers to steward and herald the canonical word today, which is very specific in both content and purpose. The fact that the spoken and written word of God serves as a basis for blessing or curse leads to my fourth argument.

Argument 4: Scripture abounds with warnings not to twist or add to God's word. Because the specific things God has spoken (both verbal and written) serve as a basis for judgment, the Scriptures abound with warnings not to tamper with or twist God's word in any way. Severe judgment follows when someone adds to or detracts from God's word (e.g., Rev. 22:18–19) or twists God's word (2 Pet. 3:16). Furthermore, the sin of presumption is serious because people are not to presume to know what God would say or think apart from the very specific testimony of what God has already said (e.g., Saul in 1 Samuel 13).

These warnings take us back to the golden rule of preaching: honesty. Recall the quote from Martyn Lloyd-Jones: "At this point there is one golden rule, one absolute demand—honesty. You have got to be honest with your text. I mean by that, that you do not go to a text just to pick out an idea which interests you and then deal with that idea yourself. That is to be dishonest with the text."[7]

Let me be clear when I talk about being honest with the text. I am not claiming that God e-mails *our sermons* to us in their entirety, but I am saying that he has given us *his word* in its entirety, which now

---

[7]D. Martyn Lloyd-Jones, *Preaching and Preachers* (Grand Rapids: Zondervan, 1971), 199.

serves as the very substance of our sermon exposition. This entrusted word is very specific in its content and purpose. Therefore, our goal should be to tether our words as closely as we can to God's word and not presume to speak for God apart from his word.

Arguments 2–4 focused on the specific content in the stewardship phase of preaching as seen in Scripture. Now we turn to the interplay between what is revealed and the person to whom it is revealed. Two defining factors are at work here: (1) the specific kind of steward who is on the scene (e.g., judge, king, prophet, priest, scribe, apostle, or pastor), and (2) the specific word from God that is entrusted to the steward (e.g., a battle plan, specific oracle, the law of God, the canonical Scriptures).

In other words, the content of revelation takes varied forms and various summary phrases depending upon the time frame of redemptive history. The channel or vehicle of God's revelation also varies depending on the time period it occupies in redemptive history. This interplay between specific types of stewards and specific types of stewarded content leads to our fifth argument.

Argument 5: Preaching in Scripture will shift somewhat according to the specific stage of redemptive history. The particular stage in redemptive history will largely dictate the specific content of stewarding and heralding. In other words, preaching in Scripture is both *content* specific and *context* specific. The content of preaching will shift according to the context of preaching. Our survey has shown that there are different types of stewards entrusted with different types of revelation throughout redemptive history.

One can recall numerous examples of this dynamic. Moses as covenantal mediator proclaimed the terms of the Mosaic covenant to Israel as God's nation. Ezra and the Levites proclaimed the terms of the Mosaic covenant in the Law of God by way of careful explanation to make the sense clear because of the gap in time from when it was spoken, then written, then rediscovered.

The prophets also proclaimed both the consequences of breaking the Mosaic covenant and the hope-giving good news of God's coming kingdom and future restoration. Jesus preached the arrival of the good news of the kingdom centered upon himself as the fulfillment of all of God's promises. The apostles testified to this very thing in their preaching as they proclaimed Christ from all the Scriptures. The Epistles make it clear that pastoral shepherds are God's stewards entrusted with the apostle's teaching.

This fifth observation and argument are important in dealing with the exceptions to which we alluded above that contain multiple passages in a single sermon. Someone may look at the preaching of the apostles in the book of Acts and say, "They did not preach expository sermons because they never took one passage and made the point of the passage the point of the sermon." Paul's sermon in Acts 17 does not even make reference to a single Scripture. These accusations are certainly true at one level, but they overlook two important distinctions between apostles and elders.

First, the apostles were engaging in evangelistic preaching as eyewitnesses of current events; they were not pastors preaching to a congregation. Second, the apostles had a different task than pastoral shepherds at this stage of redemptive history in terms of content. Let me explain that second point.

The apostles stewarded the message that Jesus is the fulfillment of all the Old Testament Scriptures, which was confirmed by what they heard Jesus say and what they saw Jesus do. They could have testified to these things by preaching a specific text, but their specific task at this stage lent itself more to the specific method of preaching broad-overview sermons of redemptive history. In order to show that Christ had fulfilled *all* the Scriptures, it made sense to preach *multiple* Old Testament Scriptures. They also had to proclaim the events that had happened among them in the present to prove that point. Jesus taught them to do this type of preaching (Luke 24:27, 44–47), and he continued to teach them for forty days after the resurrection (Acts 1:3). The preaching in Acts follows this overview method frequently (Acts 2:17–40; 3:12–26; 4:8–12; 7:2–53; 8:32–35; 10:34–43; 13:16–41).

Preachers today find themselves in a different time with a somewhat different charge. Stewards today belong to the era of the pastoral shepherd, entrusted with shepherding a local congregation with the truth of the apostles' teaching and the "faith that was once for all delivered to the saints" (Jude 3). Where do we find this teaching and this faith delivered to the saints? Answer: the completed canon of Scripture.

Peter Adam captures the logic of canonization in his three foundations for expository preaching: (1) God has spoken his word, (2) the word is written, (3) preach the word.[8] The movement from word spoken to word written to the command to preach the word is an argument for expository preaching because it follows the sequential flow of Scripture itself.

God has entrusted the canonical word of God to the people of God today. The fact that we must teach it argues for an exposition of its content. The Bible is an overall message composed of many specific messages in a specific form. God did not give us a topical book. He gave us specific books, such as Isaiah and Romans. We must give them a voice, not compile them into topics or ten-step plans.

Argument 6: Expository preaching is a multifaceted philosophy involving more than just a biblical theology of preaching. This final argument shifts to a more panoramic perspective. In the final analysis, expository preaching is both a method and a philosophy. It is a method in the sense that the methodological principles of expository preaching provide the most faithful and accurate means for ensuring the proper stewarding and heralding of God's canonical word. The method, however, cannot merely be culled from a limited number of examples or commands concerning preaching in Scripture. In other words, it is not a narrow method for preaching, but a multifaceted philosophy of preaching. The biblical theology of preaching sketched above provides the essential *foundation* of that philosophy, but many other considerations come into the picture as well. I will sketch some of these "other considerations" in part four of this book as we take soundings from systematic theology.

---

[8] Peter Adam, *Speaking God's Words: A Practical Theology of Expository Preaching* (Downers Grove, IL: Inter-Varsity, 1998).

SOUNDINGS FROM SYSTEMATIC THEOLOGY

20

PREACHING AND SCRIPTURE

Preachers have a better opportunity than anyone else . . .
to model a hermeneutically sound use of the Bible.

Graeme Goldsworthy

The fourth part of this book takes some soundings from systematic theology in order to ascertain which approach to preaching (expository or topical) best fits with other truths to which we adhere as evangelicals. The next two chapters will examine the doctrines of Scripture and sin. We could look in a similar way at any number of the traditional topics of systematic theology (God, man, salvation, church, eschatology), but the length of the book would get a bit out of hand and probably become less helpful.

THE DIVINE AUTHORSHIP OF SCRIPTURE AND PREACHING

Evangelicals say that they believe specific things concerning Scripture. Wayne Grudem speaks for many evangelicals when he says, "All the words in the Bible are God's words."[1] This doctrine has sometimes been called the verbal plenary inspiration of Scripture. Millard Erickson stresses that the process of inspiration involves the "supernatural influence of the Holy Spirit on the Scripture writers which rendered

---

[1] Wayne Grudem, *Systematic Theology: An Introduction to Bible Doctrine* (Grand Rapids: Zondervan, 2004), 73. The best book-length treatment of this theme is still B. B. Warfield, *Revelation and Inspiration*. It is volume 1 of the ten-volume set *The Works of Benjamin B. Warfield* (Grand Rapids: Baker, 2000).

their writings an accurate record of the revelation or which resulted in what they wrote actually being the Word of God."[2]

God breathed out the very words of Scripture (2 Tim. 3:16), not just topics. Therefore, which approach to preaching gives the most attention to the actual words of Scripture? My point is not that topical preaching ignores the words of Scripture, but that expositional preaching on the whole puts more stress on the meaning of words, and thus more time in the sermon is devoted to that task.

As we noted earlier, John Frame stresses that God's word is not only propositional revelation, but also *personal* revelation: "My thesis is that God's word, in all of its qualities and aspects, is a personal communication from him to us."[3] God has revealed himself *in* his word, and thus he reveals himself to us *through* his word. The personal nature of Scripture also pushes us toward worshipping over the word. One of the reasons why many people read Scripture in such a dry fashion is the way we typically define exegesis.

Most books on the subject tell us that exegesis is the search for an author's intended meaning. I do not object to this definition because of what it affirms, but I object because of what it leaves unsaid. It sounds so cerebral (i.e., recovering an author's intended meaning). We must never forget that what we find in Scripture is not just something abstract called "meaning" but One who is glorious—God himself. Consider 1 Samuel 3:21: "And the LORD appeared again at Shiloh, for the LORD revealed himself to Samuel at Shiloh by the word of the LORD." We seek God himself in his word, not just something called "intended meaning." God is the author, and he intends to reveal himself to us through his word.

This point landed on me powerfully in a dry time during my own teaching last year in my Romans 9–11 class. In one particular text, the logic behind the little word "how" began to burn within (Rom. 10:14–15). I was reading the biography of William Carey at the same time, and he further stoked the fire concerning that little word. How will they hear? Who will go? These were the questions that gripped Carey's heart.

---

[2] Millard Erickson, *Christian Theology*, 2nd ed. (Grand Rapids: Baker, 1998), 225.
[3] John M. Frame, *The Doctrine of the Word of God* (Phillipsburg, NJ: P&R, 2010), 3.

I began to reflect on my experience: "Why am I so struck by this particular text in this particular week? Why have I entered a dry spell before coming to this text?" I began to realize that I had been thinking about exegesis in a mechanical way. I had started to think that my role as a teacher of exegesis was to show students the right questions to bring to the text and then show how to answer them. It dawned on me that I had so focused on the mechanics or process of exegesis that I had taken my focus off the object of exegesis: God as he is revealed in his word. I began to see that the text has some questions for me. I am not to be a lead questioner of the text as a model for my students, but a lead worshipper over the text—modeling worshipful engagement with God through the text for my students.

Therefore, if Scripture is personal communication, which approach to preaching models the best way to handle personal communication? I believe the answer is expository preaching. If I wrote a letter to someone, I would want him or her to attempt to understand the meaning of it paragraph by paragraph, rather than by selecting topics.

THE SUFFICIENCY OF SCRIPTURE AND PREACHING

Evangelicals also believe in the sufficiency of Scripture. Wayne Grudem defines the doctrine as follows: "The sufficiency of Scripture means that Scripture contained all the words of God he intended his people to have at each stage of redemptive history, and that it now contains everything we need God to tell us for salvation, for trusting him perfectly, and for obeying him perfectly."[4]

This doctrine says that the Bible has all that we need to know for salvation, faith, and obedience. This doctrine forces us to ask which approach to preaching puts the most trust in the sufficient ability of the Bible to tell us what we need to know for salvation, faith, and obedience. Which approach to preaching puts the most trust in the power of Scripture? Topical preaching puts trust in the sufficiency of Scripture, but expository preaching makes that trust more visible and tangible in its attentiveness to Scripture. Again, the time devoted to the exposition of Scripture testifies very loudly to our belief in Scripture's sufficiency.

---

[4] Grudem, *Systematic Theology*, 127. Cf. article 7 of the Belgic Confession.

THE STUDY OF SCRIPTURE AND PREACHING

Evangelicals also believe that Scripture must be studied, not just read. Grudem says, "The doctrine of the clarity of Scripture does not imply or suggest that all believers will agree on all the teachings of Scripture."[5] Therefore, believers must engage in exegesis and study Scripture using proper principles of interpretation.[6]

Which approach to preaching best models how to study Scripture? Expository preaching best models the process of interpreting the Bible. People learn how to read their Bibles primarily from the way their pastor reads his Bible. If he preaches topically, they will think topically and read topically. If he preaches exegetically as an expositor, then they will think exegetically and read exegetically. Graeme Goldsworthy agrees: "People learn how to use the Bible mostly from their teachers in church, so preachers have a better opportunity than anyone else to teach good biblical theology and to model a hermeneutically sound use of the Bible."[7] Martyn Lloyd-Jones has this same principle in mind when he says that "honesty with the text" is the "one golden rule," the "one absolute demand" of preaching[8]

Expository preaching holds a preacher's feet to the fire with respect to the golden rule of honesty. Honesty is required because God revealed himself specifically. He did not give a general commission to the prophets (here is a message; now take it and develop it creatively by bringing in lots of other ideas). He entrusted a specific message to them. Expository preaching reflects this principle better than topical preaching. Topical preaching can be an attempt to pull together what the Scriptures teach on some topic, but it gets more of its form and creative content from the preacher, and as such it is one step removed from biblical authority. Expository preaching tethers itself more tightly to the particulars of a text. The goal of this tethering is to stay closer to the shape, content, and context of the text itself.

---

[5] Grudem, *Systematic Theology*, 109.
[6] Ibid., 108–9.
[7] Graeme Goldsworthy, "Preaching and Biblical Theology," in *New Dictionary of Biblical Theology: Exploring the Unity and Diversity of Scripture*, ed. T. Desmond Alexander and Brian S. Rosner (Downers Grove, IL: InterVarsity, 2001), 106.
[8] D. Martyn Lloyd-Jones, *Preaching and Preachers* (Grand Rapids: Zondervan, 1971), 199.

21

PREACHING AND SIN

> Just as old or bleary-eyed men . . . with the aid of spectacles
> will begin to read distinctly; so Scripture . . . clearly shows
> us the true God.
>
> *John Calvin*

The doctrine of sin is one of the most humbling of all of the teachings of Scripture. The Bible teaches us that sin is the failure to conform to God's standards in our actions and attitudes. We act in ways that break God's commands, but God also commands certain attitudes. The doctrine of sin goes deeper still. Scripture teaches that we are evil not just because we do bad things, but because we are bad. In other words, our actions are contaminated by sin the same way polluted water flows downstream from a polluted spring. Our bad actions and bad attitudes flow from bad hearts.

ORIGINAL SIN

Why does everyone have this pollution? The doctrine of original sin teaches that we receive a polluted sinful nature as a result of Adam's first sin.[1] Sometimes this doctrine is called "inherited corruption" or "original pollution."[2] Three texts are especially clear on this point. David says,

> Behold, I was brought forth in iniquity,
>   and in sin did my mother conceive me. (Ps. 51:5)

---

[1] See Alan Jacobs, *Original Sin: A Cultural History* (New York: HarperCollins, 2008).
[2] Wayne Grudem, *Systematic Theology: An Introduction to Bible Doctrine* (Grand Rapids: Zondervan, 2004), 496.

> The wicked go astray from the womb,
>   they err from their birth, speaking lies. (Ps. 58:3, RSV)

And Paul says, "We . . . were by nature children of wrath, like the rest of mankind" (Eph. 2:3).

Grudem rightly reminds us that original sin does not mean that human beings are all as bad as they could be.[3] Original sin teaches that every part of our faculties is tainted by sin, including our capacity to understand God and his world. This testifies to our need for Scripture. The Reformer John Calvin understood that the fall into sin has affected our vision, and we need corrective lenses from God in order to see clearly. God gave us his word so that we can see things as we should. Thus Calvin spoke of the "spectacles" of Scripture:

> Just as old or bleary-eyed men and those with weak vision, if you thrust before them a most beautiful volume, even if they recognize it to be some sort of writing, yet can scarcely construe two words, but with the aid of spectacles will begin to read distinctly; so Scripture, gathering up the otherwise confused knowledge of God in our minds, having dispersed our dullness, clearly shows us the true God.[4]

Scripture also teaches that the doctrine of sin applies to all of humanity, including Christians. Christians are *forgiven* sinners, but they are still forgiven *sinners*. Sanctification in this life is progressive and often painfully slow. As Charles Wesley says, God "breaks the power of cancelled sin." His power is at work, but we will not be set free from our struggle with sin until the second coming and the eternal state.

SINNERS AND SAFEGUARDS

Because everyone in the world is a sinner (forgiven or unforgiven), we can look at sin from two primary angles: the preacher's sin and the hearer's sin.

First, preachers are sinners. Therefore, the congregation needs a measure of protection against the preacher's sin. Which approach to preaching best protects the congregation against the preacher's sin?

---

[3] Ibid.
[4] John Calvin, *The Institutes of the Christian Religion*, ed. John T. McNeill, trans. Ford Lewis Battles, 2 vols. (Philadelphia: Westminster, 1960), 1.6.1.

The answer is expository preaching. The preacher will not as easily jump up on his soapboxes or ride off on his hobbyhorses if he is tethered to a text. Furthermore, a great measure of protection comes to the congregation as a preacher works through the message of an entire biblical book. A preacher must work sequentially through a series of texts while preaching through books of Scripture. When the he does depart from the text in order to ride off on one of his hobbyhorses, the congregation will see that more clearly as a departure from the text.

Second, everyone in the congregation is a sinner, and the preacher needs a measure of protection from their collective sin. Which approach to preaching provides the most protection? The answer again is expository preaching. Topical preaching always leaves one vulnerable to suspicion: why did the pastor choose that topic?

This came home to me when I was preaching my first expository series in my first pastorate. I was preaching through the Sermon on the Mount. When I came to Jesus's words on divorce (Matt. 5:31–32), I preached them. One of the most influential women in the church told me afterward that I was very brave. I asked her why she thought so. She answered, "Don't you know that four people in the congregation are divorced?" I was so thankful for the solid foothold that expository preaching gave me at that very moment as I told her that I did not pick the topic. The text dictated the message and therefore people should not be suspicious as to my motives or congratulatory concerning my "courage." All I did was preach the next text.

A final cumulative point on preaching and the doctrines of Scripture and sin is in order. Human sin is a mitigating factor that threatens all human attempts at fidelity toward the things of God. How are we to deal with the doubts that arise the further removed we are from the text? Can we be sure that we would address a topic the same way God would? Can we somehow find a way to piece things together with the right balance and emphasis and supporting arguments the way a biblical text can?

Expository preaching provides the preacher and the hearer with more objective criteria because it stays closer to the details of the text. We have confidence that God wanted a specific text to have the form it has, but we have less confidence that our way of treating a topic is what God would want. Topical preaching leaves us more exposed to our subjective crafting of a sermon and the subjective suspicions of those who hear us.

Topical preaching puts us at a disadvantage when it comes to the human element of preaching. All preaching is the proclamation of divine truth through human personality. Both points (divine truth and human personality) are proper elements in any sermon, but it should be clear that the element of divine truth should be more prominent than human personality. Focusing more on God and less on the preacher's personality becomes more difficult when the preacher has a greater hand in determining the contours of the message. The more the sermon bears his likeness in terms of content, the harder it becomes to focus on what God has specifically composed in Scripture.

Topical preaching puts the preacher in a difficult situation. As a preacher, I have to ask whether I have shortchanged the stewardship process in any way. Did I have too great of a hand in determining where to go in Scripture as I pieced together ideas from various parts of Scripture? If a text is breathed out by God, then I can have every confidence that he intended the language, the imagery, the main point, and the supporting points. I will be able to direct people's attention more to God's composition than to my own when I preach a specific text that God specifically inspired. *The focus is more on what God has composed rather than on what I have composed.* My role is to give the text a voice to be heard and emotions to be felt.

The cumulative question then is this: In the final analysis, who or what shapes the message *most*: the preacher or God? In asking this question, I am not ignorant of the fact that sermon making and sermon delivery are inevitably human products. I know that God does not write our sermons or preach them for us. And so the question is not whether the sermon will have a human element. The question is which approach to preaching allows God to shape the sermon most? I maintain that expository preaching is a method and philosophy of preaching that best allows God to shape the message.

Expository preaching attempts to honor God's choice in terms of the final form of Scripture. In the Prophets, God gave specific messages, not generic ones that the prophets had to develop. God did not give a bullet list of generic truths about himself. He revealed himself in compositional form. Do we honor these compositional forms in our preaching? Why did he take the time to reveal himself through specific things in specific contexts if he simply wanted us to take what he has said generally so that we might create specific messages? God took the time to create something specific. He did not merely reveal topics or give us outlines of his thinking. Expository preaching is a philosophy that puts great stock in the specificity of what God has revealed.

An approach to preaching that puts the greatest stress on the specificity of Scripture provides the surest safeguard from human subjectivity. The further removed the preacher is from the text, the further removed the preacher and the congregation are from the authority of the text, and the more both preacher and congregation are susceptible to sin's effects in shaping the final product. Topical preaching and expository preaching done well are both grounded in Scripture. The difference comes down to method. Our approach to preaching matters because it will represent the way we approach Scripture itself. I would argue that expository preaching models an approach to Scripture that is more faithful to the approach we would want everyone to take when studying the Scriptures.

22

TOPICAL PREACHING: FRIEND OR FOE?

You do not go to a text just to pick out an idea which interests you and then deal with that idea yourself. That is to be dishonest with the text.

Martyn Lloyd-Jones

CAN AN EXPOSITORY PREACHER ADVOCATE TOPICAL PREACHING?

I am not an adversary of all topical preaching. In fact, I am actually an advocate of topical preaching. There, I said it. I may have surprised some people by saying it. Let me explain.

Topical preaching is very vulnerable to abuse. One can do what Martyn Lloyd-Jones warned about: take a text "just to pick out an idea" and then "deal with that idea yourself."[1] I do not support that type of topical preaching.

The type of topical sermon I support is one that is a faithful summary of what the Bible says on a topic. For example, I recently preached a topical series for advent called "Behold Your King." It was a four-part series that looked at the Messiah in the (1) Law, (2) the Prophets, (3) the Writings, and (4) the Gospels. The Messiah pictured in this cross section of Scripture is (1) a King who crushes his enemies (Numbers 24), (2) a King who is crushed for his enemies (Isaiah 53), and (3) a King who crushed the last enemy (Psalm 16). The last sermon went to the New Testament for the birth of Christ to see Jesus as (4) the present King, who is with us and for us always (Matthew 1–2).

---

[1] D. Martyn Lloyd-Jones, *Preaching and Preachers* (Grand Rapids: Zondervan, 1971), 199.

THREE TYPES OF PREACHING SERIES

An important distinction needs to be made at this point. There are really three possible kinds of preaching series, depending on arrangement and method. First, the advent series was topical in *arrangement* (I chose the topic for the series and passages whose main point addressed the topic), but expository in *method* (i.e., each sermon shared the main point of the passage as the main point of the message). Second, one could preach a series that is topical in both arrangement (i.e., the preacher picks a topic for the series and passages whose main point is *not* the topic) and method (i.e., the preacher uses the text to pick the topic of his focus). Third, an expository series on a book of the Bible would be expository in both arrangement and method.

Which of the three types of series above could potentially be beneficial for the congregation and faithful to the Bible? I would argue that all three are helpful when done well. Topical preaching is not inherently sinful. I would actually encourage certain types of topical preaching—on occasion.

PUTTING TOPICAL PREACHING IN ITS PLACE

That last statement gets right to the heart of my passion. I have argued for the primacy of expository preaching, *not* for boycotting all forms of topical preaching. Topical preaching has its place, but only after it is placed below the primacy of expository preaching. My point here is simple. A preaching ministry that has a steady diet of expository preaching brings with it a much better strategy for the long-term health of the body of Christ.

Most people would agree that a steady diet of fast food is not a recipe for bodily health. In moderation, however, eating out at fast-food restaurants can be a blessing to a family. I would never advocate a boycott of either fast-food or sit-down restaurants. In the same way, I would argue that a steady diet of topical preaching is not a recipe for health in the body of Christ. The key phrase is "steady diet." I would not send a scathing e-mail to a pastor who preaches a topical sermon or try to organize a massive church-wide protest against a pastor who preaches a topical sermon.

Topical preaching (when done well) brings a *great blessing* to the body of Christ and should be an *occasional* part of a powerful preaching ministry. Expository preaching has primacy because (when done well) it brings a *greater blessing* and thus should become the *dominant* part of a powerful preaching ministry. What are the benefits and the weaknesses of topical preaching?

THE BENEFITS OF TOPICAL PREACHING

Why is topical preaching a friend and not a foe? We can answer that question by asking what topical preaching does well. We can then ask how to leverage those positive elements for maximal blessing to the body.

What does topical preaching do well? I could say many things here, but I will highlight two of the biggest strengths. First, topical sermons can show the Bible's breadth and balance on any given topic *in a single sermon*. When done well, this approach to preaching helps the hearers come to grips with the holistic nature of Scripture and how it addresses all of life.

Second, topical preaching can help the hearer appreciate the unity of Scripture amid its diversity of authors and genres *in a single sermon*. The preacher can trace out the many different ways the Bible picks up a theme at many different times and then show the common denominator in text after text. The result is that the reader is struck by a proper sense of the profound unity of Scripture, seen against a backdrop that stretches across many different time periods and genres of Scripture.

Someone may argue at this point that one can take what topical preaching does well and infuse it into expository preaching to make it more robust. I completely agree. One could argue that exposure to many years of expository preaching can have the same benefits: a profound sense of the unity of Scripture and the breadth and balance of the Bible. Again, I completely agree. All I am stressing here is that topical preaching accomplishes those things best in a *single sermon*. Topical preaching is a better medium for taking what could be said in many expository sermons and then making it more accessible by putting it in *one place*.

For example, John Piper's last preaching series as pastor for preaching and vision at Bethlehem Baptist Church was a series on theological distinctives. This excellent series covered theological themes that had been trumpeted at Bethlehem for thirty years. The series was topical in arrangement, and the sermons were a mix of topical and expository in method.

THE WEAKNESSES OF TOPICAL PREACHING

What are some of the weaknesses of topical preaching? First, topical preaching typically does not present enough of the evidence to show that one has conducted a close reading of all the texts touched on in a sermon. Therefore, the hearer is required to assume that the preacher has done his exegetical homework. The hearer has to give the preacher the benefit of the doubt. The person in the pew may have access to the generalities found on the surface of texts scanned quickly in succession, but he or she does not have the benefit of entering into the depths of the textual world with all of its intricacies.

Second, topical preaching tasks the preacher (or someone else) with the burden of picking the topic and the substance of the sermon. Picking a topic requires a rationale for choosing one topic over another. How do you discern which topic should come next? Does God tell the preacher during the week? Do circumstances dictate which topic seems most pressing?

The burden of picking the topic may even lead to suspicion. The person in the pew may begin to wonder why a given topic was chosen. As I mentioned in the last chapter, people may begin to wonder if the pastor chose to preach on divorce because of some circumstance in the church.

After the topic is chosen, the question becomes which passage or passages the preacher should read. How much should the preacher say about each one? The question of objective criteria for preaching also comes into view. How do you know whether you got a topical sermon right? How do you know whether you have strung the right texts together or struck the right balance when covering them all? In other words, the subjective element is very high when it comes to discerning what topic to talk about and what to say about that topic.

These weaknesses do not imply that topical preaching is a curse rather than a blessing for a church. I could make an argument that the strengths outweigh the weaknesses. In fact, I do make that argument, but only when topical preaching is *occasional*. When topical preaching becomes a more prominent feature of a church, these weaknesses start to make topical preaching more of a curse than a blessing. Topical preaching will hurt a church to the degree that it becomes the main mode of preaching or becomes a permanent feature of any given church.

What happens when topical preaching becomes a prominent or permanent piece in the church? Again, I could mention many things. Let me give what I think is the most decisive argument against topical preaching as the main mode of preaching. *A topical approach to preaching leads to a topical approach to Scripture.* Topical preaching from the pastor cultivates topical thinking for the person in the pew. The reason for this is simple: people learn how to read their Bibles from their pastor.

This principle came home to me in a fresh way when I became a Bible professor. I noticed that upperclassmen would lead verse-by-verse Bible studies in a way that mirrored how they learned to study Scripture in their classes. However, freshman students majoring in biblical studies would lead Bible studies in a way that mirrored how they learned to study the Bible in their churches. The results were strikingly different.

The freshman students would invariably take a text as a starting point just like the other students, but that is where the similarities ceased. After reading the text, the freshmen would quickly leave it in the interests of seeing what the rest of Scripture had to say about the topic they found in that text. The next week they would use the next text to find the next topic, but we would never get around to looking at any given text in its context.

Therefore, a class could be touted as a verse-by-verse Bible study on the book of Philippians, but *each verse* in a given week only provided the leader with the *next topic* to look up in the rest of Scripture. The result was that we never really got to hear the message of Philippians. We focused rather on what the Bible had to say about the gospel or Jesus or humility or joy or peace, depending on what topic the student found in that week's text.

This pattern became pronounced enough that I began to wonder where all of the freshman students learned to study the Bible in this way. I found the answer only when I noticed that this same pattern was what has prevailed in Sunday school classes as well. The answer became clear. Students and Sunday school teachers were doing what they learned to do from the preaching of their pastors.

CONCLUSION

The Bible does not contain the phrase *expository preaching*, but I believe with all my heart that expository preaching is the best fit for the biblical concept of preaching. The Bible itself commends expository preaching. The last three chapters have attempted to show that other systematic truths from Scripture support expository preaching.

My main point in this chapter can be stated simply: a preaching ministry with a steady diet of expository preaching is the best strategy for the long-term health of the body of Christ. Therefore, expository preaching should have pride of place in the regular rhythm of congregational life. I affirm that preachers can hold up the primacy of expository preaching without denouncing or demonizing topical preaching.

PART FIVE

CONCLUSIONS AND APPLICATIONS

23

STEWARDSHIP OF
THE WORD TODAY

And what manner of men will they be? Men mighty in the
Scriptures, their lives dominated by a sense of the greatness,
the majesty and holiness of God, and their minds and hearts
aglow with the great truths of the doctrines of grace. . . .
They will be men who will preach with broken hearts and
tear-filled eyes, and upon whose ministries God will grant
an extraordinary effusion of the Holy Spirit, and who will
witness "signs and wonders following" in the transformation
of multitudes of human lives.

George Whitefield

WORDSMITHS OR WORD STEWARDS?

In this chapter, I will suggest some ways we can be good stewards of
the fruit of this study. I will frontload the discussion of application by
focusing on some of the dangers I am trying to avoid and some of the
treasured things that I am trying to protect. One application involves
a clarification of why there is a danger in saying that a preacher is a
"wordsmith."

When most people say that preachers are wordsmiths, they mean
that preaching is largely a word-based endeavor. The term is used *for*
preachers and *by* preachers in reference to themselves. I have no strong
objection to the term *wordsmith* if I am allowed to define it, but that
is precisely one of the problems: it is a concept easy to abuse if not
defined properly. I prefer "word steward" because it is less likely to be
abused or misunderstood.

Let me explain. Preachers are *not* wordsmiths in a way that makes them the source of the words. Preachers must never lose sight of the fact that in the one great distinction between the created universe and the Creator, they are on *this* side of the divide as his creatures. Therefore, preachers are not creators of words, but stewards of *the* Creator's words.

Stated differently, if a preacher is a herald, it is important to stress that he does not herald his own words. Even though the word *herald* implies that someone has sent the preacher with a specified message to herald, the word *steward* makes that implied meaning explicit. It is not enough to say that a preacher is a herald of God's word. A preacher must first be a faithful steward of God's word in order to be a herald of it. Therefore, as creatures and not Creator, preachers are stewards and heralds of the Creator's words. God's words alone give life. The faithful pastor tethers himself to God's life-giving word as both a steward and a herald.

This focus on stewarding God's word means that the term *wordsmith* is not an apt description for a preacher if connotations of creativity, cleverness, and artistic license dominate it. Many a good book has suffered at the hands of a movie maker's "artistic license" that does not stay true to what made the book good in the first place. In the same way, many a biblical text has suffered at the hands of a preacher's "artistic license" that is not faithful to God's intent for the text. God's word does not need artistic license to improve upon it. I would like to shout that last line for emphasis, but I will settle for restating it: *God does not need us to improve his word. Our part is to give the text a voice, not a makeover.*

In this vein, it is stirring to all true stewards of Scripture to see the degree to which the psalmist celebrates the majestic beauty and manifold perfection of God's word:

> The law of the LORD is perfect,
>   reviving the soul;
> the testimony of the LORD is sure,
>   making wise the simple;
> the precepts of the LORD are right,
>   rejoicing the heart;
> the commandment of the LORD is pure,
>   enlightening the eyes;

the fear of the LORD is clean,
    enduring forever;
the rules of the LORD are true,
    and righteous altogether.
More to be desired are they than gold,
    even much fine gold;
sweeter also than honey
    and drippings of the honeycomb. (Ps. 19:7–10)

In my experience, too many people believe that making God's word real takes creative license or a flamboyant personality. That is simply not true. In fact, the very "word of the cross" thing we preach stands in opposition to these tendencies (cf. Paul's overall argument in 1 Corinthians 1–2). Many efforts to preach boil down to man-centered attempts to do something in the flesh that only God can do by his Spirit. Preachers must put their faith in the power of God's word, not in their ability to make something drab into something attractive and appealing. God's word is living and active, not drab.

MAKING MUCH OF CHRIST OR SELF?

A second danger involves a plague that can quickly sweep through the ranks of God's preachers. Pastoral ministry is already plagued enough by attraction to larger-than-life personas and the drive to become a "celebrity" pastor. Personality is not a bad thing in and of itself. True preaching involves both truth and personality (or as Phillips Brooks famously said, preaching is proclaiming "truth through personality").[1] My concern is thus not to mute personality, but to exalt truth because I believe that the balance of power has shifted in our day away from a focus on truth to a focus on the preacher's personality. Pastors as word stewards make it their sole ambition to make much of Christ with his entrusted word. We do not use his word to make much of ourselves through our words.

Putting the stress on the truth means that Christ, and not the preacher, will be exalted. This principle shines through in an illus-

---

[1] Phillips Brooks, *The Joy of Preaching* (Grand Rapids: Kregel, 1989), 26. The actual quote is, "Preaching is the bringing of truth through personality." On the previous page Brooks provided a more formal definition: "*Preaching is the communication of truth by man to men*" (his italics). He boils this definition down to its two constituent parts or "essential elements," namely, "truth and personality." He provides helpful examples of things that would not pass as preaching because they lack either truth or personality (25).

tration that I read recently. Jonathan Leeman shares the story of the different reactions people had after hearing Joseph Parker and Charles Spurgeon. Upon hearing Parker preach, they exclaimed, "I do declare, it must be said, for there is no doubt, that Joseph Parker is the greatest preacher that ever there was!" On hearing Spurgeon, they said, "I do declare, it must be said, for there is no doubt, that Jesus Christ is the greatest Savior that there ever was!"[2] This latter response is surely the ambition and hope of true preaching: to make much of Christ.

There is also a flip side of wanting to make much of Christ: taking offense when Christ is defamed. We can even go a step further. How do we respond when we see things that do not conform to Scripture? When people seek to dethrone Christ and to defame him, are you okay with them? In Scripture, men of faith and men of the word were not okay with many things they saw. Caleb tore his clothes when the other spies thought the giants were greater than God. Caleb reminded the Israelites that God's promise was true concerning the goodness of the land, and so his promise would certainly be true and good concerning their entering the land. The giants would just be bread to them—God's people should not fear (Num. 13:26–14:9)!

Likewise, David was offended that an uncircumcised Philistine giant was taunting the armies of the living God (1 Sam. 17:26). David said:

> You come to me with a sword and with a spear and with a javelin, but I come to you in the name of the LORD of hosts, the God of the armies of Israel, whom you have defied. This day the LORD will deliver you into my hand, and I will strike you down and cut off your head. And I will give the dead bodies of the host of the Philistines this day to the birds of the air and to the wild beasts of the earth, that all the earth may know that there is a God in Israel, and that all this assembly may know that the LORD saves not with sword and spear. For the battle is the LORD's, and he will give you into our hand. (1 Sam. 17:45–47)

So too, Paul's spirit was provoked as he saw the city of Athens full of idols (Acts 17:22). This deep offense at the defaming of God's name led him to stand up and proclaim that the God who made heaven and

---

[2] Jonathan Leeman, *Reverberation: How God's Word Brings Light, Freedom, and Action to His People* (Chicago: Moody, 2011), 124.

earth does not live in temples built by hands, and he is not served by human hands as if he needed anything—for he himself gives all people life and breath and everything else (17:24–25).

This sense of both faith in the unseen and offense at the seen moved Caleb, David, Paul, and many others in Scripture to action. Does faith in the unseen and grief at the seen move you to speak and act? Can you say with Henry Martyn: "I could not endure an existence if Jesus was not glorified;—it would be hell to me."[3] That our very own sinful pride would contend with God for his supremacy should also be hell to us. We seek an existence where God's glory is seen and experienced fully. We can't endure anything less! We will move forward in preaching the gospel to all the nations when the powerful wind of God's word is the driving force that fills up our gospel sails.

OTHER CONCLUSIONS AND APPLICATIONS

This whole-Bible biblical theology of preaching has shown us several realities closely tied to the central concern of making much of Christ in his word. The first such reality is the prominence that Scripture gives to the life-giving, life-sustaining power of the word. The canon opens with a dazzling display of the life-giving power of the word, and the rest of the canon continues in that same vein as we constantly see how God's word gives and sustains life. By the word of the Lord everything was made. Man does not live by bread alone but by every word that comes from the mouth of the Lord. *The ministry of the word must have pride of place in the church of Jesus Christ.*

Other ministries in the church matter—a lot. But the ministry of the word must be primary precisely because the word of God *gives life and sustains life.* Frankly, I am not sure why this point is so noticeably absent from most church-growth literature. The emphasis in Scripture suggests that we make it the centerpiece of church growth. God has always created his people by his word, and he always will do so.[4] We live by every word that comes from the mouth of the Lord.

Therefore, the application for us is to believe in the unparalleled

---

[3] Henry Martyn, journal entry, January 16, 1812, quoted in *Above Every Name* (blog), September 5, 2011, http://aboveeveryname.blogspot.com/2011/09/i-could-not-endure-existence.html.
[4] See the excellent articulation of this scriptural theme in Mark Dever, *Nine Marks of a Healthy Church* (Wheaton, IL: Crossway, 2004), 29.

authority and power of the word of God. If we believe these things about Scripture, then the only proper response is to soak ourselves in Scripture. Do not hover above Scripture. Dive into its depths. Discover its great and glorious truths for yourself. Great truths create great preachers—not the other way around. Are you more confirmed in your belief that God's word does God's work so that you are more committed to soak yourself in Scripture and preach Scripture in a way that your people will be soaked in Scripture and drenched in God's mercy?

Second, the prominent focus on God's words of life helps explain the important part played by stewards and heralds in Scripture. God entrusts his life-giving word to individuals and groups that must in turn steward and herald that word.

The application should not escape us: we must follow the instruction that comes from the example of these stewards. Every example of stewarding God's speech in Scripture becomes a useful model with helpful lessons for expositional preaching, not just texts that use "preaching" words. Faithful stewards like Moses and Ezra have much to teach us, not just "preachers" like Peter and Paul. Will you scour the Scriptures for the example and instruction of stewards and heralds who have gone before?

Third, this survey has shown that the Lord Jesus Christ is both the model and the object of our stewardship. Stewarding the word means stewarding Christ to whom all the Scriptures point. Stewarding the word also means following the model of Christ, the perfect and preeminent steward and herald of the Father's word.

Christ spoke only what the Father gave him to speak and followed the Father's word with complete faithfulness. Jesus is the very incarnation of the word so that he is called the Word become flesh. Many people spoke from God in the past, but in these last days God has spoken by his Son.

Therefore, we are to treasure the Lord Jesus Christ as the model and object of our stewardship. Perhaps more people will appreciate the profound word-based ministry of our Lord that was announced in the Old Testament and fulfilled in the New. We can always strive to preach the Savior better, but we could never preach a better Savior. Remember to preach the cross to yourself first before preaching it to others. Stand amazed that Jesus swallowed up the wrath of God as your substitute. Do you see more of the stunning glory of God in the face of Christ that causes your heart to soar with wonder and worship?

Fourth, this study has shown the vital importance of studying the Scriptures in order to rightly handle them. Stewarded speech requires the faithful transmission of God's message to an intended audience through God's appointed steward. The further removed the audience is from the original message, the more the steward is called to study the message in order to ensure that he will be "rightly handling" (2 Tim. 2:15) it so that hearers will rightly understand it. We have seen this call to study in both Testaments through stewards such as Ezra and Timothy, and we have stressed that the call to study is especially important when historical distance exists between the original text and the contemporary hearers.

Therefore, will you come away from this survey of Scripture more committed than ever to the discipline of study to help your audience bridge the gap between the details of the text and the details of their lives?

Fifth, the Scriptures highlight the terrible dangers of false teaching. Stewards and heralds must themselves guard against false teaching, and they must also rebuke false teaching sharply while remaining gentle toward those who oppose us. The opposite of "rightly handling" the Scriptures is twisting the Scriptures, and the result is destruction. Peter reminds us that people were guilty of distorting Paul's letters as well as the rest of the Scriptures: "There are some things in them that are hard to understand, which the ignorant and unstable twist to their own destruction, as they do the other Scriptures" (2 Pet. 3:16). Paul charges Timothy in the same way because the salvation of Timothy and his hearers is on the line: "Keep a close watch on yourself and on the teaching. Persist in this, for by so doing you will save both yourself and your hearers" (1 Tim. 4:16). What a clarion call to study as a servant of the word who seeks to teach it without distortion!

Will you commit to watch your doctrine closely and rebuke false teaching sharply so that you will save both yourself and your hearers?

Sixth, this survey has also shown how much the manner of the message matters! Paul states that his preaching of the message of the

308 Conclusions and Applications

cross was not in persuasive words of wisdom, but that his presence with them was in weakness, fear, and much trembling (1 Cor. 2:3). He preached in what we could call a "weak" manner that was a reflection of his message: the apparent "weakness" of the cross. He preached in a way that eschewed the "power" of human wisdom and eloquence. Nothing contradicts the message of the cross more than a manner that takes pride in highlighting human attainments of speech. Such a manner of preaching attempts to jump squarely in front of the cross and say, "Look at me and my lofty speech and wisdom" (see 2:1), rather than hide behind the cross in a way that says, "I decided to know nothing among you except Jesus Christ and him crucified" (2:2).

Paul worked hard to hide himself behind the cross so that the message of Christ would be on display because he wanted to ensure that God's power was on display in his preaching ("demonstration of the Spirit and power"), not his own wisdom and eloquence. This display of God's presence and power in Paul's preaching would facilitate a faith that rested in the power of God, not the wisdom of man (1 Cor. 2:5).

Will you devote yourself to preach in such a way that your message and manner match?

Seventh, this study has also shown that the personality of the preacher matters. Preachers give the text a voice and deliver God's truth through personality. Preaching God's word does not eliminate the personality of the preacher; God sanctifies the preacher's personality by setting the preacher apart for his purposes. The sheer diversity and variety of stewards throughout Scripture warns us against a "cookie cutter" kind of preacher.

D. A. Carson saw this principle of diversity modeled in a healthy way at the Gospel Coalition Conference in 2009, when six gifted yet different expositors preached through 2 Timothy. Fidelity to the text and diversity of styles are not mutually exclusive, but healthy and helpful to see. Carson observes, "Someone has said that if you listen to only one preacher all the time, you will become a clone; if you listen to two, you will become confused; if you listen to many, you are on the threshold of becoming wise and of growing into your own style."[5]

---

[5] D. A. Carson, preface to *Entrusted with the Gospel: Pastoral Expositions of 2 Timothy*, ed. D. A. Carson (Wheaton, IL: Crossway, 2010), 9–10.

Therefore, will you commit to say, "By the grace of God I am what I am," so that you do not endlessly try to impersonate someone else. You will not be true to either the text or God if you are not true to yourself as uniquely made and called by God for his purposes and his glory.

One can learn all of the material in this book well enough to argue for what preaching is, but miss one crucial argument, with which I conclude.

THE PROOF IS IN THE PUDDING

I have labored to present a comprehensive and cumulative argument from Scripture for expository preaching. However, I do not want to give the impression that well-placed arguments for expositional preaching will win the day alone. Do not just make arguments; *be an argument*. In other words, do not merely give arguments for expositional preaching. Let your preaching itself be an argument—indeed, the best argument—for expositional preaching.

John Piper has stated that the main reason why so many people say so many "minimizing and foolish things about preaching" is that "they have never heard true preaching; they have no basis for judgment about the usefulness of true preaching."[6]

Powerful, life-giving preaching has always been and will always be the best argument for preaching. My prayer is that this book will help preachers in the pulpit and people in the pew catch the stunning vision for preaching found in Scripture. This vision has not really been understood until it is also celebrated. True seeing in this case is savoring, or it is not seeing. That is why preaching practiced truly is always the best argument for true preaching. So let it be, Lord!

THE BURDEN OF PREACHING AND THE BURDEN BEARER

This book will fail to empower preaching if the reader regards these preaching principles as a burden piled on the preacher's back and growing heavier and heavier with every chapter. Our preaching will not change because we have stored up a series of steps or principles for effective preaching.

---

[6]John Piper, "Preaching as Expository Exultation," in Mark Dever et al., *Preaching the Cross* (Wheaton, IL: Crossway, 2007), 105.

Preaching is a high calling. It is not just difficult; it is impossible with man. Thankfully, God does not call the equipped; he equips the called. We do not preach ourselves (2 Cor. 4:5) or preach by ourselves. We preach Christ (4:5) by the demonstration of power and the Spirit (1 Cor. 2:4).

Therefore, preaching comes from a heart that savors the gospel. Sinners can be heralds because Jesus is more than the perfect bearer of good news; he is the perfect Lamb of God who bore *our sins* in his body on the tree. Sinners can be stewards and heralds because he bore our very failures to steward and herald the word.

Jesus carries *us*, not just our burden to preach. Undershepherds can be truly good shepherds only when they focus on the fact that they are sheep carried by *the* Good Shepherd. Luther understood this sweet gospel dynamic very well:

> He demands nothing of me, neither does He drive me on; He does not threaten, neither does He frighten me, but He shows me His sweet grace, and lowers Himself to me, even beneath me, and takes me upon Himself so that I now lie on His back and am carried by Him. . . . He supports me and upholds me that I cannot be lost so long as I remain His lamb.[7]

Let the experience of biblical truth capture your heart and captivate your preaching. Preach in the joy of forgiven sin; preach in the joy of our names being written in the book of life. Preach in awe of his continued mercy. Preach in the certainty that no one can snatch Jesus's sheep out of his hands. Preach in the certainty that the God who starts a good work always finishes what he begins (Phil. 1:6). Preach in the power of the resurrection (1 Cor. 15:1–3) knowing that in the Lord our labor is not in vain (15:56).

Preach in celebration that God's life-giving word brings restoration and does not return to him void (Isaiah 55). Preach in the power that he sends from on high the Holy Spirit to empower our witness (Luke 24; Acts 1). Preach in the hope of his ministry of intercession before the throne of God above (Rom. 8:34). Preach in the promise of his climactic return to restore all things (2 Peter 3). Preach in the

---

[7] Martin Luther, *Day by Day We Magnify Thee: Daily Readings* (Philadelphia: Fortress, 1982), 182.

certainty of his purpose to fill the earth with the knowledge of his glory (Habakkuk 2).

These are the truths we preach. Do you believe them? C. H. Spurgeon gives a gripping illustration concerning the certainty of the truth and the inevitability of the turning of the tide. The tide will turn. The truth will prevail. All true preaching rests on this bedrock.

> You never met an old salt, down by the sea, who was in trouble because the tide had been ebbing out for hours. No! He waits confidently for the turn of the tide, and it comes in due time. Yonder rock has been uncovered during the last half-hour, and if the sea continues to ebb out for weeks, there will be no water in the English Channel, and the French will walk over from Cherbourg. Nobody talks in that childish way, for such an ebb will never come. Nor will we speak as though the gospel would be routed, and eternal truth driven out of the land. We serve an almighty Master. . . . If our Lord does but stamp His foot, He can win for Himself all the nations of the earth against heathenism, and Mohammedanism, and Agnosticism, and Modern-thought, and every other foul error. Who is he that can harm us if we follow Jesus? How can His cause be defeated? At His will, converts will flock to His truth as numerous as the sands of the sea. . . . Wherefore be of good courage, and go on your way singing:
>
> > The winds of hell have blown
> > The world its hate hath shown,
> > Yet it is not o'erthrown.
> > Hallelujah for the Cross!
> > It shall never suffer loss!
> > The Lord of hosts is with us,
> > the God of Jacob is our refuge.[8]

George Whitefield has long been a hero of mine. His words offer a stirring picture for what it would mean for preachers to be captured by the truths they preach and thus for preachers to be an argument and not just to give arguments for preaching:

> Yea . . . that we shall see the great Head of the Church once more . . . raise up unto Himself certain young men whom He may use in this

---

[8] C. H. Spurgeon, *An All-Round Ministry* (Edinburgh: Banner of Truth, 1960), 395–96.

glorious employ. And what manner of men will they be? Men mighty in the Scriptures, their lives dominated by a sense of the greatness, the majesty and holiness of God, and their minds and hearts aglow with the great truths of the doctrines of grace. They will be men who have learned what it is to die to self, to human aims and personal ambitions; men who are willing to be "fools for Christ's sake," who will bear reproach and falsehood, who will labor and suffer, and whose supreme desire will be, not to gain earth's accolades, but to win the Master's approbation when they appear before His awesome judgment seat. They will be men who will preach with broken hearts and tear-filled eyes, and upon whose ministries God will grant an extraordinary effusion of the Holy Spirit, and who will witness "signs and wonders following" in the transformation of multitudes of human lives.[9]

A PRAYER FOR STEWARDS AND HERALDS OF THE WORD

Father, all things are possible with you. Take ownership of the pulpit by your word and turn it into the place where you demonstrably reign. In places where the pulpit has been usurped by entertainment and ear-tickling error, let the word of God run and be glorified. Let the preaching of men mighty in the Scriptures land on people once more with the force of electric shock by the power of your Spirit. Let their hearts' cry be to make much of Christ, whether by life or by death and to count their lives of no value except to finish the calling given by our Lord Jesus Christ to testify to the gospel of His grace. Let their battle cry be,

"Not to us, O LORD, not to us, but to your name give glory,
for the sake of your steadfast love and your faithfulness!"
(Ps. 115:1)

In Jesus's name,
Amen.

---

[9] Arnold Dallimore, *George Whitefield*, vol. 1 (Edinburgh: Banner of Truth, 1970), 16.

Appendix 1

THE HEART BEHIND
THE BOOK

Douglas Wilson has said that he writes in order to make the voices in his head go away. I am writing in a similar vein. I am haunted by the nagging realization that there is an identity crisis concerning preaching today. And I want it to go away.

Think about preaching for a moment. Imagine entering a typical church sanctuary. What do you see? Some may gaze around at the rows and rows of pews or look up and see stained-glass windows, lights, and a balcony, but sooner or later the focus turns to the front of the sanctuary. There, in a central location, is "the pulpit." Forget for the moment the fact that some churches have large hardwood pulpits, some have skinny, sleek pulpits of glass, and others have something in between. The burning question is, what comes to your mind when you see the pulpit? That is, what does it signify or represent? One might expect a wide variety of answers to this question. The pulpit has become a confusing symbol for many today.

I started writing this book when I was teaching a class on preaching. It quickly dawned on me that my students did not have a clear grasp of what preaching was, and so they had an even less clear grasp on how to do it. And they all expected me to have the answers. This "moment of truth" caused me to enter my study on my knees more than ever before because I began to see more clearly what was at stake.

We do not really start to think hard until we are faced with a difficult problem. My problem was that I thought I knew what preaching was because I had had many wonderful examples set before me and I had taken several classes on preaching. But now I realized that I was going to have to grade preaching! Questions began to flood my mind. Did I really know what preaching is—well enough to define it, explain it, and defend it from Scripture? What standard of assessment should I adopt? Would I know true preaching if I heard it or saw it when trying to grade my students' attempts at preaching? My high view of preaching would not let me wing it and drum up any old answers to my questions; too much was at stake. I needed a book like this one. I could not find one, and so I tried to write it.

I once read a quote by Matthew Simpson about the work of the preacher and have never forgotten it:

> His throne is the pulpit; he stands in Christ's stead; his message is the word of God; around him are immortal souls; the Savior, unseen, is beside him; the Holy Spirit broods over the congregation; angels gaze upon the scene, and heaven and hell await the issue. What associations and what vast responsibility!"[1]

How vast indeed! Who would dare claim to have mastered this task? I have not moved beyond the status of a novice who needs help.

I wrote this book also because I saw not only my own need, but also the needs of others. I have a deep-seated concern that preachers no longer tremble at the task of preaching and do not devote the time necessary for true preaching to flourish. Too many pastors get their sermons from the Internet. As a member of Bethlehem Baptist Church, I have heard John Piper preach many times. It was striking to hear some of those same sermons preached in other pulpits while I was away from Bethlehem, delivered by preachers who did not acknowledge Piper as the source. I know that the people did not come to church on those occasions wondering whether their pastors had heard from John Piper. They wanted to know whether their pastors had heard from God.

But my concern is not only with sermons downloaded from the Internet. Many faithful pastors I know try to devote time to sermon preparation, but fight a losing battle because their other responsibili-

---

[1]Quoted in Haddon W. Robinson, *Biblical Preaching: The Development and Delivery of Expository Messages* (Grand Rapids: Baker, 1980), 12.

ties eat away at their time and energy for preaching. I can certainly relate to this feeling. At one point in a church I pastored, I taught the youth as the youth leader for the Sunday school hour (hat #1). After Sunday school, the church service started and I led worship (hat #2). Then I preached the sermon (hat #3). Later in the day, after lunch, I led the small-group ministry (hat #4). These were just my Sunday hats! Needless to say, pastors have a hard time fulfilling their calling to equip the saints to do the work of the ministry (Eph. 4:12) when they spend so much of their time doing the work of the ministry themselves.

Busy, overworked pastors grow disillusioned and find it difficult to persevere in expository preaching. Furthermore, many of their congregations cannot articulate why expository preaching is important and why their pastors should devote so much time to study. The identity crisis is felt in both pulpit and pew. So, I wrote this book also with the aim of empowering expositors to persevere in expository preaching by knowing what it is and how to explain it to their congregations. I also want people who serve on pastoral search committees to know how to assess preaching candidates.

In highlighting the importance of preaching, I do not want to downplay the importance of other ministries in the church. However, I think the pulpit must be preeminent among the ministries of the church because the pulpit informs and empowers all of the other ministries. The ministry of the word must be primary because the word of God is life-giving. The life-giving grace of the ministry of the word has a clarifying and sustaining impact on the other ministries of the church. God always has created and always will create his people by his word. In this regard, Martyn Lloyd-Jones points out that a revival of true preaching has been the defining mark of every reformation and revival in church history.[2]

Therefore, I agree with Lloyd-Jones that true preaching is "the most urgent need in the Christian Church" and therefore "the greatest need of the world also."[3] Jesus promised to build his church (Matt. 16:18). He has built it and will continue to build it *primarily* (though by no means exclusively) through the preaching of the gospel (1 Cor. 1:21).

---

[2] D. Martyn Lloyd-Jones, *Preaching and Preachers* (Grand Rapids: Zondervan, 1971), 24–25.
[3] Ibid., 9.

Appendix 2

HOW THIS BOOK
IS DIFFERENT

God has blessed the church with *many* great books on preaching. I did not write this book because those books are wrong. I wrote it because few have taken the time to explore the beautifully balanced bedrock of what the Bible says about preaching. We cannot afford to be narrow or cut corners on something so foundational to the life of the church. So, I regard many books on preaching not as wrong but as incomplete.[1]

One of the reasons they are incomplete is that they focus narrowly on specific words for "preaching" instead of the wider conceptual category to which preaching belongs: the ministry of the word. This narrow approach means that many preaching books make a case for a right view of preaching based on a too-shallow foundation of word studies and proof-texting. Proof-texting also fails to make a necessary clarification between two kinds of preaching: preaching *in Scripture* and today's preaching *from Scripture*. I am convinced that many people confuse these categories or jump from one to the other too quickly.

You may wonder what is wrong with word studies and proof-texting. Concerning word studies, reducing preaching to what can be gleaned from word studies on "preaching words" can often result

---

[1] I am sympathetic about why they are incomplete. Because these books try to do so much, they allot only limited space to surveying what the whole Bible says about preaching. At the end of the day, however, this approach falls short because it leaves preaching with a flimsy foundation.

in committing the "word equals concept" fallacy. The flawed premise here is that the concept of preaching shows up only when the words for preaching are present.

However, the concept of preaching in Scripture is not drawn solely from passages that contain specific words for preaching, such as "herald" (*kērussō*) or "preach good news" (*euangelizō*). A few moments of reflection show how unhelpful this type of study is. These two words do not show up in John's Gospel or epistles. Does this mean that John has nothing to say about preaching?

This approach to studying preaching is analogous to claiming that the concept of love shows up only when words for love appear. If that is the case, then the passion narratives in Matthew, Mark, and Luke do not talk about the love of God because they do not contain any words for love in their accounts of Jesus's death.[2] This reading of the passion narratives is the polar opposite of the approach taken by Paul, who looks at the cross as the place where God demonstrated his "love" for us (Rom. 5:8).

Concerning proof-texting (supporting a point by only referring to a text without further explanation), there is nothing wrong with using a text to serve as a summary of preaching. A three-word phrase such as "preach the word" (2 Tim. 4:2) is an effective way to encapsulate the calling of a preacher. However, if one relies on proof-texting too much, preaching loses its cumulative, holistic biblical meaning, and becomes vulnerable to those who call preaching into question.

In other words, many preaching books take too many shortcuts in an attempt to explain the biblical view of preaching. Shortcuts are not necessarily sinful. When you travel, sometimes a shortcut is the fastest way to get from where you are to where you need to go. But when you are building, sometimes a shortcut is simply a way to cut corners. In the end, cutting corners can create something that will not stand the test of time. My aim is to empower expositors to persevere in preach-

---

[2] My former book shows how many have committed this fallacy when it comes to the concept of covenant in Paul's writings. Some say that the concept appears only in the eight places where Paul uses the word translated "covenant." I try to show what a more expansive and linguistically sensitive approach would look like. See Jason C. Meyer, *The End of the Law: Mosaic Covenant in Pauline Theology* (Nashville: B&H, 2009). Another illustration of this principle is the cross. The concept of the cross cannot be confined to passages that use the phrase *cross of Christ* or the terms *cross* or *crucify*. Such a study falls short at multiple levels. It ignores other terms, such as *death, blood, nails, tree,* and *curse,* as well as a host of other descriptions derived from the wider context of Scripture.

ing the word. Perseverance in preaching requires a firm foundation that does not cut any corners.

Therefore, my concern is that these shortcuts treat the Bible as if it were a textbook on preaching, which it is not. God has not given us a manual or "how to" book on preaching. He has given us a story. If we are ever to understand preaching, we have to examine what it is and what role it has played within the contours of that story. Anything less poses the danger of using Scripture to construct our own message instead of receiving Scripture's message.

We need a holistic biblical theology that focuses not just on preaching, but also on the ministry of the word. What is biblical theology? Michael Lawrence helpfully says that it is a "theology that not only tries to systematically understand what the Bible teaches, but to do so in the context of the Bible's own progressively revealed and progressively developing storyline." Biblical theology looks at not only the "moral of the story, but the telling of the story, and how the very nature of its telling, its unfolding, shapes our understanding of its point."[3]

This clarifies what a biblical theology of the ministry of the word attempts to accomplish. Within the storyline of Scripture, we can unpack the concept of preaching in an organic way in direct relation to the unfolding of divine revelation. We must keep this vital relationship between the storyline of Scripture and the concept of preaching clearly in view or preaching will lose its biblical bearings and its center of gravity.

---

[3] Michael Lawrence, *Biblical Theology in the Life of the Church* (Wheaton, IL: Crossway, 2010), 26.

Appendix 3

A CRASH COURSE ON PREACHING BOOKS AVAILABLE TODAY

C. J. Mahaney has helpfully suggested that one way to fight pride is to identify grace in others.[1] This practice is fairly easy when it comes to examining preaching books. I have not tried to hide or minimize the influence that preaching books have had on my thinking. I hope that this somewhat lengthy survey of preaching books will offer substantial evidence of that claim.

Many books on preaching soar to heights of eloquence and descend to depths of insight that I will never reach. God has blessed many of these preacher-authors with spectacular gifts and stunning influence. Haddon W. Robinson says it well: "The literature of homiletics features the names of brilliant preachers and superior teachers. One should think twice—and twice again—before nominating himself to that company."[2]

Studying the history of preaching makes one feel like Augustine's successor, Eraclius. He stood up to preach in what had been Augustine's pulpit with the full knowledge that Augustine sat behind him in his bishop's throne. He was understandably unnerved and said, "The cricket chirps, the swan is silent."[3]

---

[1] C. J. Mahaney, *Humility: True Greatness* (Portland, OR: Multnomah, 2005), 97.
[2] Haddon W. Robinson, *Biblical Preaching: The Development and Delivery of Expository Messages* (Grand Rapids: Baker, 1980), 9.
[3] Quoted in Peter Brown, *Augustine of Hippo* (Berkeley, CA: University of California Press, 1969), 408.

Serving as John Piper's successor at Bethlehem Baptist Church certainly makes me feel like a cricket. That feeling increases exponentially when I factor in how many swans have sweetly sung in the history of the church. I want to be a good steward not only of the word of God, but also of the history of great preachers and preaching that he has given to the church.

It is my conviction that the most important question to ask preaching books is this: "What is preaching according to the Bible, and how and why is it done according to the canon of Scripture?" Therefore, this brief crash course on preaching books is especially attuned to those that give answers concerning what biblical preaching is.

At the risk of oversimplification, we could divide preaching books into four categories: (1) those on the history of preaching, (2) "how to" preaching books, (3) homiletics textbooks, and (4) books on the theology of preaching.[4] The first two categories do not directly address the substance of this study, while the second set of categories comes closer. Therefore, I will treat the first two categories only briefly.

BOOKS ON THE HISTORY OF PREACHING

Some books in the first category give an overview of the entire history of preaching,[5] while others examine the preaching of influential preachers.[6] Though books on the history of preaching do not directly address the question of what biblical preaching is, they usually include a chapter on Old Testament and New Testament preachers. David Larsen devotes about sixty pages of an 861-page book to Old Testament and New Testament preachers. E. C. Dargan asserts that modern preaching developed from three sources: ancient oratory,

---

[4] One very popular genre that I am not considering here is published sermons. These are numerous, and one can learn a great deal from them as model expositions, but they do not attempt to address what preaching is.

[5] Hughes Oliphant Old has perhaps done the most extensive work in this area. He has written a multivolume history of preaching. The first volume is excellent in examining the reading and preaching of Scripture in the biblical period and the early church. See *The Biblical Period*, vol. 1 of *The Reading and Preaching of the Scriptures in the Worship of the Christian Church* (Grand Rapids: Eerdmans, 1998). David L. Larsen has written perhaps the best short history of preaching, *The Company of Preachers: A History of Biblical Preaching from the Old Testament to the Modern Era* (Grand Rapids: Kregel, 1998).

[6] Steven J. Lawson, *The Expository Genius of John Calvin* (Reformation Trust, 2007); T. H. L. Parker, *Calvin's Preaching* (Louisville, KY: Westminster John Knox, 1992); Bruce Bickel, *Light and Heat: The Puritan View of the Pulpit* (Morgan, PA: Soli Deo Gloria, 1999); John Carrick, *The Preaching of Jonathan Edwards* (Carlisle, PA: Banner of Truth, 2008); Tony Sargent, *The Sacred Anointing: The Preaching of Dr. Martyn Lloyd-Jones* (Wheaton, IL: Crossway, 1994).

Hebrew prophecy, and the Christian gospel.[7] A notable exception to the dearth of information about preaching in biblical times is the multivolume study of Hughes Oliphant Old; the first volume covers the biblical period.[8]

"HOW TO" PREACHING BOOKS

The second category contains an assortment of "how to" books. Evangelical publishers pack the market with these useful books, which address topics such as the nuts and bolts of how to construct a sermon,[9] how to preach specific parts of Scripture,[10] how sermons can reach modern audiences more effectively,[11] and how to integrate different things into preaching.[12]

Once again, I want to heed my warning not to criticize someone for not saying everything or for failing to write a book that he did not set out to write. These preaching books have a limited focus and do not devote much space to asking what makes preaching biblical, but I would be the first to say that they are still very valuable. Time and time again they offer tremendous help for the task of preaching. Therefore, we should not seek to replace them, but we do need to supplement them because they come close to begging the question.

Historical studies of preaching may have a descriptive focus that

---

[7] Edwin Charles Dargan, *A History of Preaching*, vol. 2 (New York: George H. Doran, 1905), 14.

[8] Old, *The Biblical Period*.

[9] Dennis M. Cahill, *The Shape of Preaching: Theory and Practice in Sermon Design* (Grand Rapids: Baker, 2007).

[10] Sidney Greidanus has an excellent book on how to preach the Bible's varied genres, *The Modern Preacher and the Ancient Text: Interpreting and Preaching Biblical Literature* (Grand Rapids: Eerdmans, 1988), while others books focus on specific parts of Scripture. On preaching Christ from the Old Testament, see Graeme Goldsworthy, *Preaching the Whole Bible as Christian Scripture* (Grand Rapids: Eerdmans, 2000); Sidney Greidanus, *Preaching Christ from the Old Testament: A Contemporary Hermeneutical Method* (Grand Rapids: Eerdmans, 1999). Some books focus on preaching the Old Testament itself; see Scott M. Gibson, ed., *Preaching the Old Testament* (Grand Rapids: Baker, 2006). Others focus on preaching the Pauline Epistles; see Brad R. Braxton, *Preaching Paul* (Nashville: Abingdon, 2004). Others look at how to preach individual books; see Stanley M. Saunders, *Preaching the Gospel of Matthew: Proclaiming God's Presence* (Louisville, KY: Westminster John Knox, 2010); Craig L. Blomberg, *Preaching the Parables: From Responsible Interpretation to Powerful Proclamation* (Grand Rapids: Baker, 2004).

[11] See, for example, Craig A. Loscalzo, *Preaching Sermons That Connect: Effective Communication through Identification* (Downers Grove, IL: InterVarsity, 1992), and Calvin Miller, *Marketplace Preaching: How to Return the Sermon to Where It Belongs* (Grand Rapids: Baker, 1995). Miller makes the case that sermons used to be preached in the marketplace, not church buildings. He shows how preachers can craft relevant sermons that reach the marketplace by having a creative spirit, dynamic worship, contemporary form and style, language that conforms more to "television words" or "video vernacular," and a journalistic style that allows people to make up their own minds by avoiding "you must" kinds of statements.

[12] Topics here include how to bring out the link between preaching and leadership: Michael J. Quicke, *360-Degree Leadership: Preaching to Transform Congregations* (Grand Rapids: Baker, 2006); how to use rhetoric in preaching: Robert Stephen Reid, *The Four Voices of Preaching: Connecting Purpose and Identity behind the Pulpit* (Grand Rapids: Brazos, 2006); and how to involve the Holy Spirit: Arturo G. Azurdia III, *Spirit Empowered Preaching* (Ross-shire, Scotland: Christian Focus, 1998).

teaches what a certain historical figure thought about preaching, but we are still forced to ask the normative question as to whether or not that figure was right. Likewise, teaching people how to preach presupposes that one knows what preaching is and can define and defend it according to the Bible. How can one evaluate examples from the history of preaching or "how to" methods without a scriptural means of assessment? One simply begins to judge whether such books are "effective" or not. Was the preacher an effective preacher? Did a "how to" book offer effective help in a certain area?

This consideration brings us back to the need for a standard of assessment. What basis are we using to define what makes something effective? In other words, what makes an effect a good effect? The principles espoused in books on the history of preaching or in "how to" books are very difficult to confirm or falsify without a means of measuring how faithful they are to Scripture. We must first know *what something is* before we can really know *how to do it* or whether we have *succeeded in doing it.*

HOMILETICS TEXTBOOKS

By their very design, the preaching books in the second set of categories come closer to addressing what biblical preaching is than those in the first two categories. However, they still do so in a somewhat limited way.

Homiletical textbooks contain much "how to" information like the books in the second category, but they are much broader in the sense that they offer one-stop shopping for learning what preaching is and how to do it faithfully.[13]

THREE INFLUENTIAL OLDER BOOKS

Three older books have shaped generations of preachers in the history of the English language. The authors of these books are William Perkins, John Broadus, and Phillips Brooks.

Perkins wrote one of the earliest books on preaching. It was pub-

---

[13] Here I have in mind books such as Robinson, *Biblical Preaching*; Bryan Chapell, *Christ-Centered Preaching: Redeeming the Expository Sermon*, 2nd ed. (Grand Rapids: Baker, 2005); Jerry Vines and Jim Shaddix, *Power in the Pulpit: How to Prepare and Deliver Expository Sermons* (Chicago: Moody, 1999).

lished in Latin in 1592 and in English in 1606. His preaching itself had a significant impact on generations of preachers. Perkins believed in the "plain style" of preaching. Sinclair Ferguson, in the foreword of the reprint of Perkins's book, has an apt description of this form of preaching:

> The preaching portion, be it text or passage, was explained in its context; the doctrine, or central teaching of the passage was expounded clearly and concisely; and then careful application to the hearers followed in further explanation of the "uses." Thus the message of the Scriptures was brought home in personal and practical, as well as congregational and national applications to the hearers.[14]

Perkins argues that preaching (or prophesying) is "a solemn public utterance by the prophet," which is done "in the name of and on behalf of Christ," and which aims at the hearers being "called into the state of grace, and preserved in it."[15] This kind of preaching involves: (1) reading the text from the canonical Scriptures, (2) explaining it in the light of the Scriptures, (3) gathering profitable points of doctrine from the natural sense of the passage, and (4) applying the doctrines to the life and practice of the people in plain speech.[16] Perkins develops some expository principles in two chapters ("Expounding Scripture" [ch. 5] and "Rightly Handling the Word of God" [ch. 6]) and devotes two other chapters to application ("Use and Application" [ch. 7] and "Varieties of Application" [ch. 8]). The Puritans are justly famous for their extensive and rigorous application of the word in preaching, and Perkins's model is a good illustration of this commitment.

Broadus's magnum opus, *A Treatise on the Preparation and Delivery of Sermons*, has left an indelible imprint on the history of preaching.[17] Notice that Broadus's title suggests that preaching has two elements:

---

[14] Sinclair Ferguson, foreword to *The Art of Prophesying*, by William Perkins (Carlisle, PA: Banner of Truth, 1996), ix. Ferguson revised Perkins's volume for the Banner of Truth reprint and contributed the foreword. The Banner of Truth edition is a modernized collection of two books: *The Art of Prophesying* and *The Calling of the Ministry*.

[15] Perkins, *The Art of Prophesying*, 5, 7.

[16] Ibid., 79.

[17] The first printing came in the summer of 1870. In the school session of 1894–1895, Broadus asked E. C. Dargan to make suggestions for a revision of the book. Although Dargan began these suggestions, the two men were not to collaborate on the revision because Broadus died in 1895. Dargan completed the revision with the support of Broadus's family in 1898. Although the book has gone through many editions, I prefer the 1898 revision. All citations come from the 1898 edition.

the preparation of sermons and the delivery of sermons. In the introduction to the book, Broadus does not labor to define preaching as much as he seeks to describe it. He says that preaching is "the great appointed means of spreading the good news of salvation through Christ."[18] Though the printed page has done much good for the spread of the truth, it is no substitute for preaching. The description is moving and deserves to be quoted in full:

> When a man who is apt in teaching, whose soul is on fire with the truth which he trusts has saved him and hopes will save others, speaks to his fellow-men, face to face, eye to eye, and electric sympathies flash to and fro between him and his hearers, till they lift each other up, higher and higher, into the intensest thought, and the most impassioned emotion—higher and yet higher, till they are borne as on chariots of fire above the world,—there is a power to move men, to influence character, life, destiny, such as no printed page can ever possess.[19]

Broadus goes on to stress the importance of preaching not only to "convince the judgment, kindle the imagination, and move the feelings," but also "to give a powerful impulse to the will."[20] He then identifies four requisites for effective preaching on the part of the preacher: (1) piety, (2) natural gifts, (3) knowledge, and (4) skill.[21] The rest of the book is divided into five parts: (1) materials of preaching, (2) the arrangement of a sermon, (3) style, (4) delivery of sermons, and (5) conduct of public worship.

Brooks's *The Joy of Preaching* has also made a lasting contribution to preaching.[22] This book provides what Warren Wiersbe calls "perhaps the most famous definition of preaching found anywhere in American homiletical literature."[23] The definition came in the Lyman Beecher lectures on preaching at Yale University on January 11, 1877. There,

---

[18] John Broadus, *Preparation and Delivery of Sermons*, ed. E. C. Dargan (New York: Hodder and Stoughton, 1898), 2.

[19] Ibid.

[20] Ibid., 5. He also approvingly quotes Augustine's statement that the preacher should "make the truth plain, make it pleasing, make it moving." Ibid.

[21] Ibid., 7.

[22] Phillips Brooks, *The Joy of Preaching* (Grand Rapids: Kregel, 1989). All citations are from the Kregel edition, which features a foreword and biographical introduction by Warren Wiersbe.

[23] Ibid., 9.

Brooks defined preaching as "the communication of truth by man to men."[24] In *The Joy of Preaching*, Brooks further boils down this definition to its two constituent parts: "truth through personality."[25]

TWO SIGNIFICANT RECENT BOOKS

Two contemporary books on preaching in particular have made a significant impact on my thinking. Perhaps the one that has been most formative for me is D. Martyn Lloyd-Jones's book *Preaching and Preachers*, published in 1971, which originated in a series of lectures he delivered at Westminster Theological Seminary. In the preface, he claims that this series of lectures presented his understanding of "expository preaching." He says that many had asked him to give a lecture on expository preaching, but he believed it was impossible because "such a subject demanded a whole series of lectures because there was no magical formula that one could pass on to others."[26]

This book is so shaping because it passes on not a "magical formula" but a philosophy of preaching. From beginning to end, its sustained focus is on how we should think about preaching. Lloyd-Jones has practical advice on crafting the form of the sermon, using illustrations, and the like, but he always focuses the discussion on how to think about these things at the level of principle.

He lays great stress on the priority of preaching as the greatest need today. I especially like his emphasis on preaching as an encounter with God that cannot leave us unchanged.[27] He says that the preacher is the "mouthpiece of God," sent to "deliver the message of God."[28] Lloyd-Jones also draws a vital distinction between two elements in preaching: the sermon content and the sermon delivery.[29] The message must feature an address from the whole preacher to the listener as a whole person (not just the emotions or the intellect).

In terms of the sermon coming from the whole preacher, Lloyd-Jones excels at considering the importance of God's creating a preacher by his call, not by a homiletics class. He also reminds us that all of

---

[24] Ibid., 25.
[25] Ibid., 26.
[26] *Preaching and Preachers* (Grand Rapids: Zondervan, 1971), 3.
[27] Ibid., 56.
[28] Ibid., 53.
[29] Ibid.

life is sermon preparation, and one must devote at least as much attention to the preparation of the preacher as to the preparation of the message.

In terms of addressing the whole person, Lloyd-Jones says that "the hearer becomes involved and knows that he has been dealt with and addressed by God through the preacher. Something has taken place in him and in his experience, and it is going to affect the whole of his life."[30] For this reason, the preacher must leave space for the Spirit to move freely. The preacher must pursue the anointing of the Spirit and avoid an insensitivity to the Spirit that causes one to ignore the Spirit's promptings. This process of seeking the Spirit's power does not start when the sermon manuscript is complete; it must be the focus from the first moment of the preacher's preparations. Lloyd-Jones urges us to seek, expect, and yield to this power as the "supreme thing" and to "be content with nothing less."[31] Without this emphasis, there is "always a very real danger of our putting our faith in our sermon rather than in the Spirit."[32]

Another extremely useful book in this area is John R. W. Stott's *Between Two Worlds*.[33] The third chapter is an especially helpful look at five theological foundations that inform preaching (God, Scripture, church, pastorate, and preaching). The fourth chapter helpfully provides a contextual framework for preaching. Preaching builds a bridge between the preacher's biblical text and the preacher's contemporary congregation. The fifth chapter on the need for study is also excellent.

THREE IMPORTANT ESSAYS

Three short essays get to the heart of what preaching is. Perhaps the best one I have read comes from D. A. Carson. In a two-page discussion, he makes five observations concerning what preaching is. First, he provides an exceedingly helpful definition of preaching. He says that preaching is, in an important sense, a revelatory event because it is the "re-revelation" of what God revealed in the past in his word: "[Preachers'] aim is more than to explain the Bible, however important

---

[30] Ibid., 56.
[31] Ibid., 325.
[32] Ibid., 230.
[33] *Between Two Worlds: The Art of Preaching in the Twentieth Century* (Grand Rapids: Eerdmans, 1982).

that aim is. They want the proclamation of God's Word to be a revelatory event, a moment when God discloses himself afresh, a time when the people of God know that they have met with the living God."[34] This re-revelation is not a "subset of human oratory," because human eloquence is powerless to produce this "revelatory impact." Rather, "the Spirit of God must apply that Word deeply to the human heart" in order for this revelatory event to happen.

Carson then fills out his description of preaching with four more elements. Preaching is (1) expository, (2) heraldic, (3) a faithful representation of the "Master and his message," including a "passionate commitment to make the Word wound and heal, sing and sting," which, in turn, requires (4) studying the people to whom we preach.[35]

Mark Dever also has blessed preachers with a helpful discussion of preaching as the first of the nine marks of a healthy church.[36]

Finally, Graeme Goldsworthy has an excellent chapter concerning the meaning of preaching. Chapter 4 of his book *Preaching the Whole Bible as Christian Scripture* attempts to build a basic biblical theology of preaching.[37] He claims that the New Testament clearly demonstrates that preaching the gospel is "the primary means by which the church grew."[38] So what is the content of preaching: the gospel or the word of God?

Goldsworthy sees this as a false dichotomy. Preaching the gospel of Christ is proclaiming the word of God because the Bible is about Jesus from beginning to end. Goldsworthy claims that the gospel of Christ is the only proper starting point:

> The soundest methodological starting point for doing theology is the gospel since the person of Jesus is set forth as the final and fullest expression of God's revelation of his kingdom. Jesus is the goal and fulfillment of the whole Old Testament, and, as the embodiment of the truth of God, he is the interpretive key to the Bible.[39]

---

[34] D. A. Carson, "Challenges for the Twenty-first Century Pulpit," in *Preach the Word: Essays on Expository Preaching in Honor of R. Kent Hughes*, ed. Leland Ryken and Todd Wilson (Wheaton, IL: Crossway, 2007), 176.
[35] Ibid., 176–77.
[36] Mark E. Dever, *Nine Marks of a Healthy Church* (Wheaton, IL: Crossway, 2004).
[37] Goldsworthy, *Preaching the Whole Bible as Christian Scripture*, 31–45.
[38] Ibid., 32.
[39] Ibid., 33.

FIVE ADDITIONAL BOOKS

I should also highlight five other books that have shaped the so-called evangelical consensus for expository preaching. These books were written by Haddon W. Robinson, Jerry Vines and Jim Shaddix, John MacArthur, Sidney Greidanus, and Bryan Chapell.

First, evangelical expository preaching today owes much to Robinson's *Biblical Preaching*, which was published in 1980.[40] He defines expository preaching as "the communication of a biblical concept, derived from and transmitted through a historical, grammatical, literary study of a passage in its context, which the Holy Spirit first applies to the personality and experience of the preacher, then through him to his hearers."[41]

Robinson is especially well known for his stress on identifying the main point or the "big idea" of a passage. The preacher finds the main exegetical idea of the passage, then transposes it into a homiletical idea that states "the biblical concept in such a way that it accurately reflects the Bible and meaningfully relates to the congregation."[42] The terms "big idea" or "main point" are buzzwords in the preaching vernacular because of Robinson's influence. This concept of discovering the main exegetical idea is one part of Robinson's ten-step process for developing expository messages: (1) selecting the passage, (2) studying the passage, (3) discovering the exegetical idea, (4) analyzing the exegetical idea, (5) formulating the homiletical idea, (6) determining the sermon's purpose, (7) deciding how to accomplish this purpose, (8) outlining the sermon, (9) filling in the sermon outline, and (10) preparing the introduction and conclusion.

Second, Vines produced an influential book in 1985 titled *A Practical Guide to Sermon Preparation*.[43] Vines has been an influential voice among Southern Baptist preachers. His book received a new lease on life with the help of Shaddix.[44] They define preaching as "the oral communication of biblical truth by the Holy Spirit through a human

---

[40] A revised edition is also available: *Biblical Preaching: The Development and Delivery of Expository Messages*, 2nd ed. (Grand Rapids: Baker, 2001).

[41] Ibid., 30.

[42] Ibid., 100.

[43] Jerry Vines, *A Practical Guide to Sermon Preparation* (Chicago: Moody, 1985).

[44] Vines's *Practical Guide to Sermon Preparation* and his *Guide to Effective Sermon Delivery* (Chicago: Moody, 1986) are revised, expanded, and updated in Vines and Shaddix, *Power in the Pulpit*. Shaddix has also published his own book on preaching. See Jim Shaddix, *The Passion-Driven Sermon* (Nashville: B&H, 2003).

personality to a given audience with the intent of enabling a positive response."[45] This definition highlights five *m*'s: (1) the mode (oral communication), (2) the message (biblical truth), (3) the medium (the Holy Spirit and human personality), (4) the mark (a given audience), and (5) the motive (a positive response).[46] Vines and Shaddix have a helpful seven-page survey of twenty-nine biblical words for preaching that they arrange into seven distinct elements for preaching: (1) divine revelation, (2) clear explanation, (3) practical application, (4) eternal redemption, (5) public proclamation, (6) personal confession, and (7) intentional persuasion.[47]

MacArthur has exercised an influential pulpit ministry for more than forty years. He has been a stalwart for expository preaching. He and the Master's Seminary faculty have produced a volume on preaching that also has served expositors well.[48]

Greidanus has published widely in the area of preaching and has argued strongly for expository preaching. He says, "The outstanding characteristic of expository preaching is that it uses the Bible as the source for its preaching; it seeks to give an exposition of a biblical passage. By contrast, nonbiblical topical preaching presents neither text nor exposition."[49] He rightly says that expository preaching is much more than a method; it is a passionate commitment:

> At heart, expository preaching is not just a method but a commitment, a view of the essence of preaching, a homiletical approach to preach the Scriptures. This underlying commitment, in turn, is bound to reveal itself in a method in which preachers tie themselves to the Scriptures and, as heralds of Christ, seek to proclaim only that which the Scriptures proclaim.[50]

Greidanus lists several advantages that expository preaching has over topical preaching: (1) it sets limits and will not let us invent our own message; (2) it demands integrity; (3) it identifies the pitfalls of

---

[45] Vines and Shaddix, *Power in the Pulpit*, 27.
[46] Ibid., 24–26.
[47] Ibid., 17–23.
[48] John MacArthur Jr. et. al., *Rediscovering Expository Preaching: Balancing the Science and Art of Biblical Exposition* (Dallas: Word, 1992).
[49] Greidanus, *The Modern Preacher and the Ancient Text*, 15.
[50] Ibid.

forgetfulness and disloyalty that must be avoided; (4) it produces confidence that we are preaching God's word, not our own views; (5) it causes the Scriptures to be heard in the church; (6) it gives hearers a measure of assurance that they are hearing the word of God; and (7) it provides hearers with textual limits for testing the spoken word against the written word so that they can decide more responsibly whether to accept a message or not.[51]

Chapell's book *Christ-Centered Preaching: Redeeming the Expository Sermon* has also influenced expositors, especially at Covenant Seminary and elsewhere. Chapell defines an expository sermon as "a message whose structure and thought are derived from a biblical text, that covers the scope of the text, and that explains the features and context of the text in order to disclose the enduring principles for faithful thinking, living, and worship intended by the Spirit, who inspired the text."[52] He says that other forms of preaching that proclaim biblical truth are "valid and valuable," but "no preaching type is more important than expository."[53] Chapell argues that expository preaching is a priority because the "power for change resides in God's Word," and expository preaching "attempts to present and apply the truths of a specific biblical passage."[54] Expository preaching presents the power and the authority of God's word as well as the power of the Spirit.[55]

We could add many more voices that support the evangelical consensus for expository preaching.[56] Stott will not allow expository preaching to be reduced to one "alternative among many," because he claims that "all true Christian preaching is expository preaching."[57] Robinson says much the same: "The type of preaching that best carries the force of divine authority is expository preaching."[58] Lloyd-Jones adds his affirmation of this principle and repeats it for emphasis: Preaching, he says, must "always be expository. Always expository."[59]

---

[51] Ibid., 16. Greidanus drew the first four advantages from John Stott.
[52] Chapell, *Christ-Centered Preaching*, 31.
[53] Ibid., 30.
[54] Ibid.
[55] Ibid., 30–32.
[56] Steven J. Lawson, *Famine in the Land: A Passionate Call for Expository Preaching* (Chicago: Moody, 2003); Albert Mohler and Tony Merida, *Faithful Preaching: Declaring Scripture with Responsibility, Passion, and Authenticity* (Nashville: B&H Publishing, 2009).
[57] Stott, *Between Two Worlds*, 125.
[58] Robinson, *Biblical Preaching*, 19.
[59] Lloyd-Jones, *Preaching and Preachers*, 196.

Others writers highlight the expositional nature of preaching the Bible without using the term *expository*. Al Fasol asserts that preaching is "orally communicating truth as found in the Bible."[60] J. I. Packer describes preaching as "the event of God bringing to an audience a Bible-based, Christ-related, life-impacting message of instruction and direction from Himself through the words of a spokesperson."[61]

As I stated in chapter 1, these books are treasure troves of solid information on preaching. However, because they try to do so much, they only devote a limited amount of space to surveying what the whole Bible says about preaching.

BOOKS ON THE THEOLOGY OF PREACHING

Books in the fourth category are more focused on articulating a theology of preaching. The material is more specialized because the authors do not intend for these books to be "one-stop shops" as homiletics textbooks. There are not as many books in this category, so I have included some works by nonevangelicals. Some of these books are better categorized as "theology and preaching" (rather than as "theology of preaching") because they talk about the benefits of using theology in preaching. Richard Lischer, for example, argues that utilizing theology in preaching is important because preaching may be the only medium through which parishioners are exposed to theology.[62]

Other books wrestle with how we should think theologically about preaching in the midst of a postmodern context.[63] Some utilize theological categories to address this challenge. Michael Pasquarello III looks at preaching from many different vantage points or practices (theological, traditional, ecclesial, pastoral, beautiful, and pilgrim).[64] Donald English uses categories such as creation and redemption to un-

---

[60] Al Fasol, *Essentials for Biblical Preaching: An Introduction to Basic Sermon Preparation* (Grand Rapids: Baker, 1989), 16.

[61] J. I. Packer, "Authority in Preaching," in *The Gospel in the Modern World*, ed. Martyn Eden and David F. Wells (Downers Grove, IL: InterVarsity, 1991), 199.

[62] Richard Lischer, *A Theology of Preaching: The Dynamics of the Gospel* (Eugene, OR: Wipf & Stock, 2001). He rightly stresses preaching as proclamation and worship, but in my estimation he relies too heavily on categories for preaching derived from Karl Barth. There is not enough interaction with the text of Scripture itself.

[63] Ronald J. Allen, Barbara S. Blaisdell, and Scott Black Johnston, *Theology for Preaching* (Nashville: Abingdon, 1997).

[64] Michael Pasquarello III, *Christian Preaching* (Grand Rapids: Baker Academic, 2008). He rightly argues that modern preachers have tragically transitioned from theological to technological preaching that relies not on Scripture and theology, but on rhetorical techniques and communication strategies. He also rightly calls the church back to theological and doxological preaching.

derstand preaching,[65] while Marjorie Hewitt Suchocki uses the model of Christ's incarnation.[66] D. W. Cleverley Ford has a thirty-nine-page discussion of the preaching of the word in both Testaments, but he devotes far more attention (106 pages) to the theology of preaching the word.[67] Other detailed studies are devoted to a theology of preaching.[68]

John Piper's book *The Supremacy of God in Preaching* has had a profound impact on how I think theologically about preaching. Piper stresses that preaching is "expository exultation," and thus insightfully describes preaching as worship.[69] The book takes a God-centered, Trinitarian approach to preaching that focuses on the goal (glory of God), ground (cross of Christ), and gift (Holy Spirit) of preaching. Piper also includes a discussion of gravity and gladness in the context of preaching, as well as lessons learned from the life and preaching of Jonathan Edwards.

From the specific standpoint of biblical theology, I have profited greatly from four other books.[70] What makes them so helpful is that they come closer to doing what I am attempting in this book. First, Peter Adam, in his *Speaking God's Words*, offers a practical theology of expository preaching.[71] He identifies three biblical foundations that are especially important for expository preaching: (1) the doctrine of revelation, (2) the inspiration of the written word, and (3) the command to preach the word. He develops these principles and moves on to discuss the demands upon the preacher and the preacher's purpose.

---

[65] Donald English, *An Evangelical Theology of Preaching* (Nashville: Abingdon, 1996).

[66] Marjorie Hewitt Suchocki, *The Whispered Word: A Theology of Preaching* (Tübingen: Mohr Siebeck, 1995). She argues that preaching is today's complement to Christ's incarnation. She looks at preaching through the lens of process thought to show that God's presence is in us and around us. Thus, she develops a theology of preaching from process theology, not biblical theology.

[67] D. W. Cleverley Ford, *The Ministry of the Word* (Grand Rapids: Eerdmans, 1979).

[68] Heinrich Ott, *Theology and Preaching: A Programme of Work in Dogmatics, Arranged with Reference to Questions 1–11 of the Heidelberg Catechism*, trans. Harold Knight (Philadelphia: Westminster, 1961). The first part of this work argues that theology has the "office of supervision" with respect to "gospel proclamation" (17). Ott also argues that in one sense theology and preaching are a single activity because theology is "the reflective aspect of preaching itself" (19). Elsewhere he sums up this interrelatedness by saying that theology is the "conscience" of preaching, but preaching is "the heart and soul" of theology because the theologian works with a view toward the mission of preaching (22). Theology and preaching are reciprocal because preaching focuses on the specific aspect of the text, while theology reflects upon aspects of wholeness or unity (26).

[69] *The Supremacy of God in Preaching*, rev. ed. (Grand Rapids: Baker, 2004), 9.

[70] I could add that Graeme Goldsworthy has an excellent chapter concerning the meaning of preaching in which he builds a basic biblical theology of preaching. See *Preaching the Whole Bible*, 31–45. However, I did not include his book in this category because the rest of the book largely focuses on how biblical theology and the gospel in particular enable us to preach the whole Bible as Christian Scripture.

[71] Peter Adam, *Speaking God's Words: A Practical Theology of Expository Preaching* (Downers Grove, IL: InterVarsity, 1996).

Adam's emphasis on preaching as a ministry of the word is very similar to my approach.

Second, Edmund Clowney's book *Preaching and Biblical Theology*[72] begins with a chapter on what biblical theology is. He then uses biblical theology to discuss the authority, character, and content of preaching in Scripture.

Third, Stott's book *The Preacher's Portrait*,[73] while not a biblical theology of preaching, highlights the benefits of a more expansive approach to our understanding of preaching. He does not restrict his study to the customary preaching terms but looks at five word pictures for preaching (*steward, herald, witness, father, servant*). In other words, prior studies had not looked at the preacher in terms of steward, father, or servant because these were not technically "preaching" words.

Fourth, Robert H. Mounce has written an excellent book titled *The Essential Nature of New Testament Preaching*.[74] Mounce is very exegetical in his focus and frequently engages with nonevangelical positions on preaching. He deals only with the New Testament evidence, but the book's exegetical nature makes it an excellent source for determining what preaching is in Scripture.

[72] Edmund P. Clowney, *Preaching and Biblical Theology* (Phillipsburg, NJ: P&R, 2002).

[73] John Stott, *The Preacher's Portrait: Some New Testament Word Studies* (Grand Rapids: Eerdmans, 1961).

[74] *The Essential Nature of New Testament Preaching* (Eugene, OR: Wipf & Stock, 2005). I should also mention two other authors who have provided books on the theology of preaching from the vantage point of Paul. John William Beaudean Jr. looks more narrowly at Paul's theology of preaching in his published dissertation: *Paul's Theology of Preaching*, NABPR Dissertation Series 6 (Macon, GA: Mercer University Press, 1988). Michael P. Knowles has an excellent study on Paul's preaching as well: *We Preach Not Ourselves: Paul on Proclamation* (Grand Rapids: Brazos, 2008).

BIBLIOGRAPHY

Achtemeier, Elizabeth. *Creative Preaching: Finding the Words*. Nashville: Abingdon, 1980.

Adam, Peter. *Speaking God's Words: A Practical Theology of Expository Preaching*. Downers Grove, IL: InterVarsity, 1996.

Adams, Jay E. *Preaching with Purpose: The Urgent Task of Homiletics*. Grand Rapids: Zondervan, 1982.

Allen, Ronald J., ed. *Patterns of Preaching: A Sermon Sampler*. St. Louis: Chalice, 1998.

Allen, Ronald J., Barbara S. Blaisdell, and Scott Black Johnston. *Theology for Preaching: Authority, Truth, and Knowledge of God in a Postmodern Ethos*. Nashville: Abingdon, 1997.

Ash, Christopher. *Bible Delight: Heartbeat of the Word of God*. Ross-shire, Scotland: Christian Focus, 2008.

———. *The Priority of Preaching*. Ross-shire, Scotland: Christian Focus, 2009.

Azurdia, Arturo G., III. *Spirit Empowered Preaching: Involving the Holy Spirit in Your Ministry*. Ross-shire, Scotland: Christian Focus, 1998.

Baehr, Theodore. *Getting the Word Out: How to Communicate the Gospel in Today's World*. San Francisco: Harper & Row, 1986.

Bailey, E. K., and Warren W. Wiersbe. *Preaching in Black and White: What We Can Learn from Each Other*. Grand Rapids: Zondervan, 2003.

Bailey, Raymond, ed. *Hermeneutics for Preaching: Approaches to Contemporary Interpretations of Scripture*. Nashville: Broadman, 1992.

———. *Jesus the Preacher*. Nashville: Broadman, 1990.

———. *Paul the Preacher*. Nashville: Broadman, 1991.

Bainton, Roland. *Here I Stand: A Life of Martin Luther*. Nashville: Abingdon, 1978.

Bartlett, David L. *Between the Bible and the Church: New Methods for Biblical Preaching*. Nashville: Abingdon, 1999.

Bauckham, Richard J. *Jude, 2 Peter*. Word Biblical Commentary 50. Dallas: Word, 2002.

Beaudean, John William, Jr. *Paul's Theology of Preaching*. NABPR (National Association of Baptist Professors of Religion) Dissertation Series 6. Macon, GA: Mercer University Press, 1988.

Bickel, Bruce. *Light and Heat: The Puritan View of the Pulpit*. Morgan, PA: Soli Deo Gloria, 1999.

Blomberg, Craig L. *Jesus and the Gospels: An Introduction and Survey.* 2nd ed. Nashville: B&H, 2009.

———. "Matthew." In *Commentary on the New Testament Use of the Old Testament,* edited by G. K. Beale and D. A. Carson. Grand Rapids: Baker Academic, 2007.

———. *Preaching the Parables: From Responsible Interpretation to Powerful Proclamation.* Grand Rapids: Baker, 2004.

Bradford, Charles L. *Preaching to the Times.* Washington, DC: Review & Herald, 1975.

Braxton, Brad R. *Preaching Paul.* Nashville: Abingdon, 2004.

Broadus, John A. *On the Preparation and Delivery of Sermons.* Nashville: Broadman, 1944.

———. *Preparation and Delivery of Sermons.* Edited by E. C. Dargan. New York: Hodder and Stoughton, 1898.

Brooks, Phillips. *The Joy of Preaching.* Grand Rapids: Kregel, 1989.

Brown, H. C., Jr., H. Gordon Clinard, Jesse J. Northcutt, and Al Fasol. *Steps to the Sermon: An Eight-Step Plan for Preaching with Confidence.* Nashville: Broadman & Holman, 1996.

Brown, Peter. *Augustine of Hippo.* Berkeley: University of California Press, 1969.

Bruce, F. F. *Romans.* Tyndale New Testament Commentary. Rev. ed. Grand Rapids, Eerdmans, 1985.

Brueggemann, Walter. *The Threat of Life: Sermons on Pain, Power, and Weakness.* Edited by Charles L. Campbell. Minneapolis: Fortress, 1996.

Bryson, Harold T. *Expository Preaching: The Art of Preaching Through a Bible Book.* Nashville: Broadman & Holman, 1995.

Bugg, Charles B. *Preaching from the Inside Out.* Nashville: Broadman, 1992.

Burke, John, ed. *A New Look at Preaching.* Wilmington, DE: Michael Glazier, 1983.

Buttrick, David. *Homiletic: Moves and Structures.* Philadelphia: Fortress, 1987.

Cahill, Dennis M. *The Shape of Preaching: Theory and Practice in Sermon Design.* Grand Rapids: Baker, 2007.

Calvin, John. *The Institutes of the Christian Religion.* Edited by John T. McNeill. Translated by Ford Lewis Battles. Library of Christian Classics 20–21. Philadelphia: Westminster, 1960.

Capon, Robert Farrar. *The Foolishness of Preaching: Proclaiming the Gospel against the Wisdom of the World.* Grand Rapids: Eerdmans, 1998.

Carrick, John. *The Imperative of Preaching: A Theology of Sacred Rhetoric.* Carlisle, PA: Banner of Truth, 2002.

———. *The Preaching of Jonathan Edwards.* Carlisle, PA: Banner of Truth, 2008.

Carson, D. A. "Challenges for the Twenty-first Century Pulpit." In *Preach the Word: Essays on Expository Preaching in Honor of R. Kent Hughes,* edited by Leland Ryken and Todd Wilson. Wheaton, IL: Crossway, 2007.

———, ed. *Entrusted with the Gospel: Pastoral Expositions of 2 Timothy.* Wheaton, IL: Crossway, 2010.

———. *The Gospel According to John.* Pillar New Testament Commentary. Grand Rapids: Eerdmans, 1990.

———. *Showing the Spirit: A Theological Exposition of 1 Corinthians 12–14.* Grand Rapids: Baker, 1987.

Chapell, Bryan. *Christ-Centered Preaching: Redeeming the Expository Sermon.* 2nd ed. Grand Rapids: Baker, 2005. First edition, 1994.

Claypool, John R. *The Preaching Event.* 2nd ed. San Francisco: Harper & Row, 1990.

Clowney, Edmund P. *Preaching and Biblical Theology.* Phillipsburg, NJ: P&R, 2002.

Collins, Raymond F. *Preaching the Epistles.* New York: Paulist, 1996.

Cox, James W., ed. *Biblical Preaching: An Expositor's Treasury.* Philadelphia: Westminster, 1983.

———. *Preaching: A Comprehensive Approach to the Design and Delivery of Sermons.* San Francisco: Harper & Row, 1985.

Craddock, Fred B. *As One without Authority: Essays on Inductive Preaching.* Enid, OK: Phillips University Press, 1971.

———. *Preaching.* Nashville: Abingdon, 1985.

Crenshaw, James L. *Trembling at the Threshold of a Biblical Text.* Grand Rapids: Eerdmans, 1994.

Crum, Milton, Jr. *Manual on Preaching.* Valley Forge, PA: Judson, 1977.

Daane, James. *Preaching with Confidence: A Theological Essay on the Power of the Pulpit.* Grand Rapids: Eerdmans, 1980.

Dallimore, Arnold. *George Whitefield.* Vol. 1. Edinburgh: Banner of Truth, 1970.

Dargan, Edwin Charles. *A History of Preaching.* Vol. 2. New York: George H. Doran, 1905.

Davis, H. Grady. *Design for Preaching.* Philadelphia: Fortress, 1958.

De Brand, Roy E. *Guide to Biographical Preaching: How to Preach on Bible Characters.* Nashville: Broadman, 1988.

Decker, Bert, and Hershael W. York. *Preaching with Bold Assurance: A Solid and Enduring Approach to Engaging Exposition.* Nashville: Broadman & Holman, 2003.

Demaray, Donald E. *An Introduction to Homiletics.* 2nd ed. Grand Rapids: Baker, 1990.

Dempster, Stephen G. *Dominion and Dynasty: A Biblical Theology of the Hebrew Bible.* New Studies in Biblical Theology. Downers Grove, IL: InterVarsity, 2003.

DeRouchie, Jason S. "Shepherding Wind and One Wise Shepherd: Grasping for Breath in Ecclesiastes." *The Southern Baptist Journal of Theology* 15, no. 3 (2011): 4–25.

Dever, Mark E. *Nine Marks of a Healthy Church.* Wheaton, IL: Crossway, 2004.

———. "A Real Minister: 1 Corinthians 4." In Mark Dever, J. Ligon Duncan III, R. Albert Mohler Jr., and C. J. Mahaney, *Preaching the Cross.* Wheaton, IL: Crossway, 2007.

Dever, Mark, and Greg Gilbert. *Preach: Theology Meets Practice.* Nashville: B&H, 2012.

Duduit, Michael, ed. *Communicate with Power: Insights from America's Top Communicators.* Grand Rapids: Baker, 1996.

Dumbrell, William J. *Covenant and Creation: A Theology of the Old Testament Covenants.* 2nd ed. Biblical and Theological Classics Library 12. Milton Keynes, UK: Paternoster, 2002.

Dykstra, Robert C. *Discovering a Sermon: Personal Pastoral Preaching.* St. Louis: Chalice, 2001.

Elliott, Mark Barger. *Creative Styles of Preaching.* Louisville, KY: John Knox, 2000.

English, Donald. *An Evangelical Theology of Preaching.* Nashville: Abingdon, 1996.

Erickson, Millard J., and James L. Heflin. *Old Wine in New Wineskins: Doctrinal Preaching in a Changing World.* Grand Rapids: Baker, 1997.

Eslinger, Richard L. *Narrative and Imagination: Preaching the Word That Shaped Us.* Minneapolis, MN: Fortress, 1995.

———. *Pitfalls in Preaching.* Grand Rapids: Eerdmans, 1996.

Fant, Clyde E. *Preaching for Today.* Rev. ed. San Francisco: Harper & Row, 1987.

Farmer, H. H. *The Servant of the Word.* Philadelphia: Fortress, 1974.

Fasol, Al. *A Complete Guide to Sermon Delivery.* Nashville: Broadman & Holman, 1996.

———. *Essentials for Biblical Preaching: An Introduction to Basic Sermon Preparation.* Grand Rapids: Baker, 1989.

Ferguson, Sinclair. Foreword to *The Art of Prophesying*, by William Perkins. Carlisle, PA: Banner of Truth, 1996.

Ford, D. W. Cleverley. *The Ministry of the Word.* Grand Rapids: Eerdmans, 1979.

Frame, John M. *The Doctrine of the Christian Life.* Phillipsburg, NJ: P&R, 2008.

———. *The Doctrine of the Word of God.* Phillipsburg, NJ: P&R, 2010.

Galli, Mark, and Craig Larson. *Preaching That Connects: Using the Techniques of Journalists to Add Impact to Your Sermons.* Grand Rapids: Zondervan, 1994.

Gibson, Scott M., ed. *Preaching the Old Testament.* Grand Rapids: Baker, 2006.

Goldsworthy, Graeme. *Preaching the Whole Bible as Christian Scripture.* Grand Rapids: Eerdmans, 2000.

Grant, Reg, and John Reed. *The Power Sermon: Countdown to Quality Messages for Maximum Impact.* Grand Rapids: Baker, 1993.

———. *Telling Stories to Touch the Heart: How to Use Stories to Communicate God's Truth.* Wheaton, IL: Victor, 1990.

Graves, Mike. *The Sermon as Symphony: Preaching the Literary Forms of the New Testament.* Valley Forge, PA: Judson, 1997.

———. *What's the Matter with Preaching Today?* Louisville, KY: John Knox, 2004.

Green, Joel B., and Michael Pasquarello III. *Narrative Reading, Narrative Preaching.* Grand Rapids: Baker Academic, 2003.

Greidanus, Sidney. *The Modern Preacher and the Ancient Text: Interpreting and Preaching Biblical Literature.* Grand Rapids: Eerdmans, 1988.

———. *Preaching Christ from the Old Testament: A Contemporary Hermeneutical Method.* Grand Rapids: Eerdmans, 1999.

Griffin, H. P., and T. D. Lea. *1, 2 Timothy, Titus.* The New American Commentary. Nashville: B&H, 2001.

Gross, Nancy Lammers. *If You Cannot Preach Like Paul.* Grand Rapids: Eerdmans, 2002.

Gushee, David P., and Robert H. Long. *A Bolder Pulpit: Reclaiming the Moral Dimension of Preaching.* Valley Forge, PA: Judson, 1998.

Hamilton, Donald L. *Homiletical Handbook.* Nashville: Broadman & Holman, 1992.

Henderson, David W. *Culture Shift: Communicating God's Truth to Our Changing World.* Grand Rapids: Baker, 1998.

Hoefler, Richard C. *Creative Preaching and Oral Writing.* Lima, OH: CSS, 1978.

Holmes, C. Raymond. *The Last Word.* Berrien Springs, MI: Andrews University Press, 1987.

Hostetler, Michael J. *Illustrating the Sermon.* Grand Rapids: Zondervan, 1989.

Howard, J. Grant. *Creativity in Preaching.* Grand Rapids: Zondervan, 1987.

Hugenberger, Gordon. "Preach." In *The International Standard Bible Encyclopedia*, edited by Geoffrey W. Bromiley. Vol. 3. Grand Rapids: Eerdmans, 1986.

Hybels, Bill, Stuart Briscoe, and Haddon Robinson. *Mastering Contemporary Preaching.* Portland, OR: Multnomah, 1989.

Jacobsen, David S. *Preaching in the New Creation: The Promise of New Testament Apocalyptic Texts.* Louisville, KY: Westminster John Knox, 1999.

Jensen, Richard A. *Thinking in Story: Preaching in a Post-Literate Age.* Lima, OH: CSS, 1993.

Johnston, Graham. *Preaching to a Postmodern World: A Guide to Reaching Twenty-First Century Listeners.* Grand Rapids: Baker, 2001.

Jones, Ilion T. *Principles and Practice of Preaching.* New York: Abingdon, 1956.

Killinger, John. *Fundamentals of Preaching.* Philadelphia: Fortress, 1985.

Knowles, Michael P. *We Preach Not Ourselves: Paul on Proclamation.* Grand Rapids: Brazos, 2008.

Koller, Charles W. *Expository Preaching without Notes.* Grand Rapids: Baker, 1962.

Lane, William. *Hebrews 9–13.* Word Biblical Commentary. Dallas: Word, 2002.

Larsen, David L. *The Anatomy of Preaching: Identifying the Issues in Preaching Today.* Grand Rapids: Baker, 1989.

———. *The Company of Preachers: A History of Biblical Preaching from the Old Testament to the Modern Era.* Grand Rapids: Kregel, 1998.

Lawrence, Michael. *Biblical Theology in the Life of the Church.* Wheaton, IL: Crossway, 2010.

Lawson, Steven J. *The Expository Genius of John Calvin.* Reformation Trust, 2007.

———. *Famine in the Land: A Passionate Call for Expository Preaching.* Chicago: Moody, 2003.

Leeman, Jonathan. *Reverberation: How God's Word Brings Light, Freedom, and Action to His People.* Chicago: Moody, 2011.

Lewis, C. S. *Mere Christianity.* San Francisco: Harper & Row, 1980.

Lewis, Ralph L., and Gregg Lewis. *Inductive Preaching: Helping People Listen.* Westchester, IL: Crossway, 1983.

Lischer, Richard. *A Theology of Preaching: The Dynamics of the Gsopel.* Eugene, OR: Wipf & Stock, 2001.

———. *Theories of Preaching: Selected Readings in the Homiletical Tradition.* Durham, NC: Labyrinth, 1987.

Lloyd-Jones, D. Martyn. *Preaching and Preachers.* Grand Rapids: Zondervan, 1971.

———. *Romans: An Exposition of Chapters 3:20–4:25.* Carlisle, PA: Banner of Truth, 1998.

Logan, Samuel T., Jr., ed. *The Preacher and Preaching: Reviving the Art in the Twentieth Century.* Phillipsburg, N.J.: Presbyterian and Reformed, 1986.

Long, Thomas G. *Preaching and the Literary Forms of the Bible.* Philadelphia: Fortress, 1989.

———. *The Witness of Preaching.* Louisville, KY: Westminster John Knox, 1989.

Loscalzo, Craig A. *Apologetic Preaching: Proclaiming Christ to a Postmodern World.* Downers Grove, IL: InterVarsity, 2000.

———. *Evangelistic Preaching That Connects: Guidance in Shaping Fresh and Appealing Sermons.* Downers Grove, IL: InterVarsity, 1995.

———. *Preaching Sermons That Connect: Effective Communication through Identification.* Downers Grove, IL: InterVarsity, 1992.

Lowry, Eugene L. *The Homiletical Plot: The Sermon as Narrative Art Form.* Louisville, KY: Westminster John Knox, 1983.

———. *How to Preach a Parable: Designs for Narrative Sermons.* Nashville: Abingdon, 1989.

———. *The Sermon: Dancing the Edge of Mystery.* Nashville: Abingdon, 1977.

Luther, Martin. *Day by Day We Magnify Thee: Daily Readings.* Philadelphia: Fortress, 1982.

MacArthur, John, Jr. et al. *Rediscovering Expository Preaching: Balancing the Science and Art of Biblical Exposition.* Dallas: Word, 1992.

Macleod, Donald. *The Problem of Preaching.* Philadelphia: Fortress, 1987.

Mahaney, C. J. *Humility: True Greatness.* Portland, OR: Multnomah, 2005.

Massey, James E. *Designing the Sermon: Order and Movement in Preaching.* Nashville: Abingdon, 1980.

Mathewson, Steven D. *The Art of Preaching Old Testament Narrative.* Grand Rapids: Baker Academic, 2002.

Mawhinney, Bruce. *Preaching with Freshness.* Grand Rapids: Kregel, 1997.

McClure, John S., ed. *Best Advice for Preaching.* Minneapolis, MN: Fortress, 1998.

McDill, Wayne. *The 12 Essential Skills for Great Preaching.* Nashville: Broadman & Holman, 1994.

———. *The Moment of Truth: A Guide to Effective Sermon Delivery.* Nashville: Broadman & Holman, 1999.

McKim, Donald K. *The Bible in Theology and Preaching: How Preachers Use Scripture.* Rev. ed. Nashville: Abingdon, 1994.

Meyer, Jason C. *The End of the Law: Mosaic Covenant in Pauline Theology.* Nashville: B&H, 2009.

Meyers, Robin R. *With Ears to Hear: Preaching as Self-Persuasion.* Cleveland: Pilgrim, 1993.

Millar, J. G. *Now Choose Life: Theology and Ethics in Deuteronomy.* New Studies in Biblical Theology. Downers Grove, IL: InterVarsity, 2000.

Miller, Calvin. *The Empowered Communicator: The 7 Keys to Unlocking an Audience.* Nashville: Broadman & Holman, 1994.

———. *Marketplace Preaching: How to Return the Sermon to Where It Belongs.* Grand Rapids: Baker, 1995.

———. *The Sermon Maker: Tales of a Transformed Preacher.* Grand Rapids: Zondervan, 2003.

Miller, Mark. *Experiential Storytelling: (Re)Discovering Narrative to Communicate God's Message.* Grand Rapids: Zondervan, 2003.

Mitchell, Henry H. *Black Preaching: The Recovery of a Powerful Art.* Nashville: Abingdon, 1991.

———. *Celebration and Experience in Preaching.* Nashville: Abingdon, 2008.

Mohler, Albert, and Tony Merida. *Faithful Preaching: Declaring Scripture with Responsibility, Passion, and Authenticity.* Nashville: B&H, 2009.

Mounce, Robert H. *The Essential Nature of New Testament Preaching.* Eugene, OR: Wipf & Stock, 2005.

Mulder, David P. *Narrative Preaching: Stories from the Pulpit.* St. Louis: Concordia, 1996.

Old, Hughes Oliphant. *The Reading and Preaching of the Scriptures in the Worship of the Christian Church.* Vol. 1, *The Biblical Period.* Grand Rapids: Eerdmans, 1998.

Ott, Heinrich. *Theology and Preaching: A Programme of Work in Dogmatics, Arranged with Reference to Questions 1–11 of the Heidelberg Catechism.* Translated by Harold Knight. Philadelphia: Westminster, 1961.

Packer, J. I. "Authority in Preaching." In *The Gospel in the Modern World,* edited by Martyn Eden and David F. Wells. Downers Grove, IL: InterVarsity, 1991.

———. *God Has Spoken: Revelation and the Bible.* Grand Rapids: Baker, 1979.

Parker, T. H. L. *Calvin's Preaching.* Louisville, KY: Westminster John Knox, 1992.

Pasquarello, Michael, III. *Christian Preaching.* Grand Rapids: Baker Academic, 2008.

Perry, Lloyd M. *Biblical Preaching for Today's World.* Chicago: Moody, 1973.

———. *Biblical Sermon Guide.* Grand Rapids: Baker, 1970.

———. *A Manual for Biblical Preaching.* Grand Rapids: Baker, 1965.

Piper, John. *Desiring God: Meditations of a Christian Hedonist.* Portland, OR: Multnomah, 2003.

———. *Let the Nations Be Glad: The Supremacy of God in Missions.* 3rd ed. Grand Rapids: Baker Academic, 2010.

———. "Preaching as Expository Exultation." In Mark Dever, J. Ligon Duncan III, R. Albert Mohler Jr., and C. J. Mahaney, *Preaching the Cross*. Wheaton, IL: Crossway, 2007.

———. *The Supremacy of God in Preaching*. Rev. ed. Grand Rapids: Baker, 2004.

Pitt-Watson, Ian. *A Primer for Preachers*. Grand Rapids: Baker, 1986.

Quicke, Michael J. *360-Degree Leadership: Preaching to Transform Congregations*. Grand Rapids: Baker, 2006.

———. *360-Degree Preaching: Hearing, Speaking, and Living the Word*. Grand Rapids: Baker Academic, 2003.

Reid, Robert Stephen. *The Four Voices of Preaching: Connecting Purpose and Identity behind the Pulpit*. Grand Rapids: Brazos, 2006.

Richards, H. M. S. *Feed My Sheep*. Washington, DC: Review & Herald, 1958.

Robinson, Haddon W. *Biblical Preaching: The Development and Delivery of Expository Messages*. 2nd ed. Grand Rapids: Baker, 2001. First edition, 1980.

———. *Biblical Sermons: How Twelve Preachers Apply the Principles of Biblical Preaching*. Grand Rapids: Baker, 1989.

———. *Making a Difference in Preaching*. Edited by Scott M. Gibson. Grand Rapids: Baker, 1999.

Robinson, Wayne Bradley, ed. *Journeys toward Narrative Preaching*. New York: Pilgrim, 1990.

Rowell, Ed. *Preaching with Spiritual Passion: How to Stay Fresh in Your Calling*. Minneapolis, MN: Bethany House, 1998.

Rueter, Alvin C. *Making Good Preaching Better: A Step-by-Step Guide to Scripture-Based, People-Centered Preaching*. Collegeville, MN: Liturgical Press, 1997.

Sailhamer, John H. *The Pentateuch as Narrative*. Grand Rapids: Zondervan, 1992.

Salmon, Bruce C. *Storytelling in Preaching: A Guide to the Theory and Practice*. Nashville: Broadman, 1988.

Sargent, Tony. *The Sacred Anointing: The Preaching of Dr. Martyn Lloyd-Jones*. Wheaton, IL: Crossway, 1994.

Saunders, Stanley M. *Preaching the Gospel of Matthew: Proclaiming God's Presence*. Louisville, KY: Westminster John Knox, 2010.

Scharf, Greg R. "Were the Apostles Expository Preachers? Old Testament Exposition in the Book of Acts." *Trinity Journal* 31 (2010).

Schmitt, Hans-Christoph, "Redaktion des Pentateuch im Geiste der Prophetie." *Vetus Testamentum* 32 (1982): 170–89.

Shaddix, Jim. *The Passion-Driven Sermon*. Nashville: B&H, 2003.

Shephard, William H., Jr. *No Deed Greater Than a Word: A New Approach to Biblical Preaching*. Lima, OH: CSS, 1998.

Simmons, Martha J., ed. *Preaching on the Brink: The Future of Homiletics*. Nashville: Abingdon, 1996.

Sleeth, Ronald E. *God's Word and Our Words: Basic Homiletics*. Atlanta: John Knox, 1986.

Spain, Robert H. *Getting Ready to Preach*. Nashville: Abingdon, 1995.

Spurgeon, C. H. *An All-Round Ministry*. Edinburgh: Banner of Truth, 1960.

———. *Autobiography: The Early Years*. Edinburgh: Banner of Truth, 1962.

Stewart, James S. *Heralds of God*. New York: Charles Scribner's Sons, 1946.

Stortz, Rodney, *Daniel: The Triumph of God's Kingdom*. Wheaton, IL: Crossway, 2004.

Stott, John. *Between Two Worlds: The Art of Preaching in the Twentieth Century*. Grand Rapids: Eerdmans, 1982.

———. *The Preacher's Portrait: Some New Testament Word Studies*. Grand Rapids: Eerdmans, 1961.

Strauch, Alexander. *Leading with Love*. Littleton, CO: Lewis and Roth, 2006.

Suchocki, Marjorie Hewitt. *The Whispered Word: A Theology of Preaching*. Tübingen: Mohr Siebeck, 1995.

Sweazey, George E. *Preaching the Good News*. Englewood Cliffs, NJ: Prentice Hall, 1976.

Thompson, James W. *Preaching Like Paul*. Louisville, KY: Westminster John Knox, 2001.

Towner, W. Sibley, *Interpretation: Daniel*. Atlanta: John Knox, 1984.

Tripp, Tedd, and Margy. *Instructing a Child's Heart*. Wapwallopen, PA: Shepherd, 2008.

Troeger, Thomas H. *Imagining a Sermon*. Nashville: Abingdon, 1990.

Updike, John. *Rabbit, Run*. New York: Random House Trade, 1996.

Van Harn, Roger E. *Pew Rights: For People Who Listen to Sermons*. Grand Rapids: Eerdmans, 1992.

Vines, Jerry. *A Practical Guide to Sermon Preparation*. Chicago: Moody, 1985.

Vines, Jerry, and Jim Shaddix. *Power in the Pulpit: How to Prepare and Deliver Expository Sermons*. Chicago: Moody, 1999.

Wallace, Daniel. *Greek Grammar beyond the Basics*. Grand Rapids: Zondervan, 1996.

Wardlaw, Don M., ed. *Preaching Biblically: Creating Sermons in the Shape of Scripture*. Philadelphia: Westminster, 1983.

Webb, Joseph M. *Comedy and Preaching*. St. Louis: Chalice, 1998.

———. *Preaching without Notes*. Nashville: Abingdon, 2001.

Wells, C. Richard, and A. Boyd Luter. *Inspired Preaching: A Survey of Preaching Found in the New Testament*. Nashville: Broadman & Holman, 2002.

Willimon, William H. *Preaching and Leading Worship*. Philadelphia: Westminster, 1984.

Willimon, William H., and Richard Lischer. *Concise Encyclopedia of Preaching*. Louisville, KY: Westminster John Knox, 1995.

Wilson-Kastner, Patricia. *Imagery for Preaching*. Minneapolis, MN: Fortress, 1989.

Wilson, Paul S. *A Concise History of Preaching*. Nashville: Abingdon, 1992.

———. *The Four Pages of the Sermon: A Guide to Biblical Preaching*. Nashville: Abingdon, 1999.

———. *The Practice of Preaching*. Nashville: Abingdon, 1995.

GENERAL INDEX

SCRIPTURE INDEX